THE ETHICS OF CORPORATE CONDUCT

The American Assembly, *Columbia University*

THE ETHICS
OF CORPORATE
CONDUCT

Prentice-Hall, Inc., *Englewood Cliffs, New Jersey*

A SPECTRUM BOOK

Library of Congress Cataloging in Publication Data
Main entry under title:

THE ETHICS OF CORPORATE CONDUCT.

(A Spectrum Book)
At head of title: The American Assembly, Columbia
University.
Papers prepared for the fifty-second American
Assembly at Arden House, Harriman, N. Y., April 1977.
Includes index.
1. Business, ethics—Congresses. 2. Industry—
Social aspects—United States—Congresses. 3. Big
business—United States—Congresses.
4. Corporations—United States—Congresses.
I. American Assembly.
HF5387.E86   301.5'1   77-24172
ISBN 0-13-290544-2
ISBN 0-13-290536-1 pbk.

The figure on page 99 is from George Lodge, "Business and the Changing Society," *Harvard Business Review*, March/April 1974. Copyright © 1974 by the President and Fellows of Harvard College. It is reprinted by permission.

10 9 8 7 6 5 4 3 2 1

PRENTICE-HALL INTERNATIONAL, INC. (*London*)
PRENTICE-HALL OF AUSTRALIA PTY, LTD. (*Sydney*)
PRENTICE-HALL OF CANADA, LTD. (*Toronto*)
PRENTICE-HALL OF INDIA PRIVATE LIMITED (*New Delhi*)
PRENTICE-HALL OF JAPAN, INC. (*Tokyo*)
PRENTICE-HALL OF SOUTHEAST ASIA PTE., LTD. (*Singapore*)
WHITEHALL BOOKS LIMITED (*Wellington, New Zealand*)

Table of Contents

Preface

In the nineteenth century and the early years of the twentieth, the corporation was looked on primarily as the brainchild of an entrepreneur and, as it developed, an extension of his personality. In the last quarter of this century it continues to produce large volumes of goods, to provide jobs, and, while improving the material quality of life, to make a profit when it can. At the same time it has become a major social institution and as such has responsibilities that go beyond production and traditional profit maximizing.

Yet it is apparent from national dialogue and opinion polls that the American people have shown a growing distrust of the behavior of American business in general and the large corporation in particular. There appears also to be a considerable difference between public expectations about business behavior—some new ingredient in public standards as they apply to business—and the views that corporate leaders entertain of their own activities.

As the participants in the Fifty-second American Assembly at Arden House, April 1977, pointed out in their final report (obtainable from The American Assembly), "Corporations must realize that some of their actions—actions taken in their view in the best interest of the corporation—may produce consequences on both business and the society at large that trigger disapproval."

The American people demand more of their corporations today than they did fifty years ago. Business must make the effort to reform and redesign its own behavior or risk having weighty and nonmanageable standards imposed on it from elsewhere, especially from government.

This book describes the environment in which business has operated in this century and traces shifts in ideology that have worked changes in ethical outlook and behavior of the corporation—inside its walls and outside—vis-à-vis government, other professions, and the public at large. It was first put together under the editorial supervision of President Clarence Walton of Catholic University of America as background for the Arden House Assembly, but because its subject matter touches the lives of all of us, it is expected to have a wider appeal.

The opinions that follow belong to the authors themselves and not to The American Assembly, which takes no position on matters it presents to the public. Nor is the Norton Simon Foundation Commission on the Business-Government Relationship, which supplied generous partial funding for this Assembly program on corporate conduct, to be held accountable for the views herein.

Clifford C. Nelson
President
The American Assembly

Clarence C. Walton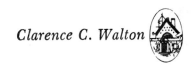

Overview

Why are there so many sad souls *in* America? Why are so many souls saddened *by* America? So to inquire is to probe neither frivolously nor flippantly; nor does it suggest agreement with that troubled segment of society who bewail such alleged misfortune. Yet even with sharp awareness of the perils of flawed polls, one cannot simply dismiss as unimportant or irrelevant the consistent reports of growing disenchantment.

Within the last decade there has emerged a new elite—well-educated, liberal and articulate—which has both fed the discontents and been nourished by them. Filled with moral indignation they are transforming government into an instrument for moral and social reform. But they must have substance to feed in—and feed on. It is to this substance, as distinguished from popular opinion, that the following preliminary comments are addressed. My interest is in "opinion-makers" from literature, politics, and business, not in polls of public perceptions.

What is relatively new, however, is that murmurings of discontent emanate not solely from youth or women or blacks, but from mature

---

CLARENCE C. WALTON *is President of Catholic University of America. Formerly a Penfield Fellow at the Institute of Advanced Studies (Geneva) and a visiting professor at the universities of Helsinki and Buenos Aires, Dr. Walton has been dean of the Duquesne University Business School and an associate dean at the Columbia Business School. He is director of several business corporations. A student of the ethics of corporations for more than a decade, Dr. Walton has written* Corporate Social Responsibilities, Big Government and Big Business, *and* Ethos and the Executive.

individuals who have operated within the system, who have adapted to the system, and who have been recognized as spokesmen for the system. While vignettes of the recently alienated do not "prove" anything about contemporary civilization, they assuredly act as semaphores.

The Faces of Gloom

Looking back nostalgically some thirty years to his early days in New York, poet Anthony Harrigan spoke of an exuberant metropolis that was clean, safe and elegant.

> Poets wrote rich symbolic sonnets about the skyscrapers and the cars moving through the city streets at twilight. The symbolism of the city has changed with time from magical opportunity and excitement to decay and disorder.

On the west coast Kenneth Rexroth now sees the whole country as an extension of the lines he once used to describe California in autumn "when the landscape has no flowers and the herbage is brittle." Said he sadly: "I don't feel at home here anymore!" Ezra Pound insisted that "we have all become rowers on the river of the dead"; and Robert Lowell lamented that "each day God shines through darker glass." Is it accident or design that prompts commentators to speak of America's entry into her third century as being "midway upon the journey"— words in the opening lines of Dante's first canto on the descent into hell?

Any temptation to dismiss these lamentations as the babbling poppycock of perennially disenchanted literati might well be checked because practical men from the tough world of international diplomacy and commerce are infected and affected too. A few examples suffice. Toward the end of the bicentennial year Edward Korry, who had served effectively as Ambassador to Ethiopia and Chile, respectively, announced intentions to sell his house, pack up and move abroad. Why? Because he had lost faith in America's political system. The second is a man with even wider experiences and larger reputation, George S. Keenan. This brilliant scholar-diplomat recalled that as a youth he had always believed it was

> a good thing that the United States had come into being and developed as it had developed. I now see all these assumptions crashing to pieces. . . . I think this country is destined to succumb to failures which cannot be other than tragic and enormous in their scope.

What of the business community? Fred T. Allen, chairman and president of Pitney-Bowes, distressed by the fact that large corporations were being viewed as "manicured hoodlums," commissioned a survey by the Opinion Research Corporation in August 1975. To Allen, the survey results of 530 top and middle managers provided a very unhappy commentary on American business ethics. It shattered his illusion that "certain nations are hotbeds of corruption into which otherwise virtuous American businessmen had misadventured and sullied themselves."

Business Week (January 10, 1977) reported that the score card on questionable payments made overseas by United States corporations indicated that 175 companies had admitted shelling out more than $300 million during the past six years. Alice T. Marlin, president of the Council of Economic Priorities, which compiled the figures, added force to Allen's judgments by observing wryly: "The problem seems to be not so much one of lower foreign corporate standards as of low standards for U.S. corporate behavior and of competition among U.S. companies." Singing the same dirges were the two successive chairmen of the Securities and Exchange Commission under Presidents Nixon and Ford. Ray Garrett Jr. wrote: "There has been bribery, influence-peddling, and corruption on a scale I had never dreamed existed." And Roderick Hills, before a Joint Economic Committee of the Congress in 1976, detailed the civil actions in various district courts against nine corporations (including some of the nation's largest with sales ranging from approximately $100 million to $1.8 billion) and noted that in each case the primary allegation was the maintenance of secret funds outside normal financial accountability systems and a variety of illegal practices. *"Always there was direct involvement and participation by senior management officials."*

One may therefore legitimately ask whether it was masochism or honesty which brought a standing ovation to J. Irwin Miller, chairman of Cummins Engine, when he told one hundred top executives at the Conference Board in January of 1977 that we are "losing our freedoms" not because of the appetite of some monster government, but because we (businessmen) "have abused our freedoms when we had them." The clear inference is that there have been some very low shots, even by the ankle-high standards of certain American businessmen: Lockheed's misadventures nearly shoved Italy to the Communist camp and *did* materially influence the fall of a government in Japan; the Kepone scandal rocked Allied Chemical; Vepco built a nuclear plant over a geological fault; Gulf's payoffs brought down its chief executive in disgrace; AT&T was shaken when its southern affiliates sought to buy political favors; the CIA and ITT had soiled hands in Chile. The moral canvas seems black indeed.

Not all agree. Frederick Collins, president of Sperry and Hutchinson, asked for perspective:

> Let us not forget that 495 of the *Fortune* 500 companies did not bribe foreign companies, that thousands of companies did not make illegal political contributions, and that thousands of companies did not attempt to interfere in the internal affairs of Chile. That's kind of like bringing you the news that thousands of planes landed safely yesterday. However, that news is worth recognizing every once in a while.

Pennwalt Corporation ran a full-page advertisement in the New York *Times* on June 30, 1976, to proffer the modest suggestion that the wrongdoings of the few should not blind us to our strengths.

In a society where Everyman is his own philosopher it is seldom easy to distinguish heavy-handed hyperbole from hard-headed realism or fiction from fact. Even when appropriate distinctions are made the challenge to make correct ethical choices is still difficult. We are all heirs to a complicated and sometimes contradictory set of moral traditions. Indeed it may be argued that the corporate malfeasance head-lined in recent years is simply the peak of an ethical iceburg the dimensions of which none of us really comprehend. Ethical imperatives are sometimes ambiguously stated, often wrenched from the historical context in which they were formed, and asserted in different ways at different times by different groups. Censure of corporate executives too quickly when the rules-of-the-game are in considerable flux may itself constitute unethical behavior.

I would argue, therefore, that no one can have a sense of what ethics is all about without a sense of historical perspective. To provide a measure of perspective I propose to do four things:

1. Enter the ethical thicket to derive a working definition of business ethics;
2. Extract the major values which evolved throughout Western civilization into two major typologies (classical and modern) which guide our moral decision-making;
3. Assess the health of contemporary American democracy and the free-enterprise economy; and
4. Note briefly the condition of other basic value-forming institutions—family, church and school.

Into the Ethical Thicket

Few executives subscribe to the notion that business ethics means only conformity to law; they would agree with the philosophy expressed by Caterpillar Tractor Company in its *Worldwide Business Conduct:* "The law is a floor. Ethical business conduct should normally exist at a level well above the minimum required by law." Quaker Oats expressed its understanding in the following way:

> A reasonable and practical standard of ethical behavior in business decisions and actions is that which would not be embarrassing to you, your family, or our company if it were revealed publicly and, more fundamentally, that behavior which would seem right to those who live by the best standards and moralities.

The same idea captured Fletcher Byrom, Koppers' chairman, when he said to his co-workers in June 1976:

> Possibly the best test—for a person with a family—might be to think whether you would be happy to tell your spouse and children the details of the action you are contemplating or whether you would be willing to appear on television and to explain your actions in detail.

The test of disclosure is the key to ethics under this definition. Reflecting on his IBM experiences Ralph Pfeiffer said that while clarity of definition is helpful and while visibility and disclosure are great disciplinarians, he had developed a simple guideline to "smell" danger: "Show me a company that is careless in accounting for money disbursed for travel expenses and I'll show you a company in—or heading for—ethical trouble."

Frank Cary, IBM chairman, attempted no definition in his preface to that company's guidelines but suggested that ethical standards are related to "excellence and fair dealing." Fred Collins of Sperry and Hutchinson is convinced that, despite quantum leaps in education "there has been no appreciable moral and emotional growth among men. The mind is a fearfully fine instrument for analysis but the mind is totally amoral." Collins would root his personal and business ethic in those Judeo-Christian admonitions that were commonplace in our early religious traditions: "Subtle definitions and sophisticated codes cannot improve those standard religious precepts," he insisted. This theme was shared by GM's Thomas Murphy: "I believe that the ethical standards that have come down to us from the world's great religions and through our Judeo-Christian traditions are surprisingly comprehensive in their applications and even more surprisingly practical."

Agreement on the essential meaning of ethics itself is difficult to achieve. When professional philosophers talk of deontological ethics, theological ethics, meta-ethics and the like, executive ears wax heavy as professional tongues wax eloquent. After all, what the manager wishes to know is this: in a given concrete situation what *ought* I do—and why? The question is unambiguous. The answers are not. Awareness of the ethical thicket through which the decision-maker walks induces, understandably, a hesitancy to reach for definitions. Yet a beginning must be made and it is to that end that the following is offered:

1. Ethics involves critical analysis of human acts to determine their rightness or wrongness in terms of two major criteria: truth and justice.
2. Business Ethics extends the range of criteria whereby human actions are judged to include such things as societal expectations, fair competition, the aesthetics of advertising and the use of public relations, the meaning of social responsibilities, reconciling corporate behavior at home with behavior abroad, the extent of consumer sovereignty, the relevance of corporate size, the handling of communications, and the like.

Some of the criteria by which business ethics seek to judge are not necessarily ethical under the narrower definition of the root term noted above. For example, conflict-of-interest questions are measured as often by appearance as by substance, big enterprises are held to tighter standards than small ones, and disclosure is mandated only for items deemed material to the company's sales and profits.

It must be remembered that ethical principles carry, according to their nature, different powers of persuasion. On a primary level, there is little doubt that ethical judgments can be formulated which command well-nigh universal assent. Among these *first-level* ethical propositions are the following:

1. Human life is more precious than animal life.
2. Basic needs must be satisfied before desires for luxury are satisfied.
3. Creative and dignified labor is a good.

4. **Laws must be fair, applicable to all, and applied in an even-handed manner.**
5. **A just peace is preferable to war.**

In addition there are important "secondary" principles which have been refined through human experience and which still command allegiance. Among such secondary principles are the following:

1. Obedience to legitimate civil authority is obligatory.
2. There may be occasions when a higher unwritten law justifies the breaking of unjust laws—provided always that the violator is willing to accept the civil consequences.
3. Private property is a right which always carries social obligations.
4. Economic power, once viewed as flowing from property ownership, need not be based exclusively on property to be ligitimate.
5. Greater economic power is paralleled by greater moral responsibility.
6. The contemporary corporation must be viewed not simply as a profit maximizing unit but as a moral entity which can give dignity to work, just wages to employees, and needed goods and services to the community.

In applying ethical principles it is important to distinguish between *command* and *exhortation*. The former insists that the action be done —or not done—under severe ethical censure; the second counsels people to behave in a certain manner. An example of the former would be the obligation of a corporation to fulfill its warranties, to discharge its economic obligations to workers and stockholders, and to pay taxes to the government. Examples of ethical counsels include that range of activities which normally fall under the rubric of corporate social responsibilities—supporting education, participating in community affairs, aiding the performng arts or encouraging citizens to vote.

Even when principles are clear, decision-making sometimes is not. At times there may be an absolute necessity to take action with the foreknowledge that both good and bad effects will occur. In such cases, a general three-pronged rule exists to help: (1) the action may be performed if the doer does not really desire the bad effect; (2) the doer does not use the bad result as a step toward even good purposes; and (3) the prospective results suggest that the good effect will outweigh the evil. *This principle of double-effect is often the one that confronts corporate decision-makers.* It is always difficult to handle, sometimes difficult to justify, and occasionally used as a pretext for irresponsible behavior. Sometimes, therefore, choices must be made between two goods or even two bads and not the black-or-white options which are often portrayed after the fact.

When a person seeks to act morally some justification is sought. Understanding how such justification comes about is a fascinating exercise. While there are others, the following "justifiers" are worth noting.

Motivation—The argument here is that if one is well-intentioned then one has behaved ethically. The right spirit and the right purpose give rectitude to the act: to lie blatantly out of the spirit of love is good, whereas to lie from desire to hurt is evil; to bribe for the corporation's good is proper but to bribe in order to harm the organization is wrong; to have an abortion out of concern for a child likely to be born crippled is good, but to have an abortion to spite the husband is evil. Respect for proper motives encourages tolerance and respect for differing opinions.

But resting the case for ethics on motivation alone has its limits. The most heinous examples of good intentions gone amok come from attempts to "civilize" alien peoples—by persuasion if possible and by sword if necessary. The motives of a Hitler or Stalin to make Germany or Russia the supreme nation of the world may have been well-intentioned but the results were tragic. Good people may have mad motives and madmen may have pure ones.

Practicality—The practical ethic asserts that the workable is good and the unworkable bad. But *a priori* judgments are made on what is workable and what is not. Is biologist Garrett Hardin a proper moral mentor when he advocates his practicality "lifeboat ethics" in these terms:

> Metaphorically each rich nation amounts to a lifeboat full of comparatively rich people. The poor of the world are in other much more crowded lifeboats. Continuously, so to speak, the poor fall out of their lifeboats and swim for awhile in the water outside, hoping to be admitted to a rich lifeboat. What should the passengers in the rich lifeboat do?

Hardin answers: Nothing. To admit more would risk sinking and the practical wisdom is to "save your own skin." Applying this concept to starving peoples of the world, Hardin concludes that to be really ethical the poor must be abandoned to their starvation so that the more prosperous can survive. Otherwise, posterity is not served because the world is ultimately peopled by more and more who are poorer and poorer. The persuasive force of this morality rests on the common-sense action that people can only do certain things. But following Hardin's ethic, a mining company could determine, for example, that where possibilities for quick profits exist but where also political instability prevails, the proper ethical course is to get—and get out—even if the "getting" produces exploitation and misery for the abandoned people. The point is simple enough: practical ethics may produce results at the price of innocent third parties; practical ethics calls for no substantial sacrifice; practical ethics is invariably self-serving.

Opinion—Another criterion used to justify an action or ethic is opinion. In one case, it is *public* opinion revealed by polls or by the maxims of a marketing ethic which enjoins business to give customers what they want. Business is hard put, at times, to find a better moral maxim, but business is equally troubled when pornographers use the same apologetic to justify their merchandise and their selling techniques. In short, the majority rule is the best moral justification for the political society but is not a fool-proof one; consumer sovereignty is the best moral justification for free enterprise but it, too, is not fool proof.

In the second case, *personal opinion* is held to be the appropriate determinant of matters ethical. It is expressed in the maxim that one person's opinion is as good as any other person's opinion. Yet even "pagan" Cicero scorned this view by saying that only a madman maintains that the distinction between the honorable and the dishonorable, between virtue and vice, is a matter of opinion and not of nature.

Two World Views

How an individual makes ethical judgments is influenced by the way he perceives himself in relation to society, the cosmos, or God. These relationships touch on the nature of human nature, the meaning of individual dignity, the purpose of human existence, the reality of human suffering, the presence of evil, and almost all other issues subsumed under three powerful words: "the human condition." They also touch the meaning we give to such key words as *community, society* and *state*. That the first of these is overworked in contemporary idiom is shown by the way we speak of the business community, the academic community, the political community, and so on. Yet some of our wisest contemporary philosophers (one thinks of Martin Buber and John MacMurray) insist that community has a precise and narrow meaning in that it always involves a *personal relationship* based on friendship. The motive power of the community is love, the binding force is equality and its *raison d'etre* is found in itself.

Society, on the other hand, involves functional relationships based on self-interest; roles are created on the basis of the division of labor in order to promote that society's particular good. A labor union and a business partnership are good examples of a society based on reciprocal self-interest. Because of role differentiation the society operates through superordinate-subordinate relationships and equality is not one of its hallmarks. Instead of the famous "I-Thou" involvement (which was Buber's way of defining the community) the society creates more usually an "I-It" relationship. Whereas community involves the total personality, society involves only a part of the personality—one's brawn and muscle, intelligence and shrewdness, working capacity or commitment. It comes about, then, that love and charity hallmark the community whereas justice becomes the central goal of a society.

When society becomes large and impersonal, complex and interdependent, the normal contractual modes for organizing functions to produce justice start to weaken. Needed now is another institution to insure justice and this form of society is called a state. The more complex the nonpolitical societies the more complex becomes the state. To promote justice, the state resorts to the progressive income tax, sponsors social security and welfare programs, provides employment benefits, establishes courts of criminal justice to suppress violence, and creates various regulatory bodies to assure fair play in the market. Ironically, the ultimate moral aim of a society and of a state is to become a community and yet the likelihood of achieving it is remote. Yet we judge societies too often—and unfairly—by the criteria of a community.

How modern man goes about creating community and society is influenced profoundly by the traditions which form his culture and share his world view. Our moral legacy has been influenced by Greco-Roman thought, by the Judaic and Christian religion, by the Enlightenment philosophy and by the Scientific Revolution. To understand that tradition requires a comprehension of that vast historic landscape called Western Civilization. Few of us possess such magistral knowledge. The required fact base is enormous, the necessary interpretive skills are vast and the desired objectivity is marred by a cultural bias. Eventually, however, we are all driven to seek some sort of conceptual framework which yields those basic beliefs that together give legitimacy to what we do and how we do it.

More often evocative rather than definitional, certain words—justice, equality, liberty—help form our particular mind-set. These words, which I call "concept-captions," will be used later to demonstrate some of the contrasting and contradictory values under which we operate. To employ concept-captions is not to ignore the flaws which mar them. For example, we speak of the medieval period as the "Age of Faith" yet the twelfth and thirteenth centuries were among the most legal-minded and rigorously logical periods in Western history. Even the dominant theology emphasized reason over blind faith. We also think of men in earlier times as being inclined more toward justice than liberty when, in truth, they prized physical safety above all else. Martin Luther correctly captured the spirit of his own and earlier times when he said that "peace is more important than justice and peace was not made for the sake of justice but justice for the sake of peace." If the examples are many, the point is singular: concept-captions are useful but frequently inadequate and with this caveat in mind we can now address ourselves to the two great moral typologies which have evolved in Western society—the *classical* and the *modern*.

THE CLASSICAL VIEW

The *classical* world view holds that the universe has meaning and value quite apart from the meaning and value given it by man. Man's own life has a specific value and purpose and his ethical obligation is to live in accordance with that value and that purpose. Man fulfills his obligation in this dispensation by respecting his own nature because creation is good and man is sacred. The normal result of this philosophy is to accept God as creator and lawmaker.

Irving Kristol, co-editor of *The Public Interest* and a member of *The Wall Street Journal*'s board of contributors, said that modern man's penchant for talking about values instead of about moral beliefs arises "out of a very simple purpose, namely to divorce morality from religion. That is why we talk about values and why we don't talk about moral beliefs and moral convictions." All previous civilizations have rooted morality in religion; ours does not. "But if there is no God," persists Kristol, "how can anyone tell genuinely what is right and what is wrong?" Religious precepts are the symbolic statements of the moral beliefs and moral convictions of human beings over many generations.

The assumption is that the experiences of all of these peoples over all of this time adds up to something wiser than any one of us could possibly be.

> This collective human experience . . . has an implicit inarticulate reason behind it. Inarticulate is the word—that is, it knows more than it can say. There is a reason why religions say "do this" or "don't do this"—even if they canot tell you the reason. Perhaps the reason is not philosophically sayable, but simply comes down to profound human intuition developed over centuries by generations of people who are no stupider than we are.

Kristol is quick to recognize that since the classical view rests on respect for tradition and since our civilization is geared to progressive change, there is little likelihood that the classical view will be resurrected. That refusal explains, in part, why another critic would say that this nation has so many John Deans—"men without a center." Martin Mayer assessed our situation this way: "We see ourselves sprung full-panoplied from the brow of Henry Ford, Thomas Edison and Harvey Firestone—the memory goes no farther back. They the seed; we the stalk; our little ones the fast-fading flower children."

THE MODERN WORLD VIEW

Since a *modern* world view dominates, it is well to note that it, too, has contradictory strands. It is largely a product of eighteenth-century Enlightenment in Europe. But one must always ask which Enlightenment? For there were two—one born in French intellectual soil and the other in the Anglo-Scottish traditions. Rousseau and Voltaire, Diderot, and Condorcet were the big names in France and from their pens flowed words creating a moral excitement the likes of which the modern world had not before experienced. The French invented a new God, a new calendar, a Republic of Virtue, and a revolutionary elite endowed with impeccable credentials. To the French, the assignment was nothing less than the "universal regeneration of mankind."

The English and Scots were less exuberant, less confident over the capacity of governments to produce men of virtue, less sure about the future, and less certain of the inherent goodness of human nature. Adam Smith was a fairly representative spokesman on the foibles of men when he observed wryly that jurists like "to reap where they have never sowed," employers are drawn "to practice collusion," corporate directors neglect "other people's money," lawyers (when paid according to the length of the brief) "multiply words beyond all necessity." The ambivalence regarding human nature—so strikingly lacking among the French—plagued Adam Smith and John Stuart Mill in England, and plagued our forefathers. The American Enlightenment *was* different in important respects from both the French and the Anglo-Scot movements.

In Europe the Enlightenment's energy was invariably directed against the medieval world with its feudal and ecclesiastical structures. It questioned religious orthodoxy, opposed any established church, denounced all forms of censorship, demanded an end to aristocratic privilege, and scoffed at tradition. Little of this was found in America. There was no established church and the feared "papists" had no Catholic bishop before 1776. There was no pervasive censorship, no aristocracy, no great centralized state, no standing army and no heavy tax burdens. In America the Enlightenment was a relatively bland affair which drew strength from its own experiences to develop its specialized version of the Enlightenment. In Europe Enlightenment ideas undermined the existing order whereas in America they validated what was already commonly believed. But here, too, different interpretations existed.

In a sense we created our own separate versions of what an enlightened society should reveal. The difference between John Adams and Thomas Jefferson is illustrative. The two men first met in Philadelphia during June of 1775 where the Second Continental Congress had convened. Legend grew that Jefferson was "the mind," Adams "the tongue," and Washington "the spirit" of American independence. Despite their personal friendship, Adams and Jefferson differed profoundly. The former, a product of New England, always felt that the fundamental institutions established by the Puritans—schools, army, town-meeting, and congregation—must remain the pillars of the community. No government could survive unless it made use of these intermediary institutions. Calvinism colored his theory of human nature. In 1776 he said: "There is so much rascality, so much banality and corruption, so much greed and ambition among all ranks and degrees of men in America, that I sometimes doubt there is public virtue enough to suport a Republic."

Jefferson, the Virginian, presented a sharp contrast. Whereas religion was an ally to Adams, the Anglican Church was an enemy to Jefferson. He felt no need to maintain the centrality of religion because man was inherently good and essentially creative. He wrote in the Virginia Statute, "that our civil rights have no dependence on our religious opinion."

When it came time to form the new government Adams thought that while Machiavelli and Hobbes were too hard on human nature, they were nevertheless right in believing that self-love was the dominant passion and that governments must restrain it. Jefferson, on the contrary, believed that there was a moral sense which led men to seek the good of others, to live soberly in society, to be instinctively concerned with justice. Adams saw man as a political animal seeking power; Jefferson saw man as a social animal seeking community.

The two men died within hours of one another on the fiftieth anniversary of America's independence—July 4, 1826. For a half century they had engaged in a dialogue and had, as Daniel Webster declared in his eulogy for the deceased patriots, profound influence on all of us.

Why this modest excursion into the byways of history? Because their differences are our differences, their ambivalences are our ambivalences. Perhaps it cannot be otherwise. But no one can think, for example, of the popularity given to Douglas MacGregor's theory x and theory y for business organization without realizing how the ghosts of Adams and Jefferson still walk among us.

The practical consequence is that even though we share the modern world view our value perspectives are generated from different angles: some trust men and distrust government; others trust government and distrust men. And these perspectives bear heavily on debates regarding the future role of government in private affairs. In short, the contemporary world view seems to lack power in proving the kind of unified conceptualization that made medieval man comfortable in his beliefs. Lacking a transcendental source man is driven to create a natural one; lacking a moral consensus man creates one through laws as a substitute for voluntary agreement; lacking an objective ethical base man relies on his subjective judgment.   License to steal!

SCIENCE

Inexorably man is driven to seek a surer ground than motive, practicality, or opinion in order to legitimize an action. Frequently science is summoned to fill the moral void. It was probably in renaissance Italy that the learning style of scholasticism was converted to modern science and engineering. Science would replace ethical relativism by providing objective data against which things could be measured. Consequently science would liberate man from ignorance, superstition, religious servitude and dull routine. And surely science would add to our ease of living and to greater wealth-creating capacities. One thing seems certain and it is this: whether in developed, developing or decaying societies, science has had one consistent effect, namely to corrode tradition. Western tradition has dealt with values which should govern human behavior so that future salvation would be assured. Science fixed man's eyes on the operations of the physical world and in that fixation Voltaire could say properly that there was "no such thing as better or worse in things that are indifferent." And so Voltaire hailed the victory of fact over doubt. In the very act of emancipation, however, science shook man from his moral moorings and, at the same time, created its own subtle form of imprisonment. Science builds boundaries around the imagination, cannot deal with mystery, distrusts symbols and dislikes metaphor. By seeking physical causes for human aberrations, it contributes to a weakening of the sense of sin. In anti-social acts today the victim is often blamed for having conspired with society and the criminal is deemed innocent because he has been the true victim. A sinless person is an irresponsible person yet persistent efforts have been made to make man either the product exclusively of environment or genes.

This interest in "evolutionary ethics" is long-standing. In the eighteenth century one Lord Monboddo (the Scottish judge who joined Adam Smith in forming the "Select Society" in Edinburgh in 1754) published an essay arguing that no strict demarcation between men and animals exists. Rules for conduct gradually emerged through evolutionary change. In the nineteenth century Herbert Spencer set the scientific pattern of ethics by holding that the good can be identified with the concept of the "more highly evolved." In the present controversy over abortion, cytogeneticists like Jerome Lejeune and Gunther Stent seek to establish precise scientific data to determine when human life begins. The assumption is that scientific evidence then settles ethical debates.

An example of how the discussions are advancing occurred in the fall of 1975 when Harvard University Press published a book by zoologist Edward Wilson entitled, *Sociobiology: The New Synthesis.* Wilson asked whether genes *might* exist which favor the development of specific social behaviors; he then speculated what the consequences of these genes might be and how they could express themselves. Wilson bravely suggested that if human nature could be defined in terms of behavioral motivators and censors inherited from early stages of evolution, then a neural understanding of the human brain will provide a firm foundation for ethics.

Those sympathetic to the Wilsonian interpretation feel that since evolution has undermined that transcendental foundation for ethics which guided western civilization for a millenium, a new scientific way out of the dilemma between unlimited moral relativism and supernaturalist absolutism must be found. Wilson hinted at an *objec-*

tive ethic based on science which alone can restore effective consensus. Note how cautious Wilson is: he suggests, he hints, he hypothesizes. Yet his caution did not save him from stinging rebuke. The *New York Times Book Review* noted that "Wilson has joined a long parade of biological determinists whose work has served to buttress the institutions of their society by exonerating them from responsibility for social problems." My own hunch is that science will move us farther along in our understanding of men as moral agents but that science alone cannot provide the objective basis all seek for ethics. Science exemplifies a morally neutral ideal and can foster a world where, in Robert Hutchins's words, "everything valuable is now value free."

While it is dangerous to select one spokesman for the classical and the modern world view, respectively, interesting insights are given by St. Thomas Aquinas and René Descartes. Whereas Aquinas felt that the "slenderest knowledge that may be obtained of the highest thing is more desirable and precious than the most certain knowledge obtained of lesser things," Descartes insisted that truth-seekers should not "bother with any object of which they cannot have a certainty equal to the demonstrations of arithmetic and geometry." Those skeptical of the all-embracive claims of contemporary science claim that the Cartesian and Newtonian revolutions have provided excellent guidelines to the flatlands of knowledge but that the highlands of the spirit remain untouched and unexplored.

What, then, has the Enlightenment produced? A short-hand answer would be this: a rationalist libertarian society. Lineaments of a libertarian society include the free market system with its emphasis on self-interest, profits and competition, representative government, social roles filled by autonomous professionals, a secularist civilization, a people who are self-critical and prepared to debate first principles. The dilemma of the American libertarian society is the fact that liberalism's traditional function, namely, criticism of the existing order, cannot go forward in the face of collapsing values and of collapsing institutions. Tearing down needs to be balanced, to say the least, with shoring up.

CONCEPT-CAPTIONS

We are now prepared—and with full awareness of limitations—to draw sharp distinctions between the classical world view and the modern world view.

CLASSICAL WORLD VIEW *(Greco-Roman and Christianity)*	MODERN WORLD VIEW *(Enlightenment Philosophy and Science)*
Religious Faith (God Is)	Religious Skepticism (God Is Not—or May Be)
Future-World Orientation	This-World Orientation
Ends (Teleological)	Means (Instrumental)
Mystery-to-Be-Accepted	Problems-to-Be-Solved
Centralized Authority	Diversified Authority
Language of Metaphor	Technical Terminology
Intuition	Rationalization
Religious Obedience	Religious Dissent
Blessed Are the Poor	Blessed Are the Prosperous
Sense of Community	Sense of Individualism
Charity	Self-Interest
Compassion	Survival-of-the-Fittest
Justice	Liberty
Status	Contract
Routine	Innovation
Individual Stability	Individual Mobility
Static Economy	Growth Economy
Just Price	Market Price
Cooperation	Competition

If one stops for a moment to consider how the moral patrimony, outlined above, was translated into realities by the American people, several interesting observations can be made. In the first instance, the Founding Fathers fashioned for us a form of government that was not designed to make citizens virtuous—as the Greeks sought to do—but to assure justice for free citizens. The market system, operating on the same premise of freedom, sought to make men richer. Liberty was the cord which bound the ideologies of the two systems together even as each operated with its own autonomy. Note how both the political and the economic system had the limited aims which go with the meaning of a *society*. Building a *community* was the assignment of churches, schools and families—all operating in the small-town ambience of neighborliness, mutual respect, and a certain measure of affection. Since the political system was fueled by a passion for equality that no other nation had ever equaled, democracy encouraged the belief that the communitarian ideal could be reached.

New questions—and possibly historic ones—now confront us. Are democratic governments and market systems equal to the original assignments placed upon them? Are they strong enough (in both their operations and in the public confidence they command) to bear the demanding dialectic seemingly being placed upon them today to wed the functions of the society and the goals of the community into a new synthesis? Is the expectation implicit in the hunger for a new dialectic a reasonable one? Or an unreal one? A rather hasty view of the present state of democracy and the free enterprise economy provides no answers but clues to answers.

Democracy—Past and Present

Ever since the appearance some twenty years ago of Arnold Toynbee's monumental history on the rise and fall of civilizations, commentators have regularly used the Toynbean technique to depict current institutional realities. If one does not succumb to overgeneralization this analytical device has some merit. In this context a review of American civilization (and the democratic government it created and sustained) provides interesting contrasts.

For two centuries Americans regularly did the impossible—and with relative ease: torrents tamed, farms from forests, the mighty metropolis from a tiny town. Their inventiveness was not restricted to things material; in matters spiritual and philosophical no people excelled Americans in their capacity to reconcile the irreconcilables. They believed in God's laws but moral transgressions were so rarely considered that, from Jonathan Edwards to Josiah Royce, no major philosopher ever faced squarely the problem of evil; when they thanked God for His gifts they praised themselves for what they had wrought with them; eyes uplifted toward heaven never lost sight of earth; the hereafter never blotted out the here-and-now. Nonfiction writers who gained greatest popularity were those who plausibly wedded the precepts of kings spiritual with those of kings temporal. For example: one William Makepeace Thayer wrote a 354-page tract called *Tact, Push and Principle* and concluded with this ethical prescription:

> It is quite evident that religion requires the following very reasonable things of every young man, namely: that he should make the most of himself if possible; that he should watch and improve his opportunities; that he should be industrious, upright, faithful, and prompt; that he should task his talents, whether one or ten, to the utmost; that he should waste neither time nor money; that duty, and not pleasure or ease should be his watchword.

Orison Swett Marden advised youth (in a book called *Pushing to the Front*) to remember that the "law of prosperity" is just as definite as the law of gravitation: "It is a mental law. Only by thinking abundance can you realize the abundant prosperous life that is your birthright." While literary critics gave short shrift to such authors of high conviction and low talent, the populace thought differently. Marden's book alone sold more than three million copies.

In the American belief system the gospel of democracy and the gospel of capitalism were nicely wedded because representative government and free-enterprise were seen as sides of the same freedom coin. This ability to unite democracy and capitalism arose partly from an underlying logic and partly from a practical assessment by ordinary folk that, despite flaws, both systems were eminently successful. In 1902 Brooks Adams received an enthusiastic response from America's leaders when he published *The New Empire*. Adams hammered home a single cheerful theme: the future belongs to us. He was simply noting that between 1890 and 1900 the world had experienced a major alteration in social and political equilibrium when the center of energy shifted from Europe to America. The twentieth was destined to be "the American century." "We are not at the cock crowing and the morning star," wrote Emerson earlier. Every American believed him.

What, then, of today? Writing from a British perspective the respected Norman Macrae concluded that the United States is undergoing a change similar to that which occurred in Britain around 1880 when world leadership began to pass to other hands. Yet Americans, said Macrae, seem to be singularly insensitive to the portents. Having been born free, Americans expect to escape scot free.

To suggest that Adams and Macrae are engaged in debate when they are so separated in time is patent nonsense. Juxtaposing their position, however, has the merit of intensifying reconsideration of the historical question raised by Elie Kedourie in the November 1976 issue of *Commentary:* Is democracy doomed? The answers are not encouraging. A report sponsored by the prestigious Trilateral Commission (and prepared by Michael Crozier of France, Samuel Huntington of America and Joji Watanuji of Japan) was called *The Crisis of Democracy.* The authors quoted Willie Brandt, who observed that

western Europe has only twenty or thirty more years of democracy left in it; after that it will slide, engineless and rudderless, into the surrounding sea of dictatorship, and whether this dictation comes from the left or from a junta on the right will not make that much difference.

So far as the United States is concerned Professor Huntington predicted a substantial increase in governmental activities and a substantial decrease in governmental authority.

Coupled to the decrease of public authority foreseen by Huntington is a diminished effectiveness by the two major political parties. Walter Dean Burnham, one of our best analysts, said that such basic realignments are currently at work, that we have a *caesura* in American political evolution which marks the end of two-party politics in the traditional sense. Huntington's (and possibly Burnham's) assessments take us full circle to George Kennan's frightening observation: America's democratic government is destined to failure.

But are these analysts right? Is it simply perverse optimism to believe that those who wallow in the dank jungle of discontent have lost perspective? This is not the first time that America has been at a watershed and, as with all watersheds, the landscape is blurred. 1890 provides an instructive example from American history when, in the face of great changes, intellectuals behaved in ways analogous to the behavior of certain scholars and writers today. If Rexroth and Korry speak of leaving their homeland forever, Henry James and Bret Harte actually did leave for England and Lafcadio Hearn became a Japanese citizen. To listen to Kennan is to hear again the musing of William Dean Howells, then the dictator of literary America: "after fifty years of optimistic content with civilization and its ability to come out all right in the end, I now abhor it."

Society, always fluid in America, seemed then to be in a process of disintegration; yet the persistent and effective reintegration which actually occurred was less obvious. Consider three historic responses. To meet the dangers of corporate concentration Congress produced the Sherman Antitrust Act of 1890; when Melville Fuller became Chief Justice of the Supreme Court no one anticipated that he would bring a radical reinterpretation of the Fourteenth Amendment to nullify State autonomy in many economic and social areas; the Populists produced a program for social and economic improvement which the major parties gradually adopted to meet new conditions. And all three developments marked the road toward greater centralization of power in Washington. Trade-offs had to be made then and trade-offs will have to be made now.

This is not to say that there is little to worry about. In 1977 the budget for Congress' own work topped, for the first time, the billion-dollar figure and is four times higher than it was in 1960: an activist Congress passes 34,000 to 38,000 bills every congressional session, many so ill-conceived that business has constant jitters; greater activity by the Internal Revenue Service, the Federal Trade Commission, the Securities and Exchange Commission, and their sister agencies is evident; Court decisions often reject hallowed rules-of-the-game for business; government is slow to tackle energy problems perceived long ago even by nonexperts; the shift of population to the South and West (of the ten largest cities, five are in Texas and California) has brought no legislative relief from a massive outflow of funds, estimated at $28.5 billion annually, to the declining Northwest and Northeast regions.

On the other hand, there are signs of hope. Disenchantment with regulatory bodies will produce reforms; the General Accounting Office is serving as an efficient watchdog over the bureaucracies; zero-base budgeting will be tried; Congress is reducing its overload of committees and has taken a more responsible stance toward its own budgetary and allocations process; there is awareness that the number and amount of transfer payments are not limitless; there will be housecleaning in the welfare programs; the two-party system proved equal to the challenges of the 1976 election. Reading lessons from history is a high-risk venture but one is especially worth considering; *our ancestors handled historic confrontations not so much by blueprints but through innovative institutional mechanisms which permitted decisions to be made as specific challenges arose.*

THE FREE-ENTERPRISE SYSTEM

Worry over dismal prospects for democracy's future is paralleled by concern over the unhappy state of a free-enterprise economy. It was not atypical when the *New York Times* began 1976 with bicentennial essays addressed to the problem: will capitalism survive until the year 2000? And the celebration year ended with the very same question still being asked. Alfred Malabre of the *Wall Street Journal* wondered aloud whether the economy was "manic depressive or excessive-recessive?"

While it is difficult to catalogue all of the expressed concerns over the future of free enterprise, five are worth noting:

1. Fear that having gone so far down the welfare road, the required capital for growth will be grossly indequate and a static economy will exacerbate social tensions.
2. The feeling that because we have so plundered the earth's resources the future must be geared to limited or near-zero growth.

3. Worry that if we continue to misread the real nature of our economy as profit-oriented only—to the neglect of the public and not-for-profit private sector—the wrong questions will be asked.
4. Concern that the system simply is not adapted to provide the necessary long-range planning for problems hurtling against us, and
5. A sense that capitalism is losing the ideological or semantic war.

The net effect of these troubled assessments raises a most serious question: do we understand the economy in ways which provide analytically correct descriptions of its operations and morally satisfying criteria for judging the behavior of the system's managers of large corporations? In short, do we know what we have and do we have what we want? Do the values which once legitimized free-enterprise's existence—private property and contract, competition and constrained government—still provide the criteria for assessments? Does big government and big business operate more comfortably together than their respective rhetorics suggest?

Business did not create the work ethic; it used it. Business did not create the idea of a living wage; it accepted it. Business did not invent the idea of contract; it lived by it. Business did not produce the scientific revolution; it employed its technological byproducts to create an affluent society. What does all this mean in terms of values by which the performance—efficient and ethical—is judged? Failure to answer creates a sense of drift. And it is this sense of drift, more than any basic failures, that produces the expressions of consternation catalogued earlier.

OTHER VALUE-FORMING INSTITUTIONS

What permits a society to *work* is its government and its business; what legitimizes that work is a commonly shared set of values. But what, then, of those other major institutions which have historically shaped personal and social values? The three most important value-forming institutions are family, church, and school. All three are in varying stages of disarray. Yet it would be rash to assert the *degree* of disarray when experts differ sharply.

Family—So far as the family is concerned, the evidence is inconclusive. Urie and Rolf Bronfenbrenner of Cornell report that the family has been so changed within the past generation that the consequences, for both the young and for society at large, are calamitous. According to their version the "extended family," still in place until 1950, provided both stability and socialization for the young. One out of every ten families had another adult relative living under its roof; divorce rates were low; mothers were at home; children were born within the marital bond; parents sought a better education for their offspring; magazines spoke of "togetherness." All this has vanished. More mothers are working; more divorces are occurring; more children are going to preschool; desertions are more common; more children are born out of wedlock; more training is given the child during daylight hours by parent surrogates. The net result for the child is value formation by peer groups while for those who remain aloof, there is alienation or loneliness.

Against this is the interpretation of sociologist Mary Jo Bane who argues that the "good old days" never existed. While the divorce rate has risen, more children today are living with at least one parent than ever before; divorced persons remarry; children are conceived as they are wanted and not as they are "produced"; women have wider options and working mothers are good mothers. Which way the evidence will fall is hard to discern. Certainly the Bronfenbrenner's dismal interpretation received reinforcement in January 1977, when an Illinois study revealed that crime by fourteen to eighteen year-olds was not known by the vast majority of parents, and that the greatest influence on the child was not parent or the church or school, but peers.

The consequences are not limited to the young. Speaking before the annual meeting of the American Association for the Advancement of Science on February 25, 1977, Dr. Alasdair MacIntyre of Boston University decried "the rootlessness and isolation, in death as well as life." Past cultures permitted people to die "garrulously," meaning that dying people talked freely of their approaching death to their children and grandchildren. Not only did a garrulous death allow the dying to pass on advice and wisdom to family members, but it better prepared them for a death they were more willing to accept. "Death is to be accepted, it should be looked on as a task that is completed," MacIntyre said. "It is a time to complete the transmission of the past to the future."

At the same meeting Harvard University's Dr. Thomas Schelling said that a "good" death today is viewed by many Americans as a sudden death with little or no time to prepare for it. Schelling said this view reflects at least in part the rootless and mobile lives led by a growing number of Americans. "A rich life should include that part of living that is concerned with death," Dr. Schelling said. "The right to speak out at the time of death and have others listen is part of that rich life."

Church—The position of the church is similarly hard to assess. While regular attendance is down, while internal divisions have erupted into external debate, and while authority has been flaunted, churches show surprising strengths in the political and business spheres. Civil rights was never an exclusively political or economic movement but a profound church involvement as well. Signs of spiritual reinvigoration are noted, and the overwhelming commitment to social justice has been one of the most remarkable developments within Christian churches of the last fifteen years. Businessmen have been particularly aware of the support given Caesar Chavez by distinguished churchmen.

Yet the present real impact by the Church on conscience-maturation and on value-formation is impossible to determine precisely. Business will likely receive no refurbished Protestant ethic which was so individualistic in emphasis; it will receive a doctrine of "social sin" which faults institutions more than individuals. This will not be easy to handle.

Schools—That leaves us with the school where blanket indictments are common enough. One may ask, however, whether parents and church leaders have not put too heavy a burden on teachers? Declining scores in standardized tests, disciplinary problems within the classroom, rising youth violence in the playground, growing use of drugs, and teenage pregnancies do suggest that the schools are simply not up to the challenge posed by a changing social order.

Implications for Business

The foregone survey—necessarily long to avoid oversimplification and yet too abbreviated to prove certitude—has been designed to provide some answers to this question: What does it mean to corporations whose executives must operate within a cultural milieu they have not completely created, do not effectively control, and cannot fully direct? By what moral standards should they be judged: the ethic of liberalism, the ethic of science, the ethic of religion or the ethic of some new ideology? America is at a watershed. Inaction means disaster and precipitous reaction means the same thing.

The first obvious step is to seek understanding of those basic forces at work within the government, in the marketplace, and within the family, church, and school. Once having catalogued the major transformations which characterize this historic watershed, steps can be taken to respond constructively to them. Among the generalizations that can be drawn for business at the international, national, and corporate levels are the following:

I. Global
   A. The finite biosphere of water, soil, and air is producing a revolution in thought comparable (said anthropologist Margaret Mead) to the Copernican revolution. "Selling more" may yield to "selling less—but better."
   B. Mankind is more interdependent than ever before and a parochial nationalistic view by corporate or government executives will not help. Economist Harold Isaacs has said that

   > we are experiencing on a massively universal scale a convulsive ingathering of men in their numberless groupings of kinds—tribal, racial, ethnic, religious, national. . . . Yet the more global our science and technology, the more tribal our politics; the more we see of the planets the less we see of each other.

   Perhaps this is the great moral paradox of the century.
   C. A fundamental problem is the lopsided distribution of the world's resources, both material and human. Definitely needed are mechanisms whereby the world's resources can be better identified, better managed and more equitably distributed.
   D. A consequence of the uneven distribution of resources is the need to cope with the growing power and growing demands of third-world countries—defined mainly as non-Caucasian people largely in Africa, the Caribbean, India, and the South Sea Islands. In a talk to the Wharton School alumni in 1976, Reginald Jones, General Electric Chairman, put the matter simply:

   > Managers of the future will be less provincial, more world-minded. . . . Right now there is a struggle for world markets between world corporation headquarters in Europe, Japan and North America. Executives will have to think and plan in global terms.

   E. These third-world people, determined to overthrow cultural and political domination by the West, will influence the formation of a new transcultural ethic. The new imperative will be neither "do in Rome what the Romans do" nor "do in Rome what Americans do in America."
   F. To find a new ethic of compromise Western man must begin

to understand their literary and philosophical traditions. For third-world writers, the most exciting Shakespearean play is *The Tempest;* to the surprise of Westerners, the important character is not Prospero, the exiled royalist who controlled an island with magic, but Caliban, the uncivilized native whom Prospero tried to educate but could not control.

G. Critical to all efforts to increase prosperity and share it with others throughout the globe is the multinational corporation whose power must be channeled into mutually satisfactory efforts.

II. Domestic

A. The older sense of "Manifest Destiny" for America has been rejected in favor of a more modest view of both our capabilities and our rights vis-à-vis those of other nations.

B. The legitimacy of American capitalism, based on the moral system of rewards rooted in the Protestant sanctification of work, is under increasing strain.

C. If the politicalization of social decision-making continues at present rates the point will soon be reached when ethics will be defined simply as obedience to the law—and this would be disastrous.

D. Neither the free-enterprise and pluralistic economic system nor the political democratic system have yet developed instruments for coping with long-range problems. Illustrative is the report of January 21, 1977 from the Joint Economic Committee of the Congress which said that the federal performances are suffering from two major shortcomings:

> a lack of integrated policy-making within both the executive and legislative branches which has caused the nation to tackle problems in bits and pieces, and a lack of foresight in averting problems because they simply do not have the mechanisms to anticipate, analyze, and understand them.

Hazel Henderson of the Princeton Center for Alternative Futures said that we are "drowning in irrelevant data, inappropriately collected, using old models based on confused goals."

E. Because the need for large-scale organizations is explicitly recognized, the meaning of competition must be redefined.

F. Despite the remark by W. Michael Blumenthal, Treasury Secretary in the Carter Administration that business and government have developed an interdependence and involvement with each other to a degree which a great many of his colleagues find difficult to accept or even understand, labor and government are clearly accepted by business as having legitimate roles to play in a free economy.

G. Key value-forming institutions—church, family, and school—are themselves in such disarray they may not contribute significantly in the near future to ethical reinvigoration; if this assessment is correct heavier burdens fall on businessmen's shoulders.

III. Business

A. The distinction between old-fashioned capitalism and modern enterprise is basic and the corporate executive accepts his obligations to the larger society.

B. The identifying mark of the new enterprise system is professional responsibility defined as the sophisticated balancing of claims by various interest groups—stockholders, employees, customers, and the larger public.

C. A renewed emphasis on human values requires the corporation to develop a working climate wherein each individual can constructively translate personal aspirations important to him into performance and results important to others.

D. Moral improprieties by the few have given a black eye to the entire corporate community so that ethical renewal is essential. But the norms for making ethical assessments are not static but changing—sometimes clear and often ambiguous.

E. Professions other than management (notably law and accounting) also bear a heavy responsibility for the effective and ethical performance of the modern corporation.

F. The clamor for corporate reform will encourage large enterprises to reassess the composition of their boards to assure a greater range of competence and of representation.

The Challenge

To conclude: a sense of expectancy permeates America—a feeling that new socio-philosophic fields remain to be explored, boundary lines demarcated, mechanisms for ethical trade-offs established, and a new human fulfillment made possible. The basic perception is that America and the world confront a watershed. It is a personal judgment—and possibly a mistaken one—that behind the clanging cymbals, rumbling rhetoric, and clamors for instant reform is an unstated issue which relates to our priorities for justice and freedom. Comment on this subjective viewpoint is essential.

For the longest period of human history great thinkers—from Socrates, Plato, and Aristotle in the Greek traditions to Thomas Hobbes in the modern philosophic idiom—emphasized justice. Since the eighteenth century, however, the tendency has been somewhat in the "opposite" direction to favor liberty. Whether one examines the thought of Europeans (Locke and Smith, Rousseau and Kant), of American constitutionalists (Adams and Jefferson), or of the classic essays by John Stuart Mill, the constant and emphatic theme is liberty. The results of this philosophic emphasis are important. Corporations became legitimate not simply because they were efficient but because they represented a voluntary response by free individuals who, acting together, could do more than anyone could do singly. Democratic government was good because it, above all, recognized the importance of liberty as the expression of individuality.

But the social order is shifting. Paul Johnson, who served as editor of the respected English journal *New Statesman,* remarked in November of 1976 that if, even ten years ago, someone had said we are going to have to undertake a vigorous battle on behalf of individual liberties, he would not have believed. Johnson believes now! In our country Milton Friedman keeps reminding us of the fragility of freedom and that, contrary to the popular view, it is not the natural state of man.

The new emphasis is on equality with a novel twist: it is equality in sharing rather than equality of opportunity. Is this, therefore, the wave of the future or a vulgar aberration? Is it a variation on the theme of justice? For misguided or not, the egalitarian drive is one of the most potent forces in the world today.

Even here discussions are inconclusive; for to dwell on notions of justice, liberty, and fraternity is to recognize how much and how long Western man has talked of the first, more recently of the second, and almost never of the third. Even James Fitzjames Stephen, who published the classic study in 1876 on *Liberty, Equality and Fraternity,* confessed that he could understand men wanting liberty and justice. But brotherly love? Scarcely, because fraternity is not conveniently translated into reality by law and politics. Indeed, it is quite possible that contemporary liberal political thought which supports egalitarianism is essentially individualistic and unfraternal, and that fraternity is discussed by moderns in the sense of Cain and Abel.

There is a spiritual thirst for justice, freedom, and fraternity. One knows it. In this moral maelstrom executives will either find refuge or give refuge. But their power precludes ethical evasiveness; they will be involved in the one great decision every society must make from time to time: *how to live in society and community?* No society can exist unless people agree fundamentally on what is decent and indecent, reasonable and unreasonable, offensive and inoffensive. The question always to be asked is the one raised of old by Pericles: "Are we people who pride ourselves more on this than on that?"

As America moves toward a new century and a new millenium others will surely ask Pericles' question. So shall we. But primarily on Americans rests the awesome responsibility for answering it.

PART ONE:
THE MORAL ENVIRONMENT

Carl Madden

1

Forces Which Influence Ethical Behavior

One of the themes struck in the opening in "Overview" is the clash of values which Western moral tradition has brought to contemporary corporate leaders. In the following two-part analysis, Carl Madden expands and clarifies this theme. He concludes that the heart of the liberal position, expressed in a utilitarian ethic, lacks a definable posture toward the end of human action. The business "game" is therefore played according to its own rules, chief of which is the performance ethic. The jurors (investment analysts, credit analysts, and loan officers, insurance companies, and managers of other people's money) judge performance by the bottom line and not by the process. The other great juror is government which, through regulatory agencies, looks more at the process (assure competition) and less at the results.

Each set of jurors may not even agree on the criteria whereby business should be judged, yet each exercises a powerful force on the corporation. Difficult ethical questions arise: Is "winning" the name of the game? Does a successful business career require a hard head and a harder heart? Are business schools inculcating an ethic of conformity in their graduates? Are the ultimate ethical answers to

---

CARL H. MADDEN, *Professor of Business at American University, was Chief Economist of the U.S. Chamber of Commerce, 1963–76. He has also been economist for the Senate Banking Currency Committee and consultant to the U.S. Treasury Department. He was Dean of the College of Business Administration, Lehigh University, 1960–63. A former president of the National Association of Business Economists, Dr. Madden has edited and written many books on business topics, including* Clash of Culture: Management in an Age of Changing Values.

*be found in science and its quest for objective truth? The interesting
questions elicit from Madden interesting answers.*

C. C. W.

I. External Factors

Few are prepared to argue that reported business scandals have
not had considerable effect on the declining public credibility in what
corporate executives say and do. Faith in the free enterprise system
and even in big business has been reasonably constant; trust in the
ethical behavior of executives has plummeted.

It is pointless to repeat the charges. What is essential is to note
the social changes America is experiencing and to ask what fundamental forces, as distinct from symptoms or occasional behavioral
aberrations, are at work shaping our ethics.

This chapter will be divided into two main sections. Emphasis in
the first is placed on those *external* forces, past and present, which
influence the moral conduct of business leaders. The second section
incorporates certain internal factors that significantly influence business values and the ethical criteria employed to judge executive conduct.

In the first section I propose to argue four things—

1. that advanced industrial societies are caught in an ethical dilemma where
   the old ethic of liberalism is inadequate and where the new one, based on
   the role of science, is not clearly perceived;
2. that when society approves ever-increasing wealth-creation it imposes upon
   businessmen this powerful ethic: performance for results;
3. that big government is a consequence of big business and must serve as
   an external constraint on corporations; and
4. that trade and industry associations generally exert a benign influence and
   that even those geared to lobbying (the Chamber of Commerce and the
   National Association of Manufacturers) are less likely to induce unethical
   behavior than the so-called "Washington Representative."

The Ethical Dilemma of Scientific Societies

Frank Knight, perhaps the most elegant spokesman for the ethics
of free enterprise, observed that "the problem of ethics is the most
baffling subdivision of the social problem as a whole." Knight was

referring in 1947 to a problem that Walter Lippmann had addressed earlier in his brilliant 1938 study, *Essays in the Public Philosophy*, but it still haunts the modern world and, in particular, the United States. While society depends on, or indeed, almost consists of, moral like-mindedness, the 1960-1970 period of social transition found the society divided and sadly lacking in what could be called "moral common sense," or what Lippmann called "a public philosophy."

The two hundred-year epoch of modern economic growth, despite its complex causation, has had as its major source—generating radically different patterns of the last two centuries—the emergence of modern science. *The dilemma for ethics that besets scientific societies such as the United States concerns the role of science itself in defining, conditioning, and shaping ethics; in my view, this issue represents the central ethical dilemma of the last two centuries.* Further it is my conviction that while learned debate rages over the question, still the power of scientific concepts, discoveries, and tests of truth—tests that appeal to evidence of the senses—are sufficient to change ethical standards before our eyes.

STATING THE THESIS

The late Jacob Bronowski, one of our great physicists, lucidly (in *Science and Human Values*) states the issue of science and ethics:

> Is it true that the concepts of science and those of ethics and values belong to different worlds? Is the world of *what is* subject to test, and is the world of *what ought to be* subject to no test? I do not believe so. Such concepts as justice, humanity, and the full life have not remained fixed in the last four hundred years, whatever churchmen and philosophers may pretend. In their modern sense they did not exist when Aquinas wrote; they do not now exist in civilizations which disregard the physical fact. (Emphasis added)

The argument of this essay on the ethics of the lead actors can now be stated: *the rise of science and its eighteenth century concomitant—the advent of the free society—has yielded undeniable and growing power of production, through the evolution of economic processes. That advance, in turn, redefines ethical norms.* It increases the ability of the human species to survive by doing good through greater justice for its own betterment; or to become extinct by eschewing knowledge, by doing ill, leading to its own decline and threat of species-death. The ethical imperative of scientific societies can be read in the subtle evidence, daily multiplying around us, brought by science and its spirit at work in people, of ethics derived from the structure of life itself.

We live today in a clash of cultures, the culture of science and the culture of traditions unwilling or unable to face the reality of stubborn, brute, irreducible fact. It is the sanction of experienced fact that has changed and shaped all the concepts of people who have felt the Scientific Revolution. That sanction clashes with the sanction of revered but outworn belief about facts or principles that, relying on tradition, cannot withstand the test of fitting into the context of reality created by the novel enterprise, seen over the centuries and seen as a whole, that science has constructed.

When, therefore, the constraints and empowerments of our lead actors, corporate executives, are subsequently examined—both the external forces operating on them, and the internal forces they must deal with—the theme of this chapter should be kept paramount. The modern world is haunted not so keenly by the vision of heaven as by the Faustian realization that a static and fixed heaven cannot be the home of those who have eaten richly of the fruit of the Tree of Knowledge. Our universe will not sit still for mere humans. It rages over eons of light years with dynamic energy of awesome power, stretching from black holes that suck light itself back into their innards, to galactic fireworks displays of supernovas that to us seem to light the sky.

Says Bronowski: "The gravest indictment that can be made of our generalized culture is, in fact, that it erodes our sense of the context in which judgments should be made." There can be no ethical justification for simple scoundrels, to be sure, wherever they are found— and whether their scope is petty or grand. But more than that, whether we like it or even know it, we are responsible for the future of the earth and of all life on the earth. We are the custodians of mankind's cultural evolution.

In examining the forces at work on the lead actors in corporations, we need not settle for either naive outrage or resigned bafflement. Rather, we need to create a context in which to answer such questions as: What happened to our society in the 1960s and the 1970s? Where does it seem to be heading, willy-nilly? By what test of authority or evidence of the senses does informed and wise judgment of experience persuade us where we should head for? And what is the role of economic enablement, of economic power, at this stage of the evolutionary journey of the human race?

Part of the current wide-scale ignorance that exists in the United

States today concerning business and economics—reflected in survey after survey of public opinion—is a lack of appreciation for the ethical implications of the politico-economic system. A review of the main ethical assumptions involved in free enterprise as a social-economic form allows an evaluation of recent corporate conduct according to the norms that ought to be accepted by supporters of that system.[1]

The Ethics of the Liberal System

LIBERTY AS THE CORE

Liberal, laissez-faire economic organization holds that each individual (really meaning each family) should be free to use his own resources in his own way to satisfy his own wants. The primary ethical claim of the system is that each gets the consequences of his own activities; that is, he takes out of the social enterprise what he puts in. At its ideal, people contribute their resources of skill or property to a joint product and each takes from it the "equivalent" of what he puts in. The measure of equivalence is the exchange value or money price of the contribution. It may appear arguable that such a system leaves little or no place for ethics. The thesis here is, on the contrary, that such a social system embodies a genuine ethical ideal and that, once understood, it is clear and defensible, though assuredly not closed to adaptation and change, nor is it devoid of inconsistencies.

Its essential socio-ethical principle is that all relations between people should rest on mutual consent and not coercion, either by other people or by the state. The ideal function of the state is to prevent the use of coercion by one group or person against another. This idea of the state as a vehicle of using coercion only negatively is separate from the issue of what may be right or wrong in individual conduct.

It should be made clear that laissez faire has never been advocated in a strict or absolute sense. Every advocate has recognized the need for restrictions on individual freedom and for positive action by the state—such as for defense, the administration of justice, and many other public functions. Indeed, these functions for Adam Smith explicitly included public works and education "for all ages." Taxation by the state was favored, not in accord with benefits received, but to equalize the tax burden. And liberalism has always supported the doctrine that every member of society is entitled by right to live at some

---

[1] The following account is largely based on Frank H. Knight, "Ethics and Economic Reform," *Freedom and Reform* (New York: Harper & Brothers, 1947).

minimum standard provided by society as a whole, from revenues of taxation levied as described when the individual is unable to provide such subsistence through personal efforts or the voluntary sale of services, or from family help or private charity. Finally, liberals since Adam Smith have always recognized as a legitimate state function the provision for the education of youth and, in varying degrees, for activities designed to promote the diffusion of knowledge, the general advancement of science and art, and the general culture.

The nineteenth-century liberal advocates of laissez faire held as their ideal that of mutual consent applied in all relations of life. Indeed, historically the early struggle for freedom related to religions even more than to economic freedom. Their concern with this particular freedom arose from an assumption, right or wrong, that the major opportunity for coercion of individuals by other individuals arose in the sphere of economic life. The liberal argued that economic life is pragmatically nearly inseparable from other forms of social life and, therefore, that social and economic systems are mutually interdependent and interactive. To this view, it is a fact of experience that every form of human association gives rise to power relations and conflicts of interest, to rivalry and struggle. Cultural rivalry and personal clash are far broader in scope than the purely economic. From Olympic gymnasts to ballet, from opera singers to chess players, rivalry seems to be inherent in human activity.

The essence of the liberal position—an essence hard to grasp without reflection—is that it has no position. It is not logically committed to any particular conception of the nature or the content of the good, individual or social. It is the heart of the liberal position, the utilitarian ethic, to have no concrete position regarding the end of action. The end of action is whatever the individual wants and strives to get, to do, or to be. The view is that the individual is the best judge of his own goals, albeit not a perfect judge since there are exceptions to his freedom in respect to consensual restraints or illegal activities. But it is held that the individual is a better judge of personal goals than "the government" or some other coercive corporate body.

The upshot is that, in this view, a greater total achievement of ends actually desired and pursued comes about (and therefore in that sense a greater realization of the "good") when there is widespread and general application of the principle of freedom, within the limitation of mutual consent, than from the application of any other general rule of conduct. What is more, these principles involve no moral obligation on anyone to practice efficiency. Indeed, efficiency is not a norm of laissez-faire doctrine. People are free to pursue "poverty, chastity, and obedience" universal "love," or any other form of ascetic or extravagant practice, so long as they do not attempt to coerce others or infringe on their similar freedom. Liberalism allows economic life to be organized by any collection of individuals as they choose through any type of cooperation and any mode of apportioning burdens and benefits. Liberalism means that individuals and groups should not coerce others, not merely in economic life, but throughout all aspects of life.

INSTRUMENTALISM

Even though the logic of liberalism envisaged no position about the content of the good life, it did create simplistic views of values and motives because it was, historically, mainly instrumental. That is, the main argument for laissez faire was to increase efficiency. So, in fact, it took the individual's actual possession of means as a datum, as a given fact. Indeed, so doing is the main weakness of the system because freedom is the freedom to use power, of which a given individual may possess much or little, and still be designated as equally free. Anatole France stated the dilemma: "In capitalistic societies, both rich men and tramps are free to sleep under bridges." But even so, the implication of utilitarian philosophy, however crude its statement, is that freedom may be, and often was considered, not merely as instrumental but as an end or value in itself.

The instrumental view toward achieving productive efficiency was highly developed by associated economic theory and is today a dominant criterion of public policy. The idea is that individuals (given their ownership of productive services of human skill, tangible capital goods, or land, insofar as they behave in accord with the principle of economic rationality) apportion their productive capacity among all the alternatives of use open in order to maximize the total "return" in all forms of return, expressed in, or reduced to, common units on the individual's own scale of values. In short, a person uses his means to maximize his utility by engaging in exchange with others to increase his total income. And, as economic theory demonstrates—given these and other restrictive assumptions—the outcome of rational behavior is the maximum provision to each individual, under the given conditions, of the "means of life."

The effect of this theory of economic organization which we call the free enterprise system—by freeing the urge to self-advancement from Christian canons and proscriptions about self-aggrandizement—created a separation of "business" from other areas of life. There developed a feeling that it was "right" to play the business game according to its special rules; that it is not just ethically legitimate but even positively virtuous to desire to maximize one's income, subject to the sweeping constraint of mutual preconsent in all relations with others. Liberalism cast no light on what to do with income, why it was wanted, or whether any obligation existed beyond honesty and non-predation. "Business" was "business"; business was not "charity." The primitive notion of equity, the *lex talionis*, eye-for-an-eye, tooth-for-a-tooth principle of reciprocal exchange gave way fully to the idea of exchange through markets with flexible prices. While the notion of a "fair" price, and even of a considerate or humane price, has persisted in modern civilization, traditional judgment gave way to free adjustment in markets of exchange prices.

The liberal view of government was that, above all, it is a coercive force and must be limited. As seen by liberalism, government is not individuals, but is essentially "the Law." What was wanted was "a government of laws and not men." The difficulty about this notion of law as an ethical principle is that its content can never be taken as beyond dispute; it has to be interpreted, enforced and, on occasion, made afresh. As to coercion of individuals, the primary duty of the state to prevent, was to proscribe "force and fraud." From such simple concepts came recognition that monopoloy is a form of coercive power and inadmissible in a free society. However, the liberal doctrine and its "individualism" expressly include, rather than exclude guidance over one individual's activities by another's when it means increased efficiency through more competent direction. Rather than ruling out the private corporation, individualism actually promoted such voluntary association.

A CRITIQUE OF LIBERALISM

Three unclear areas of liberalism should be noted: contract, persuasion, and free mutual relations. The freedom of an individual to contract away, to alienate his own freedom had to be restricted in its enforcement on individual labor contracts if liberty in any pragmatic sense was to be preserved. But this meant that people whose only resource is their own labor power were put in an especially weak position because they were dependent on opportunities open in the market to use their services to earn a livelihood.

Next, there was doctrinal trouble about the whole area of persuasion

—advertising. To the degree that products were not standard but capable of differentiation, market dealings inevitably became entangled with efforts to persuade by both buyer and seller. These phenomena were doctrinally excluded from liberalism except insofar as persuasion consisted in the provision of information. So, the task of law in avoiding force and fraud was made difficult in this area.

Third, the primary principle of liberalism, namely, free mutual relations, took no account of inequality in economic position. Freedom to accumulate carried the possibility of cumulative increases in the inequality of economic power, and this has been realized in individual and corporate accumulations. In addition, economic power brought other forms of power, especially in politics. To the extent that free association is the *only* means to control modes of action and social behavior which do not involve force or fraud, free association itself may be used to aggrandize power by practice of exclusivity. It also means that all notions of the effective purposes of social processes are excluded from evaluation or discussion.

Even when evaluated by its own standards, the single biggest defect of liberal individualism is that it takes the individual as given. It views the social problem as one of right relations among individuals. But this runs counter to clear and unalterable facts of life. The individual, as a matter of logic, cannot be taken as given for purposes of social policy for the very reason that individuals are largely formed in and by the social process. In modern society there is no such animal as the self-made man or woman. Therefore, since the nature of any individual is affected by social action, social policy has to be judged by the kind of individuals it produces. The paradox for liberalism is that it never meant individualism and could not do so, given the unalterable facts of life about organized society.

By taking the individual—that evanescent phenomenon that comes into the world destitute and helpless—as being given, the doctrine of liberalism contains the fallacy of also taking society for granted. The canon of free association by given individuals overlooks the paramount question which is this: what are the long-run consequences of freedom itself? What will people do with freedom? Indeed, what kind of people is freedom creating? What consequences will their acts have on society as a whole? Market dealings do create efficiency. We have still to appreciate how much efficiency. But they leave unprotected wide areas of contemporary individual interests. It is not that we should not cheer the market but that, as Arthur Okun suggested, it deserves only two cheers, not three. Some values are too dear to be priced through markets and for the very reason that markets are so powerfully effective. The society has some obligation for compulsory coordination of valued activities by some inclusive group organization when the individual cannot possibly know except within an extremely narrow segment of time and space, the effects of his transactions even upon living persons and their interests—still less on "civilization."

The Impact on Wealth Creation

Having put forth a sketch of the ethics of enterprise economics, it only remains to take a brief look at its impact on wealth creation before examining the impact and force of its effect on the ethics of corporate executives. No apologies should be needed for striving to define contexts in which balanced and informed appraisal of corporate ethics can be attained.

In a nutshell, science and the enterprise economy during these last 200 years have created, have invented, a new form of wealth. To begin with a simple fact: up to about 1776 the human race had always been poor. Awareness that the history of hominids stretches back 3.5 to 4 million years ago and that farming is only 8,000 years old puts a two-century period in perspective as relatively short. Because the world has been poor, the process of changing it is hardly over. But it is changing. In a crude estimate, Buckminster Fuller noted that it was not until 1907 that 9 percent of the world's population could be said to live under conditions of adequacy; by 1970, it was perhaps 40 percent, counting the Chinese.

Without modern wealth invented in the West, all would still be poor; life expectancy would be about thirty years; nine of every ten human beings would be consigned to a short and hard life of unremitting toil on the land.

The basis of modern wealth is, in one word, knowledge. It is tested knowledge of nature, transferred to technology—the knowledge of means—which enables man to produce more with less effort and with less material and energy. But knowledge of means extends beyond its application to physical tools; it includes new forms of organization which enable men to use technology effectively.

TWO FALLACIES

There are two erroneous notions about the nature of our new wealth. One is that it must come from exploitation of some by others. Before the advent of science and the Industrial Revolution that was true. Amid a severely limited total output with little prospect of growth the rich grew rich by taking from the poor. But modern wealth is different. It comes from producing more tomorrow with the same amount of resources as used today. Exploitation quite literally does not pay. What does pay in a modern laboratory, plant, or office are trained, educated, healthy, safe, and voluntarily willing human beings —not ignorant, ill-fed, threatened and coerced slaves.

The second error about the new wealth is that it depends on natural resources. The new wealth, by using the growing knowledge of the structure of nature—its physical, chemical, biochemical, and physiological configuration and behavior—has literally created natural resources from previously "useless" material. While one can grow rich by finding gold, oil, chrome, or copper, every one of these resources has a potential substitute. Even the wealth of Nauro Island and its guano, or the Arab Emirates and their oil, depend on outside markets —on reliable and continuous outside contractual demand.

Japan's success illustrates dramatically that it is not natural resources but knowledge and markets—know-how and study of other's desires— that is the key to gaining new wealth. A close parallel to Japan is Israel, with its powerful thrust toward labor-force skill and knowledge, its heavy emphasis on science-based industry, and its astute diplomacy directed to widening markets and reducing barriers to trade and investment for goods produced there, whether by Israeli or foreign investment or producers.

There is a related point. Having been a colony does not make a country poor. Most colonies were better off when they became independent than when they became colonies. Singapore, Korea, and Brazil were all once colonies whereas Ethiopia and Liberia, never colonies, are not doing as well. One form of exploitation is that of the swindler. His gain is his victim's absolute loss. Another form is when the stronger deals with the weaker to their mutual advantage but with more of that advantage going to the sronger party. Here, although the weaker still gains more than if left alone, such exploitation may be unfair or reprehensible. But it does not make the weaker poorer.

Are rich industrial countries holding back the poorer areas of the world or using up the world's resources? My answer is emphatically in the negative. The rich are not holding back the poorer areas; rather, they startle the poorer areas into cultural conflict and growing awareness of the power of knowledge to yield wealth. They are using up some few exhaustible resources because these resources are still cheap relative to substitutes that are yet to be fashioned or perhaps are more greedy of energy. We need to be far more careful in our use of exhaustible resources. But there is no solid reason to beleive that advancing knowledge will not furnish new resources and new resource-saving techniques. On the contrary, present theoretical understanding of nature reveals that we have nowhere nearly approached the limits of what is possible within the known principles of nature's structure. A United Nations study, headed by Nobel Prize-winning economist Wassily Leontief, concluded that the world has enough resources to support both a growing population and rising living standards.

The key to understanding the new wealth of the last two centuries is to realize that, increasingly, resources are the result of knowledge embodied in physical capital and new forms of organization. Indeed, this relatively new enterprise economy has created a new and unique economic epoch in the history of humankind. The major sources of its efficiency—its growing productivity—have been investments in intangible capital employed to improve the tangible capital stock. These chief determinants of growing productivity have been investments in —and this list can be surprising—education, research and development, the health and safety of the labor force, and the increasing ability to move about the nation and the world on the part of people, jobs, money capital, information, and capital plants.

The Impact on Corporate Executives

The external forces at work on the behavior of corporate executives can now be examined. By external forces are meant forces involved in the operation of the marketplace, construed broadly, and forces outside the marketplace. The internal forces facing the executive are those impinging from within the corporation and its internal disciplines, constraints, and avenues of choice.

THE ETHICS OF COMPETITION

As to the forces of the marketplace, perhaps the first issue of ethics, based on the standard of liberalism itself, is whether corporate executives are acting unethically when they practice monopoly. First, everyone knows that Sherman (1890) and Clayton (1914) Acts plus their amendments (1936, 1950) have through practice become a well-knit body of rule and precedent. The two basic classes of monopoly behavior they attack are (1) cooperation among firms to restrict markets and so to reap "excessive" profits; and (2) market dominance which permits a firm to withhold output and force up prices above their level if there were competition, in order to gain "excessive" profits. Since 1914, the Federal Trade Commission has enforced antitrust laws through administrative action. Some parts of the economy are exempt from antitrust laws—agriculture and fishing, labor unions, regulated industries, baseball and football, newspaper mergers, and agreements (cartels) among exporters to share overseas markets. In these cases, it should be clearly understood that public policy has approved monopoly behavior.

Second, we should realize that in a broad sense the United States economy must be viewed as competitive. In two hundred years, real output per capita has doubled every generation. From 1872 to 1972, output rose fortyfold, allowing a sevenfold rise in output per person to $5,600 per head in 1972 and, since then, to over $7,000 per head in current dollars. Transport and communications gains, still going on, both widen markets and choices that reduce place-monopoly. In this sense metropolitan America today is more competitive than small-town America of yesterday. The number of United States businesses per 1,000 people in the population is rising, not falling. And the share of the top 200 or 500 large corporations in sales, assets, or value added has not risen significantly.

To be sure, assets are concentrated in major corporations just as population is concentrated in major cities or doctoral degrees granted are concentrated in major universities. In economics, nearly every significant aspect of activity is skewed toward rewarding effectiveness with growth. Still, corporations have not expanded their role in American life during the past fifteen years, though government has. Most people do not now work and never have worked for large corporations; most production does not now take place and never has taken place in large corporations; manufacturing provides jobs to only 18.5 million out of a work force of more than 85 million. The top 200 such corporations employ less than a third of all manufacturing workers, or less than 9 percent of the work force, and the proportion is declining as the service industries grow. Concentrated industries in the United States manufacturing from 1960 to 1970 earned 11 percent profits on equity capital invested, compared with 10.68 percent on equity earned by nonconcentrated manufacturing such as food, apparel, leather, and printing-publishers where many firms exist in these industries and compete with one another.

Are Major Corporations Too Big?—It is surely debatable whether very large United States corporations "should be" broken up. In Congress, the late Senator Hart of Michigan introduced in 1973 the "Industrial Reorganization Bill" to create such a presumption for seven major industries—chemicals and drugs, electrical machinery and equipment, electrical computing and communications, equipment, energy, iron and steel, motor vehicles, and nonferrous metals. After voluminous testimony by experts the bill got nowhere. The claim was that the structure of these industries creates a *prima facie* case for monopoly results, enough to justify that the firms in these industries should assume the burden of proving to a proposed new government agency that they are not monopolies. But the evidence of monopoly results was not convincing. Further, foreign-based large companies have recently (until the 1974-75 recession) grown faster than American-based companies. And, in twelve countries, the same high-technology industries that gain cost economies by large-scale output were concentrated to about the same degree. Surveys of public opinion show that a large majority of Americans do not favor the break-up of large corporations.

It is difficult to make the case that corporations and their executives fail to meet the test of the marketplace in producing goods and services people are willing and able to buy. It is even difficult to sustain the view that concentrated industries—many that compete in world markets—generate monopoly profits or fail to respond to changes in taste or technology or withhold ontput. At least, the broad majority of the public does not agree with the view. Still, public opinion of such consumer activists as Ralph Nader, is approving, moderate, and sophisticated. People like and admire Nader. They believe he does good as a corporate gadfly. They believe Nader errs on occasion. But they do not wish to see Nader's efforts inhibited. The public, however, takes for granted the marketing efforts that preoccupy corporate executives.

Turning to the impact on corporate executives in meeting the marketplace test, most people who do not follow the investment markets have little awareness of the volatility of markets or the genuine risks that discipline corporate executive behavior. Among investment bankers, surveys have shown that, of one hundred proposals for financing, only about three are worth a second look. Of the three worthy of serious consideration, about half are actually financed. And of those financed, scarcely more than half yield significant returns—usually aftei several years. Among new retail products, about one out of seven yield profitable returns after test marketing; a good rule-of-thumb for product lines actually being marketed is that 80 percent of profits are derived from 20 percent of products.

Salesmanship—Something should be said explicitly about the ethics of salesmanship. Successful sales efforts, varying between tangible and intangible products, require special personality traits: the ability to tolerate frequent rejection, persuasiveness against resistance, self-motivation, and the ability to negotiate under pressure. Bargaining is normal for big ticket items. Sales and distributive middlemen add value to products by supplying information about markets and by providing convenience of place and of adaptation to customer needs. Abuses in stock and bond sales led in 1934 to creating the Securities and Exchange Commission, which regulates securities transactions through rigid requirements of information disclosure in order to assure honesty in dealings and self-policing.

Much retail sales activity relies on brand names, national advertising, and packaging to create point-of-purchase sales appeal—as in supermarkets, discount stores, and other self-service stores—that sharply economizes on sales personnel and leaves much choice to consumers. Mail order sales, such as of the 45,000 items in Sears catalogues, rely wholly on precisely accurate information and the right of exchange or refund without question. Consumer laws have moved to shift liability to manufacturers of branded products widely distributed. Sales by big business to business or government—big capital items, large contracts and the like—have involved in some instances excessive entertainment expenditures, bribes and even procuring.

The competitive picture inferred from textbook models of the economy, though useful for short-run analysis, is a misleading caricature of competitive reality. Modern economic price theory, or microtheory, rests for much of its validity on assumptions that taste and technology are constant, that markets consist of single-product firms, that products are more or less standardized, and that firms are small relative to markets. The theory has moderate usefulness in providing basic understanding of market behavior. But "pure" or "perfect" competition not only seldom, if ever, existed but is hardly a standard for the real world of evolving tastes, technology, industries, economic processes, and regions. Such theoretical competition could never exist, given the nature of today's technology, without huge economic waste caused by neglect of economies of scale.

Innovations—Modern corporate executives face a far more pervasive form of competition than suggested by these theoretical models. It is the competition of innovations. Few informed Americans have to be reminded of the great half-century waves of innovation that swept over the society: First, 1790 to 1840 was the era of steam power and textile machinery that produced the flowering of New England. Next, 1840 to 1890, the railroad and the telegraph opened up the Middle West and made Chicago the city of railroads and hog butcher to the world. From 1890 to perhaps 1940 was the age of the dynamo that lighted American homes and wired the farms into electric power, the automobile which created the suburbs and put Mom at work as a taxi driver, and the airplane which put Dad on wings. Since World War II, and as these forces strengthened, the age of the Scientific Revolution emerged. New insights and methods reduced the empirical content of scientific study and made research systematic, first in great industrial laboratories of General Electric and Bell Laboratories, and later, in massive organized enterprises such as the Manhattan Project and the space effort. The Scientific Revolution of our century is still gathering force and changing, worldwide, the structure of industry.

It is not too much to say that modern competition in markets represents an analogy to biological evolution, where new economic processes are tested for their survival value against people's preferences and incomes. Corporate executives are leaders of species and subspecies of technology and social organization in an innovative process of technological evolution. Steel competes with cement and plastic, copper with laser-beamed glass fibers, printing with Haloid copying and magnetic tape, and so on. Indeed, in family budgets children compete with cars, cars with homes, homes with travel or education, and so on. One of the grossest canards against modern business is that, somehow, the real risks have been removed from production. Far from being removed, the risks of competitive decline or extinction from innovative forces require of executives ever more systematic methods of anticipatory risk sharing or aversion through research and development, new forms of marketing, and new forms of anticipating changing expectations. As Reginald Jones, Chairman of General Electric, said, "The basic strategy for corporate survival is to anticipate the changing structure of society, and serve it more effectively than competing institutions." Corporations are being forced into forecasting not merely economic, but social, political, and technological change in order to remain responsive and responsible.

THE PERFORMANCE ETHIC

The major societal force acting on corporate executives, then, is the market mechanism of the enterprise economy itself. These managers of resources, responding to highly complex signals of cost and price, of demand and supply in markets, of changes in opinion and in values in technology, and in world events, are as much shaped in their behavior as are other individuals in society by the demands and the environment where they make their lives.

The spirit needed to economize resources on behalf of themselves and others is of necessity adventuresome, rational, calculating, analytical, and acquisitive. Emphasis perforce is placed on corporate self-interest and aggrandizement, whether long or short-term. Of necessity, management action is accomplished through others and, therefore, requires tough and objective judgments of the results of other people's action. Strong appeals to the acquisitive and self-centered instincts of others are reflected in financial rewards and penalties shaping corporate personnel behavior. Power over others is made real through incentives and is exercised without apology.

Because corporate executives themselves are evaluated by results, ultimately through markets, these people are strongly results-oriented. Because they must assume burdens of risk and uncertainty they are selected for skill in evaluating and apportioning such risk. The management of advancing technology itself is risky. It requires a reasoning and agnostic mind incompatible with acceptance of—or obedience to —social canons of authority. Innovative and enterprising personalities are sought by growing firms as avidly as conformists are rewarded in stable or declining firms, or in routinist occupations. Energy is directed to sophisticated appraisal of people's factual demands, as distinct from people's protestations or claims about their tastes. Vigorous business leadership seeks growth in market shares; such growth, in turn, enlarges the scale of activity; enlargement of scale leads to impersonality in judgment, objectivity in organizing activity, and above all, results-oriented design of functions. However, since a modern corporate work force involves people chosen from a ladder of wide-ranging skills, great attention is paid in progressive corporations to human aspects of motivation and incentive out of the need for achieving efficiency.

Corporate executives themselves are evaluated strictly and diligently by a relatively little known group in business—the investment analysts of investment banking firms that manage individual, corporate, union, and other trusts, and by credit analysts and loan officers of commercial banks, insurance companies, and other managers of people's and institution's savings. Huge quantities of information are made available to these business appraisers of business in extremely efficient ways. Such persons are highly and broadly educated, rich in business experience, and are themselves rewarded by their results in choosing to invest in more rather than less profitable companies. They continuously study broad trends: social, political, and technological. They make detailed studies of individual firms: they visit plants, talk to managers, force chief executives to report to them on prospects: they compare industry and company results. And they dominate the process which determines the financial value of corporations—that is, they dominate the buying and selling of equity and debt shares and issues in specific corporations in the fast-moving and efficient capital markets of the country. Indeed, they are the agency, considered together, which expresses the final force of market appraisal on the corporations themselves and therefore on their executive. The viewpoint of securities analysts is typically oriented to "the bottom line" within a short time span.

Generalizing about the details of market influence on corporate executives can itself be dangerous. Corporations range in size from giants such as American Telephone and Telegraph to firms with fewer than twenty employees. Not only that, corporations exist in rapidly growing, stable, or declining industries of greater or less stable or cyclical demand for their output, in product or service industries, in high or low technology industries, and serving mainly industrial or consumer markets. Enormous variation occurs in executive behavior depending on individual corporate characteristics as to size, growth, location, nature of market, ownership, and many other variables. Guiding the destinies of a firm such as Thompson-Ramo-Wooldridge (TRW) which at one time had 2 percent of the nation's and 1 percent of the world's physicists, can hardly be compared to managing a separately-incorporated fast-food franchise except as to the principles of response to broad market forces and marketing, personnel, and financial principles. The scope of knowledge, however, that surrounds the successful food-franchiser, through guidance from the parent company, engages the best efforts of competing multinational firms.

GOVERNMENT

"Free enterprise" may correctly describe the United States compared to communist state-owned capitalism or even democratic-socialism in Europe and elsewhere. But the United States has a pluralistic system in which profit-making and not-for-profit sectors work interdependently to produce what people want. The liberal ethic is the bench mark for understanding our predominant social values, but its dilemmas and defects are equally important in having opened avenues for government and other not-for-profit activity. Scarcely more than two-thirds of employment was in the private sector in 1977 and nearly one-third, equally divided between government and nongovernment, was in the not-for-profit sector. The total direct share of the not-for-profit sector was 31.9 percent of employment and 26.3 percent of the gross national product. In government itself, the fastest growing sector was in state and local, not federal, employment.

By traditional American standards and values, government plays a very large role in the economy. Government at all levels—federal, state, and local—receives an amount equivalent to nearly 40 percent of the value of the nation's yearly production, buys more than 20 percent of it, and redistributes from some people to others about 11 percent of total personal income. In fact, if in-kind government transfers are counted as if they added money income to the recipient (which, in effect, they do tax-free), the 11 percent figure would be larger. A 1976 government study for Congress showed that, if in-kind transfers such as the equivalent monetary, after-tax value of medicaid, food stamps, and the like are counted, we had 50 percent fewer officially-designated poor people—5.4 million families and single people, or 6.9 percent of the total—rather than 10.5 million families and single people, or 13.8 percent of the total, as counted by Census data relying entirely on money income.

Government is a force of large and growing effect on corporate executive behavior; it exercises influence over business through legislation, law enforcement, administration of justice, taxation, spending, and regulation. Government and the non-for-profit sector have grown because of the irreversible process of social transformation involved in economic growth. Rising urbanism, population growth, and increasingly large-scale industrialism have all—as consequences of and part of economic growth—increased a demand for government services. Once the American people had made the choices for strong defense, more access to higher education, improved medical care, and suburban life, the die was cast.

In a very real sense, nothing about the growth of government for such purposes is inconsistent with the views of Adam Smith and other classic liberals. However, the scope of government action required by the institutional and ideological changes linked to the growth process itself were not foreseen. And they are still confused by some modern "conservatives." There is no way that the nation can accommodate a rising population and an irrepressible demand for the amenities of suburban life unless all levels of government expand, given limitations on the ability of private business to provide such goods and services. Business has expressed more concern about "stopping government growth" than it has shown ingenuity in offering in its stead private market performance.

A second aspect of government growth flows from defects of liberalism. Frank Knight, for one, points out that liberalism takes the individual as given and does not consider the inequality of power that may exist between individuals. The imbalance of power between management and labor generated the labor union movement. Another defect of liberalism mentioned by Knight is its assumption that individuals will be informed. Economic theory requires, in order to prove that choices in a market system are preferable to choices in other systems, that the choices be rational. If choices are to be rational, they must be informed. The consumerist movement derived from failure by corporations to supply accurate information on which rational consumer judgment could be based.

Indeed, the irreversible character of social transformation generated by economic growth is well illustrated by the history of early consumerism. The railroad and the telegraph created the prospect of mass continental markets. To serve them, corporations developed trademarks, brand names, and the idea of national advertising to identify and create appeal for distantly manufactured products. The mass magazine, marketed to serve as a vehicle for such advertising, in its efforts to generate circulation, turned to vivid writers. One such magazine, *McClure's,* accepted Ida Tarbell's article on terrible abuses in oil trusts. Thus, the school of journalism called "muckraking" went national. The resulting furor of public opinion helped pass the first consumer-oriented business regulation, the Pure Food and Drug Act of 1907. And "consumerism" was born as a national political force.

PERFORMANCE ETHIC VERSUS REGULATION

Regulation of business, beginning with the Sherman Act of 1890 passed to control monopoly behavior, then burgeoning during the 1930s, generated many administrative agencies—the so-called "ABC" agencies—that regulate utilities (such as telephone, electric power, natural gas, transportation, communications), finance, and to a growing degree, financial aspects of housing. These "old line" administrative agencies have come under increasing criticism from economists and others of various political persuasions.

The story is a long one, filled with esoterica, but is not abused by mention of two factors. One is the doctrine of the "natural" monopoly, a justification for regulation as a substitute for competition which crumbles under the onslaught of advancing science. It was thought, for example, that railroads were a "natural" monopoly, that is, an industry in which the largest firm is *naturally* the most efficient because of economies of scale. Therefore, the Interstate Commerce Commission was established to grant railroads territorial monopoly and to regulate rates. Today, not only railroads but even American Telephone and Telegraph face competition from alternative technologies, and confusion exists over their continued regulation. If AT&T is not a natural monopoly, then it is hard to see how there are any at all.

The second reason, related to the first, is that in many cases empirical evidence suggests that government regulatory agencies actually behave as government cartels. Just as in a private agreement among corporations, the agencies divide the market through official territorial or other franchises, prevent competition, and set prices higher than competition will yield. The effect is to keep the supply less than competition will provide. Harvard professor and former presidential adviser Hendrik Houthakker wrote about "forty-five sacred cows" for President Ford's 1974 summit meeting and urged that forty-five regulatory agencies be abolished or drastically reorganized.

On this question business opinion is divided. Affected executives are generally opposed to regulatory reform. Notably divided are transportation executives over the question of abolishing the Interstate Commerce Commission. Truckers like the high rates set for railroads; barge line operators like the ICC protection of their rates; railroads have learned to live comfortably with the ICC. So none of the ground transportation modes want change. Indeed, a further charge against ABC agencies is that they are staffed by personnel who, the more they learn about industry, the friendlier they become. For example, while it is widely thought that network television is a "private, competitive enterprise," a strong case can be made that the Federal Communications Commission perpetrates monopoly or quasi-monopoly through restrictive granting of licenses. The networks are a government-sponsored cartel.

Besides ABC regulation, business executives face a proliferation of other forms of regulation to deal with civil rights of employees (Equal

Employment Opportunities Commission), safety (Occupational Safety and Health Administration), the environment (Environmental Protection Agency), and many others, including from time to time regulation of wages and prices. Since the 1960s, it is fair to say that there has been an explosion of consumerist and environmentalist legislation.

To illustrate what has happened one can use the *Catalog of Federal Regulations Affecting the Iron and Steel Industry* published by the federal government's Council on Wage and Price Stability in December 1976. It considered regulation of the industry in the following categories: (1) environmental (water, air pollution); (2) safety (occupational safety and health regulation); (3) civil rights (Equal Employment Opportunities Commission); (4) industrial relations (including general labor disputes and liability to employees, plus regulation of pensions through the Employee Retirement Incomes Security Act of 1974); (5) antitrust regulation (including the Department of Justice merger guidelines, enforcement of antitrust by the Department of Justice and the Federal Trade Commission, and statistical regulations requiring line-of-business reporting to the Federal Trade Commission); (6) foreign trade regulation (including Treasury, Commerce, State Departments plus the International Trade Commission—the old United States Tariff Commission); (7) federal income tax regulation; (8) energy regulation (including coal use and conservation of energy); and (9) miscellaneous regulation (including wages and prices, securities, procurement, and potent regulation).

The conclusion of the study drawn by the then Acting Director of the Council on Wage and Price Stability is striking:

> Steel is an industry whose production procedures are to some extent prescribed for it by government, whose costs are substantially influenced by government, whose market share exists at the sufferance of government, and whose profitability has a good deal less to do with innovation and enterprise than it does with what government decides to let it keep. [p. iv]

The council's study documents the recent rapid growth in the volume of federal regulation of business. It lists 5,600 regulations from twenty-seven different agencies that have some impact on the manufacture of steel. At one time, the steel industry had to concern itself only with tariffs, taxes, and antitrust laws; to compare the old to the list of twenty-seven agencies in 1976 tells the distance traveled.

Edgar B. Speer, Chairman of United States Steel, in a speech on February 7, 1977, had this to say about the OSHA regulations which went into effect in January of 1977:

These new requirements run from the ridiculous to the extreme. For example, the performance standard says that no employee can be exposed to more than 0.15 milligrams of particulates per cubic meter of air during an eight-hour period. And that 0.15 milligrams is roughly equivalent to an ounce of material dispersed in an air space twenty feet high and three football fields long.

Other requirements call for collecting air samples at every coke battery—perhaps a minimum of 600 samples a month at our Clairton Works and 14,000 a year across our entire company . . . providing annual and semi-annual physical examinations for coke oven employees . . . supplying work clothes and laundering them every week . . . making employees take a shower before they go home . . . forbidding them from eating or using tobacco on the job . . . and like mother of old, requiring them to wash their hands and faces before they eat their lunch.

The growth and spread of regulation deeply disturbs results-oriented and cost-conscious business executives. They are broadly supportive of some measures to cope with the problems brought on by recent concern about the quality of life. They are genuinely puzzled and frustrated about how to create government-business relations that allow reasonable trade-offs of quality and economic objectives. They are acutely bothered by the costliness of regulation, both in delays and in creating added work.

GROWTH AND WELFARE

Besides competitive markets and government, a great external force affecting corporate executives is the state of the distribution of income and wealth. As discussed above, one great defect of the liberal ethic is that it takes the individual as "given," when, in point of fact, individuals are almost wholly the creatures of society. Their freedom is limited by their power to do what they can. To what extent are they really independent?

For many years the argument has been made that the degree of inequality in the distribution of income and wealth in the United States was necessary in order to achieve economic growth. After all, it was held, this is the richest nation on earth and inequality is the price we have to pay. However, the United States has been surpassed by Kuwait in per capita GNP since the early 1950s; has been surpassed by Sweden and Switzerland whose per capita GNP is about 20 percent above ours at current exchange rates, and is about to be surpassed by Denmark, Norway, and West Germany.

In the United States, there are significant disparities in income.

The richest 10 percent of the population receives about 26.1 percent of income. The poorest 10 percent receives about 1.7 percent of income—mostly in government income transfer payments. As to physical wealth, 20 percent of the population owns about 80 percent of all the wealth that can be privately owned, while the bottom 25 percent owns no wealth and may have debts exceeding its assets.

While the highest living standard in the world is used to justify these arrangements, that is called into question by the better records of other countries. The degree of inequality in income distribution is such that the richest 10 percent receives fifteen times the income of the poorest 10 percent in the United States. In Sweden the figure is 7 percent; in Japan, 10 percent; in West Germany, 11 percent. Long-run living standards are largely determined by productivity growth. Yet for the past two decades, Western European productivity gains have been twice those of the United States. The argument that gains in productivity in Western Europe and Japan would slow down when their economies caught up with ours is not borne out by the facts.

It is worth recalling that the liberal-individualist doctrine ideally called for consensual relations among individuals, taken as given, in all aspects of life. The conditions of individual life in America during the nineteenth century provide the security of a farm or of a small business or of a craft for larger proportions of the population than today. It was not merely security that the small farm or the craft offered; it was ownership of the means of production, and therefore, personal independence. The idea of bargaining and of exchange ideally implies some sort of rough equality of status. The question, therefore, arises whether, in a society where the top 20 percent have 80 percent of the physical wealth and where the bottom 25 percent holds none, the assumed conditions of liberalism concerning rough equality of status hold to nearly the same extent as in the nineteenth century. How independent and secure are individual Americans when compared to those in the nineteenth century?

The argument for speeding growth, often derived from liberal doctrine, is that this country should "liberate free enterprise" and reduce social expenditures. However, the United States is being surpassed by Sweden, which has the world's biggest social welfare expenditures; by West Germany, where labor unions share corporate directorships with corporate executives; and by Japan, where government dominates the economy. Indeed, the fastest growth rate was achieved during the 1940s at a 36 percent increase when wartime conditions of a command economy prevailed. The second fastest decade was the 1960s when the economy grew 30 percent during a period of expansion of government social-welfare programs. Before the era of government intervention, the decade of fastest economic growth was 1900-1910, when the country grew 22 percent.

An argument of some validity can be made that the United States carries a larger defense burden than Western Europe and Japan; it spends 7 percent of GNP on defense, whereas Western Germany and Sweden spend only 3 percent, and Japan 1 percent. However, defense spending could be used to drive forward the level of technological attainment, as has been done by other nations in the past. Our recent productivity record does not suggest we are succeeding at that job. In any event, the long-standing basis for resistance to examining seriously the question of equity in sharing income and wealth is surely weakened by the nation's fall from the chosen position as the richest and highest-income land on earth.

ETHICAL INFLUENCE OF "PROFESSIONAL" ASSOCIATIONS

A potent force on corporate executive behavior is that of traditional business organizations, such as Chambers of Commerce and the National Association of Manufacturers. In addition, more recent groups such as the research-oriented Conference Board and the Committee for Economic Development have been important. Finally, among such nonindustry oriented business associations, the Business Roundtable, made up of chief executive officers of 150 very large corporations is very important because of its size and quality and because its members have committed themselves to lobby personally on critical issues.

These broadly-based business organizations are joined by as many as 1,700 national "trade associations," which represent the interests of the trade or industry before Congress and the federal bureaucracies, serve to educate the members of the industry, and maintain communications within the industry.

A commentary on the major groups is important since their scope is not always appreciated. The U.S. Chamber of Commerce has over 60,000 members including 2,000 of the nation's 3,000 local Chambers, about 1,500 national trade associations, and the rest made up of business firms. Its monthly publication, *Nation's Business,* has the largest circulation of any business magazine; it holds week-long institutes for training trade association and Chamber executives on eight different campuses across the country each summer; it sponsors hundreds of conferences and meetings each year for its twenty-six standing committees and its ten to twenty *ad hoc* committees. Its major job is to express the views of its members in Washington. But of course, doing so means also informing, communicating, debating, analyzing, studying, evaluating, and judging opinion in respect to its members. Finally, it means lobbying to have its views put into effect rather than opposing views.

While the U.S. Chamber of Commerce represents businesses of all kinds, including United States business located abroad in thirty-five different countries, the National Association of Manufacturers represents about 11,000 firms engaged only in manufacturing. It is, so to speak, "Pittsburgh" business compared to the Chamber's "Main Street" business. NAM has powerful state subsidiaries made up of leading manufacturers, just as the Chamber has State Chambers of Commerce as members.

The Committee for Economic Development, organized after World War II, is made up of 150 trustees, including 10 college presidents and 140 high-ranking business executives from large corporations. It is, so to speak, "Wall Street" business. (Of course, there is difficulty with these analogies in all three cases. Manufacturing is hardly limited to Pittsburgh or the Industrial Crescent; business is hardly flourishing only on Main Street, when compared to the suburbs; and Wall Street experiences competition from uptown as well as non–New York City headquarters.) The CED conducts studies on major policy questions and publishes its results. Although the CED does not lobby like the Chamber and the NAM, it is often influential with top-level government officials because of the prestige of its members or the cogency of its research.

The Conference Board, a large, business-sponsored research organization of about one thousand big-business members and others, is effective most often in producing management and economic research for business over a wide range of subjects. The quality of its work is highly respected, partly because the Conference Board does not expose itself to the hurly-burly of policy debate.

The influence of these groups on business ethics is not easy to assess. There is no doubt that trade associations have raised ethical standards of performance for corporate executives by encouraging them to become better educated and by keeping them better informed. In the same way, both the CED and the Conference Board have provided useful and informative research on questions of the most fundamental economic importance. By doing their studies and research with top business executives, the CED and the Conference Board have exposed many opinionated executives, long accustomed to agreement from subordinates, to differing business views and to the best academic thought. Similarly opinionated academic experts are chastened by the realistic knowledge of executives who possess keen intelligence, wide education, and rich experience.

When it comes to business lobbying groups, however, the impact of these groups on business ethics is harder to assess. First off, it should be noted that the specific behavior of these groups is highly ethical; large national business lobbies avoid lavish spending and unlimited expense accounts and Internal Revenue Service audits (usually conducted during Democratic administrations and often lasting two to three years) seldom, if ever, reveal tax discrepancies. No improper pressure is placed on officials or groups through these organizations.

In the second place, these groups consist to some degree of secular theologians of business conviction. But assessing their ethical influence on corporate executives is somewhat like trying to measure the Vatican's effect on the Catholic priesthood. These organizations tend to promote policy judgments favorable to their own and frequently truncated views about "free enterprise." The expressions are most often abbreviated because of pressure by some important group within the membership that wishes to concentrate on some notable freedom offered by free enterprise. These organizations are often used by corporations, industries, regions, or other business alliances to take strong legislative positions on questions when, for reasons of possible retaliation by government, threat to sales, or damage to an "image," the group within these organizations prefers to remain in the background. In such cases, the U.S. Chamber of Commerce or the NAM are "front runners."

These organizations, somewhat like the Vatican, properly serve as sources of prestige, psychological support, and ceremony for their leading members. They excel in a kind of ritual behavior at conferences and meetings not unlike the rituals of religious observance. To some degree the ceremony, prestige, and ritual renew the support of members for deeply-held values of the society, inculcating ethical energy and will. And to some degree, also, the ritual lends to the prevailing views of members an aura of rectitude which sometimes borders on the sacred. To that extent ritual is resistant to change and even to reflection.

Like the Vatican, too, the business lobbying organization is technically expert but understandably not overstaffed with dispassionate observers. The consequent ethical danger to the business lobbying organizations—unlike the Vatican which specializes in theology—is self-deception that is simplistic. The danger is not always, though it is increasingly, checked by wide outside consultation.

Another ethical danger is staff passivity and complacency. It is easy for staffs to believe that these organizations are protectors of the dominant societal influence; they see themselves—and often act—more as part of the judgmental faculties of the society whose approval is required before change may be tolerated than as participants with others in a changing process of consensus. Therefore, these organizations seldom propose and often oppose legislation; they seldom assume responsibility for social ills addressed by proposals of others. While recent years have seen exceptions to this generalization, most exceptions have been painful to leading members and risky to involved staff.

The plain truth of the matter is that the ethics of leading business organizations rarely extend to acknowledging criticism of the business community or of specific members for inappropriate conduct, or even to expressions of moral outrage regarding events such as Watergate. While this policy of noncriticism of members is wholly understandable in membership organizations, it leaves something to be desired. Business lobbying groups are more likely to respond to criticism of business by moving to "reform the critics" or "improve their education" than by addressing the criticisms directly. However, like other power groups, business organizations have been forced by the pressures of changes to adapt to criticisms by consumerists and environmentalists. They simply lack political power to prevent a deluge of legislation, much of which they fail to foresee.

In summary, the aim of the ethics of business lobbying groups is governed by one "commandment" over all others: increase business power and influence and preserve a continuity of its ideologies in educational and ritual activities. Very seldom do such groups undertake policy initiatives outside a highly predictable and conventional sphere. In this sense, it would be difficult to sustain the case that these groups provide significant ethical leadership to business beyond an occasional study or analysis containing facts that soften or temper the visceral reactions of powerful and assertive members. Unlike the Vatican, business lobbying organizations do not have an organizational structure that generates a single charismatic leader or a college of cardinals for any long period. The organizations are fundamentally staff-led and to a considerable degree find themselves in the same relationship individually to staff as stockholders to corporate management. Ethical leadership of scope and innovative power is unlikely to come from paid staff management.

Perhaps the focal point of pressures for unethical conduct in Washington is the Washington representative of the corporation. It is in his office that relations with government converge. The "Washington Rep" is responsible for following legislative developments, keeping contact with government personnel, influencing legislation affecting his company, getting government contracts, and making contacts for top company executives with top government officials.

While old line business lobbying organizations and trade associations have to be above suspicion, the Washington representative moves in a less public context. Further, the budget of lobbying and trade association groups is rigorously controlled by budget committees at annual meetings whereas the budget of Washington representatives is less exactly specified. The "Washington Rep" is more likely to enjoy an unlimited expense account, to be required to buy the $100 tickets or the $1,000 table for some political dinner, to entertain this or that government figure on behalf of top company officials, and to place corporate interests above all because he is directly accountable to corporate headquarters. All these factors make it more likely that when specific acts of unethical conduct occur, they will come through the Washington corporate offices of specific corporations rather than through lobbying organizations or trade associations.

Aside from Washington representative offices, there are various important ancillary groups such as public relations firms, labor relations consultants, Washington lawyers, and others whose conduct in specific acts may turn out to be unethical. In the aggregate these groups provide an essentially shadowy element of corporate action in Washington. Each has its own ethics, some of high integrity, and others of questionable merit. Press reports on International Telephone and Telegraph, on its Washington representation, and on its approach to gain influence are illustrative of the potential for improper influence on government officials, as well as on others.

II. Internal Factors

In the concluding part of this analysis attention is focused on certain forces within the business community which generate a predictable type of ethical behavior. Specifically, I shall suggest that

1. professional preparation and a "club" psychology engender a conformity ethic long before the individual arrives at the top and that this preconditioning reinforces a bottom-line morality, and

2. nothing more dramatically illustrates the tension between the free-enterprise ethic and the ethic of science (truth) than the present status of American television.

Calculus of the Bottom Line

There is no doubt that, day in and day out, the single biggest influence on the executive from inside the company is the calculus of
the bottom line. How it becomes expressed, though, is more complex
than might appear. Do big corporations maximize profits? Or do they
maximize growth? Or survival? Do they maximize profits in the next
reporting period or in the next five years? Do they maximize profits
for shareholders? Or do they keep things on an even profits keel to
gain significant independence from directors and shareholders?

Certainly the Wall Street investment analyst puts pressure on the
corporate executive to make earnings look good in the very next
reporting period, and from then on. The relatively short tenure for
chief executive officers, five to ten years in many large companies, leads
these CEO's to believe that the "future is now." In the late 1960s the
"go-go" standards on Wall Street for growth companies and the relatively short tenures for many CEO's put on powerful pressures for
speculation, merger, and growth through acquisition. It created a
short-run perspective of corporate objectives and emphasized maximizing short-run advantages.

At the same time, the separation of ownership from control in
major corporations has become so great that many managements of
large public corporations have enormous discretion in meeting the
bottom-line requirement. Some of them jokingly suggest the criterion
of shareholder relations that the late Yale football coach Herman
Hickman put forward to deal with alumni: "I try to keep them surly
but unrebellious." This is particularly true of financial and banking
executives whose firms are in heavily regulated industries. But the
practice is not limited to the regulated firms.

The absolute discretion open to top management is very large, although it is often seen as relatively minor. For example, an individual
having a $10,000 annual income may have a bank balance of $100.
That sum draws no interest and is hardly worth investing in Treasury
bills. A firm with $1 billion of annual sales, holding 1 percent in cash
would have a bank balance of $10 million. Interest at 6 percent a year
on a 360-day basis on this amount is $1,650 for one day. This example
illustrates economies of scale. The same factors that yield economies

of scale also provide the firm's executives the potential scope for absolutely large discretion that conveys power.

The liberal theory of individualism, as Frank Knight pointed out, has always contained a doctrinal difficulty in respect to inequality of power among people. The legal tradition of treating the corporation as a "person" itself set in motion a train of power inequalities among the spectrum of corporations that ranges from AT&T to the smallest individual proprietorship. AT&T's 950,000 employees represent more than one out of every one hundred workers in the labor force. Working through its affiliated companies AT&T should in principle have no difficulty in, let us say, assigning a company executive living in each of the 435 congressional districts to every representative and everyone of the 100 senators to monitor and influence his behavior—a practice that could not be held improper. However, there is no way to avoid conceding that it represents power. There is the argument to be made that AT&T (amounting to assets of more than $50 billion, having 950,000 workers and around three million stockholders) *deserves* to have power consistent with its responsibilities. However, the question is this: who represents AT&T's interests? Is it always, of necessity, management? How does the liberal ethic deal with such a question? The answer has to be that the traditional liberal ethic largely begs such important questions.

The evolution of corporations, from national scope in the latter nineteenth century to multinational in the mid-twentieth, and the rise in scale of organization that has substituted franchising or chain stores for independent merchandising or that has all but eliminated manufacturing of less than national scope, has corroded and weakened the power of local leadership in all but a few regional centers of the United States. Local business leadership today is noticeably branch plant or office leadership; it lacks decision-making power, is often indifferent to local problems, and consists frequently of executives with short tenure and with ambitions elsewhere. Even banking is now afflicted because of the advent of state-wide branch banking or holding company banking.

BUSINESS SCHOOL EDUCATION

Collegiate and graduate business schools, a United States innovation, began a modest invasion of reluctant universities dominated by clerics and liberal arts professors at the turn of the twentieth century. The Wharton School at the University of Pennsylvania led the way.

After that, for one student generation after another, business schools cranked out young people—mostly young men—who were familiar with the rudiments of finance, marketing, production, management techniques, and economics. After Harvard's creation of a business school based on the case method, and the growth in prestige of schools at Columbia and Pennsylvania, the business school gained further respectability on academic campuses by World War II, despite the lack of job opportunities for young graduates during the depression-riddled 1930s.

After World War II, the postwar boom brought the business school in its own. A stronger market for its graduates arrived just when modern quantitative advances in analysis, made known by intelligence and logistics problems of the war itself, enlarged the conceptual base of management technique and moved the schools toward their long-sought goal of "professionalism." By the late 1950s, spurred by the Ford and Carnegie foundation studies, American business schools looked hard at their curricula, reduced the degree of narrow vocationalism they contained, tried again (and with some success) to integrate their educational program content, and raised the standards for entrance and graduation, especially the conceptual and quantitative standards.

By 1960, if not earlier, graduate business schools were attracting top-quality college graduates from science, engineering and the humanities. Their graduates had begun to compete vigorously with holders of law degrees for strictly managerial jobs. The "MBA" (as the holder of a Master's degree in Business Administration came to be called) developed a strong market that held up when engineering demand sagged, that was independent of demands for lawyers in business, and that commanded a steady premium over holders of bachelor's degrees. The "MBA" knew his way around business; he knew the institutions, the techniques, and the principles. But more than that, the MBA was quick to see and enjoy management problems imbedded in specific company environments and the best were quick to seek to take them on. The MBA was not intimidated by age or status; he had analyzed a lot of cases about getting around this or that "old Joe" of whatever rank or specialty. And the MBA was not intimidated, either, by relative lack of familiarity with the business. Somehow, he had been imbued with the doctrine that management principles are the same, whatever the institution, and further, that he was born to the mantel of management.

Yet there was a curious omission in the business curricula. In the years since World War II, ethics has not been a notable feature for emphasis or analytical treatment. Not until the 1960s had ripened did leading graduate schools restively insert programs on urban or other social issues into curricula. It would, however, be a mistake to make business schools the flak catchers for unethical behavior in business. Business schools, like the populace generally, have taken the enterprise system more or less as given and for granted. They have seen and have accepted the utilitarian ethic, along with its defects and fallacies, which they have tended to ignore because of lack of knowledge and interest. They saw their educational assignment to educate managers much the same as medical schools educate doctors or law schools educate lawyers, inculcating skill and confidence at the mechanics and the accepted spirit of the profession. They produced students who had learned a common language, had acquired a relatively common outlook, had built up a common stock of ideas. But they were—and I do not wish to stretch the criticism—somewhat like the older law schools as exemplified by Yale which, according to one of its most distinguished graduates, Robert M. Hutchins, did not provide understanding of "the common good of the political community in which we were to function. . . ."

Some exasperated faculties have tried an "Ethics" course about once every business cycle, on the up side when speculative behavior strains a few rudimentary business consciences. Most educators believe, however, that success will only come from a fully integrated business program that implicitly teaches ethical behavior. By that, they seem to mean that a fully integrated course would reveal a results-oriented ethic of liberalism capable of defense.

It is by no means clear that business leaders of today, even though they are better educated than before, are any less able to rationalize cheating when the external and internal forces converge on their conduct than their less well educated predecessors. The increasing influence of quantitative analysis in business schools can deaden certain ethical sensitivities, but this does not have to be the case.

THE CLUB—CONFORMITY TO GROUP BEHAVIOR

The internal pressure on executives to conform only begins in business school. The technique is well known in the case-study classroom. "Smedley," says the instructor dolefully, "your solution to the ABC Company's succession problem was to promote Mr. Competent over Cousin Ratskeller, even though the Ratskellers hold controlling interest on the board." A significant pause, then, "Well, what do you other fellows think?" This technique gives enough time to the canniest supporters of the reality principles to wipe out Smedley's position, along with the issues of ethics or competence that may be lying around, meanwhile, ingratiating themselves with the instructor at Smedley's expense. And, of course, even if there is always a Smedley, sometimes Smedleys can be sleepers, once they really get the message, and may even arrange an honorary degree for Ratskeller as well as the corporate succession.

Such thoughts aside, the exclusivity appeal of business management advancement is surely powerful. John O'Hara, James P. Marquand, and others have fictionalized some of the realities of life in the wardroom, the officer's quarters, the fraternity, and the club whose ethics are powerful enough to provide self-esteem for those of weak ego whose need to win satisfies self-doubts and builds evidence of prowess. The life of the club strengthens the power of its leaders through the threat of withdrawal for nonconformity. "Smedley is a great guy, Bill, but someone ought to tell him about that hair." Even if Smedley is the star salesman or holds patents, there are plenty of businesses that cannot tolerate the nonconformist equivalent of long hair, whatever it may be. Groucho Marx once observed: "I do not want to be a member of any group or club that would accept *my* qualifications for admission." Besides its brilliant wit, the statement lifts social climbing above mere logic to possibly an ethic. That such an ethic has enormous practical significance for behavior can be illustrated in the following scenario.

Suppose a fictitious fund-raiser of a hypothetical political party with a background as a highly successful, social-climbing executive of the self-made sort comes to town to meet the local powers-that-be at the oak-paneled dining room of the Old Boys Club. While there, the conversation about the party's needs flows toward imaginary threats (or hints of mysterious problems) that could arise in Washington—or worse yet, postulated visions are involved of the havoc that could befall if "the others who are not friendly and certainly not our kind" are victorious. If all this happens, the result could be an illegal corporate campaign contribution. But there is no way—no way at all—that any legal inference can be drawn as to intent of either the party spokesman or the corporate donors. The rationale is simple: "Everybody is doing it, absolutely everybody—and who the hell are they kidding with their sudden, sanctimonious morality?" Memory invokes that most poignant television pronouncement, "Your President is not a crook!"

Indeed, if the laws on corporate donations are changed unexpectedly after years of subterfuge and dissembling; the embarassment to the Old Boy mentality is thoroughly comprehensible even if top corporate executives can seldom be envisaged by ordinary folk as underdog victims. Exclusivity signals power. The chauffeur-driver limousine, the private dining room, the unmarked driveway, the unlisted number, the private jet, the private social set—all reinforce the Old Boy ethic. The very rich owners of an earlier era used the doctrine of private property to justify exclusiveness. Perhaps the most notable practitioners were Paul Getty and Howard Hughes. Today, some top executives have supplanted the owners in assimilating aloofness. Yet, that aloofness contains the seeds of doctrinal difficulty since executives of top corporations represent power without property. Is the aloofness a key to effective power? Even the practice of baboon troops, thought to reflect primate social behavior of a million years ago, suggests that it is. Dominant males among baboons remain aloof, using only threat-posturing to control bickering, and reserve genuine involvement for serious threats to the troop. Yet aloofness, among other things, reduces the credibility of executives in the eyes of the public. Does the public intuitively recognize that today's corporate executive no longer presides over doctrinally pure private enterprise, that big corporations are inevitably tinged with a public interest, and that the corporate executive lacks the legitimacy to mimic the earlier captains of industry?

The Club mentality also raises questions about the business judgment of relying on classic sanctions of legitimacy too far into a period when social change demands new sanctions. The biggest corporations, where ownership and control are fully separated, when management is just another profession among others, where the public interest has already been expressed through regulation, where the corporate charter is all but an anachronism of by-gone days of state sovereignty, and where public opinion of executive credibility is at an all-time low, are hardly secure enough in their present political legitimacy to invoke "rebelliousness from the already surly"—to revert to Coach Hickman's phrase. How high a price do executives wish their corporations to pay for their own "perks" of aloofness, exclusiveness, the Old Boy lifestyle, and general inability or unwillingness to stand up and be heard? On the other hand, how far into the hustings dare they go without beginning to look like politicians and risk further loss of credibility?

THE CAREER LADDER—UP THE ORGANIZATION

How widespread is pressure on managers to compromise personal ethics for corporate goals? A January 1977 survey of Pitney-Bowes, Inc., the Stamford (Connecticut) manufacturer of business equipment and a leader in campaign for business ethics, gives a depressing answer.[2] A majority of Pitney-Bowes managers, surveyed anonymously by the company, reported that they do feel pressure to compromise personal ethics to achieve corporate goals.

Business Week concluded that "such pressures apparently exist widely in the business world." It cites the 1976 study by Uniroyal and by University of Georgia Professor Archie B. Carroll III, who queried a random sample of corporate managers throughout the country. Seven out of ten Uniroyal managers and 64 percent of Professor Carroll's respondents perceived company pressure on personal ethics, when questioned anonymously. Most managers believed that their peers would not refuse orders to market off-standard and possibly dangerous products (although an even larger majority insisted they would personally reject such orders), and a majority thought young managers automatically go along with their superiors to show loyalty.

At both Pitney-Bowes and Uniroyal, nine out of ten respondents considered it unethical to turn in an incomplete report or charge an expense account with a meal eaten in a relative's home. Half or more of both groups would market an off-standard item if it was not dangerous. Overall, 90 percent in both companies answered that they favored a code of ethics and the teaching of ethics in business schools. Seventy percent of Pitney-Bowes respondents thought that press reports revealed a valid cause for business concern about unethical business practices and did not represent merely evidence of antibusiness bias. Most respondents also thought that business ethics were as good as or better than the ethics of society at large.

Internal forces on top executives reward results. Salaries matched by bonuses based on profits, stock options, other deferred compensation related to equity value, all push managers toward cost-cutting, moving fast to save costly time, toward open-mindedness to change, and toward sympathy for proved—not promised—technological, organizational, marketing, or other forms of effectiveness. Current public criticism of corporate executive conduct is mainly of bribery abroad and illegal campaign contributions at home. *Both actions, viewed inter-*

2 *Business Week*, January 31, 1977, p. 177.

nally and instrumentally, are aimed at corporate effectiveness and are based on a worldly realistic acceptance of things as they are.

A TYPOLOGY

Of greater significance is the fact that concern about corporate ethics does not go to crude self-enrichment and flagrant violation of the rules of the business game itself. The concern goes to the interface of public-private relations, to the power in politics here and abroad of corporations and their managers, to the social responsibility of corporations and to what meaning should be attached to it, and to what should be the standards of disclosure from corporations, that is, how public they should be.

In early 1977, the psychoanalyst Michael Maccoby published a book called *The Gamesman* which was based on six years of Rorschach tests, dream analysis, and interviews with 250 managers (4 percent of them women) at twelve elite United States corporations.[3] The interviews were conducted by Harvard University's Project on Technology, Work and Character. The thesis of this book is that four types of people become managers in today's well-run corporations. The first is the "craftsman," a gentle holder of traditional values, an admired worker but so absorbed in a specialty—engineering, finance, or sales—that he or she is inadequate to lead a complex organization. Next comes the "jungle fighter," a dog-eat-dog destroyer of peers, superiors, and eventually of himself. The "company man" is the third type; he is occasionally effective but is dominated by caution and fear. The fourth, "the gamesman," simply loves glory and winning not so much to gain wealth and power (though he may achieve both), but for the sheer joy of victory and distaste for losing.

Of course, Maccoby acknowledges that no person studied was fully encompassed by these types nor was he a pure exemplar of any one of them. But his studies showed that the higher into the corporate structure he went the more executives he found who showed gamesman characteristics, even though most were a mixture of one or two types. The gamesman, typified in public life by John F. Kennedy, loved taking calculated risks, was fascinated by new techniques, was simultaneously cooperative and competitive, playful but compulsive, a team player but with the desire to be a superstar. A gamesman is not strongly loyal to the corporation, is skilled at finding short cuts and on his way up, tries to get corporate superiors to leave him alone. He

[3] *Time*, February 14, 1977, pp. 57-58.

is mainly interested in getting power in order to build a team loyal to himself. The gamesman, according to Maccoby, is cheerfully willing to build what will sell, whether polluting products, weapons, or whatever else although, at the same time, he may be a closet liberal in politics.

The chief trouble the gamesman finds, and what sets him off from the findings of William H. Whyte, Jr. (*The Organization Man,* 1955) or Douglas McGregor (*The Human Side of Enterprise,* 1960) is that the gamesman's work does little to satisfy or even stimulate what Maccoby calls the "qualities of the heart": loyalty, a sense of humor, friendliness, compassion. The gamesman is not inner-directed in the same sense as the earlier prototype, nor is his satisfaction to be found in achieving ideological conviction or ethical fulfillment.

The danger of stereotyping and of over-generalizing about American business executives from a sample of twelve elite corporations is surely obvious. However, the effect of partly accurate stereotype, as was true earlier of the "organization man," is that the symbol serves to replace an unknown reality for millions of people for whom the reality is out of reach of personal experience. And for lack of a better one, the symbol can serve as a hypothesis to use on testing limited personal experience.

Perhaps the key aspect of Maccoby's study is to note the decline since 1950 of an ideological or ethical basis for action among the generation of executives born in the 1930s and after and a lack of satisfaction with business results as representing any events of broad human significance. Oversimplified, the descriptive phrase is negative—the absence of a strong ideological or ethical commitment to the meaning of work, except to the commitment of "winning." Winning then turns out to be, as forecast, "the only thing."

No one who has worked long, while sharing family responsibilities, in any kind of organization—business, government, or academia—can be unaware of social pressures of peer groups. No doubt, elaborate psychoanalytical studies of diplomats, government officials, congressmen and congresswomen, university faculty, union managers, or almost any other occupational peer group might show private attitudes, human motivation, and psychic rewards and disappointment differing from the prevailing myth about that occupation. Not known is whether these other occupations have as their leaders people like the corporate gamesman in their approach or attitude.

Still, looking back at this review of internal forces at work on the ethics of executives, the quality of Adam Smith's early judgment remains broadly intact. Like him, we still rather expect that whenever a few merchants gather together they may well be plotting some conspiracy against the public and that, as a consequence, we have to rely on the broad theory that competition must check self-interest and direct it into channels of social advantage. And, to be scrupulously fair, we have to recall immediately the observation of the late Henry Simons, Chicago University economist, who noted that all professions are in significant part conspiracies against the public. He meant, of course, that monopoly of knowledge or skill when practiced anywhere commands a value of scarcity otherwise absent. The forces of education, group behavior and career incentives all reinforce, for the executive, the ethic of the bottom line. They generate no added accountability beyond instrumental effectiveness, attained in the face of the given sum total of individual self-interests expressed in markets and coexistent with whatever consensus may be reflected in public policy. We need not fully rely on the dangerous conviction that the brightest in business must perforce be the morally best, or that business financial success ought by its nature to confer corresponding moral stature; not any more, one must hasten to add, than the tendency for a person to excel in any instrumental skill should confer independent moral stature. George Bernard Shaw put a crushing truth about human beings in these gentle terms: "Men differ as to their virtues, but they are similar in their vices." To make the case that business leaders are not paragons of ethical grace is not to concede that other professionals are superior.

There is to be marshaled the classic rhetorical inquiry: Where would be the priest absent the sinner, the cop without the criminal, or the teacher without the unlearned, the proper without the rake, the middle class without the poor, the woman of virtue without her fallen sister? The context of judgment concerning revelations of corporate misbehavior would be shallow indeed if it invoked, as the ground for corporate culpability, the inferior moral quality of business leaders. Who is to assert the individual moral superiority of the closeted cleric over the honest cop—certainly it could not rest on quantity of real incidents of temptation. People of large affairs experience large issues. But ethics is principle or nothing at all in principle. And whatever social systems may have rested on divine right in the past, certainly the liberal ideal and the United States system did not. The legitimacy of the business system has never rested on any implied moral superiority of the rich or powerful, except in the Calvinist theology, which has hardly gainsaid the stoic eloquence of Jeffersonian doctrine in American social history.

The Issue of Structure

PUTTING SOME PIECES TOGETHER

External and internal forces do not exhaust the influences on the executive. There remains the question of the structure within which the executive functions. In our survey, we have seen how the public is critical, not of the political and economic system, but of "corporate morality," because it is distant, impersonal, aloof from human concern, subject to hidden motive. The still-dominant "liberal" ethic of laissez faire has, as its major concern, the right relations among individuals (really families). It will be recalled that the liberal ethic, by taking the individual as given, slips into almost a fallacy, because it ignores the fact that individuals are largely the creatures of their social environment. Since freedom is the freedom to use power, large differences in individual power amount to denial of instrumental freedom to those lacking such power.

The ethical appeal of liberalism is that it offers people their just deserts: "From each according to his free will, to each according to his contribution." The record of this ethic is breathtaking. The last two centuries are an epochal innovation in human history when everything economic took off. Using knowledge the West invented a new form of wealth where, for the first time in history and in a world that had always been poor, the rich could get rich without taking from the poor. Science and the enterprise system combined to get the process started in the eighteenth century. And both, we remember, sought freedom—science from religious authority and enterprise from political constraint—to seek the truth of nature and to put that truth to use.

The ethic of liberalism starts with self-interest, supports relations of mutual consent among individuals in all areas of life, seeing the best use of the coercive force of government in avoiding coercion of some individuals by others. But it refuses to take a position on the goal of action. The modern corporation is the major institution of economic enterprise. Its executives, the lead actors, are impelled by the outside force of competitive markets to be efficient in using resources in order to match people's expressed demands—what they in fact will buy—not what they may want to want. Such efficiency is an ethical principle of note. The executive is forced by his own self-interest to give people *what they want and not what he thinks they should want,* forced to serve people as buyers whether he likes or even knows them, forced to get results and not pious sentiment or expressions of good intentions. Indeed, the ethic does not require of the executive morally superior motivation.

The province of the liberal ethic is power. The modern corporation is a repository of power—economic power which commands the use of resources of humans, of raw materials, of land—and seas—and, in its own discretion, organizes these resources to some predetermined purposes garnered from the marketplace where fluctuating prices signal changing demands and supplies. The corporate executive is responsible for this process.

The modern corporation exploits the Platonic dictum that knowledge is power. It traffics on knowledge; know-how, and more and more, know-why. Theory and experiment suggest invention. Invention rearranges the *status quo* in some area of knowledge. It is technological reform. The patent system confers ownership on invention but also makes inventions known and allows "engineering-around" inventions in order to gain further technological reform. Corporations use knowledge that is in the public domain. They also pay to use proprietary knowledge, to get the services of people who "have" knowledge, to buy machines that "embody" knowledge, and to recruit people of creative ability to work at producing still other "new" knowledge that may be either public or proprietary, or a combination thereof.

However, knowledge—as Whitehead once wrote—is like fish: it will not keep. This was vividly illustrated by the secrecy hassle over the atom bomb. Scientists kept telling the military that there was no secret, that the very existence of the bomb demonstrated that atoms could be split and a bomb could be made. What remained was only developmental technology to solve the how-to-do-it-now-that-you-know problem. Development takes only resources and time. Because knowledge will not keep, it has a peculiar economic quality. Once new knowledge is discovered, further use of the discovery does not involve additional cost. Knowledge, in this sense, is a public good which once produced, involves no marginal cost for added units of output; once extant, it cannot be exclusively possessed or consumed by using it. To remain a private good, knowledge must be kept secret.

If external forces drive the executive to meet the challenge of innovative competition, the internal forces push the executive towards learning how to use power to achieve the ends set by the external environment. To repeat a key theme: *the internal master of the executive is the bottom line, guarded relentlessly by the investment analyst.* The school, the club, the career-ladder all point toward the value of winning at the gamesmanship of power on behalf of the bottom line. Business trade and policy organizations connect the external and the internal corporate world, supportive in ritual and action of the convictions of the collective executive corps—of management.

The separation of ownership and control in corporations, however, has placed enormous responsibilities on the executive. Seen in the context of a liberal ethic of individualism, corporate management "represents" large aggregations of economic power. The individual or family lacking ownership of the means of production is increasingly dependent on continuous employment to gain the promised fruits from the system. Senior corporate management will not promise full employment; the liberal ethic itself argues implicitly that government should do so. And government has done this through the Employment Act of 1946.

THE ETHICS OF KNOWLEDGE

The ethics of power structured in the corporation through management may become inconsistent with the ethics of knowledge. Let us return to Bronowski's observation:

> Is it true that the concepts of science and those of ethics and values belong to different worlds? Is the world of *what is* subject to test, and is the world of *what ought to be* subject to no test? I do not believe so. (Emphasis added)

It cannot be so that, for example, there is no ethical imperative in the knowledge that fire burns, or that ropes strangle—or, indeed, that protein deficiency in pregnant females and infants produces mental retardation.

Knowledge enlarges human ethical responsibility when it reveals that "acts of God" can be placed under human control. More precisely, knowledge of nature carries the imperative of abiding by nature's laws, or ignoring them at peril. The argument of this chapter needs restating in order to illuminate the structural aspects of the ethical dilemma: Although the rise of science and of the free society yielded undeniable and growing power of production, it also redefined ethical norms by increasing the power of the human species over its own future evolution. Any society that feeds on knowledge cannot suffer power to trample or suppress it. *Unethical behavior, at its root, takes the form of some attempt to suppress truth.* Too many times we have seen that "might makes right," and that sheer institutional power can overwhelm the opinion of the individual.

Suppression of truth is threatening for two reasons. First, by so doing institutions and nations retard their own growth. Post–World War II Soviet agriculture, wedded to the anti–Mendelian theory of Lysenko, and derived from Stalinist dogma, was inconsistent with what Bronowski called "the physical fact." In 1859, John Stuart Mill in his *Essay on Liberty* published three classic arguments against the suppression of the opinion of the individual; to me they are of such major importance that their full restatement is warranted:

1. If the repressed opinion is true, one loses the opportunity of discovering the truth.
2. If the repressed opinion is false, discussion of its falsity strengthens the opposing truth and makes the grounds of truth evident.
3. The truth may be divided between the prevailing opinion and the repressed one, and by allowing expression of both, one makes recognition of the whole truth possible.

The second reason why truth suppression is the great unethical art is that it permits truth-suppressors to inflict damage on individuals who step out of line. Too often, the executive motivated by self-interest and possessing almost absolute discretion, suppresses the truth about corporate acts which, if known, would encounter the proscription of the liberal, utilitarian ethic against force and fraud. The same principle applies in government as well. The tragedy of the "Old China" hands, such as John Service, is not limited to the false attack on a courageous man's character; the real price was an ill-founded China policy until 1973.

It is not surprising, then, that many reform movements of the last decade take the form of truth-releasing measures. These include: the over-throw of Nixon, the Freedom of Information Act, the Truth-In-Lending and Truth-In-Packaging and Labeling Acts, increased requirements for corporate disclosure by the SEC and FTC, the case of the Pentagon Papers, the State Sunshine Laws and similar congressional moves through amendments to regulatory agency powers in 1976, the Kennedy/King/Kennedy assassination controversies, the FBI/CIA disclosures, the Metcalf Report on corporate audits by CPA firms, the consumerist movement bills, the environmental impact statement, and others.

Arranging for the release of the truth from the too-warm embrace of executive self-interest is seen in proposals from the business community that would encourage "ethical" corporate behavior. Former Dean Courtney C. Brown of Columbia University's Graduate School of Business gives an excellent example. He proposes that the board of directors of a company be separated from its executive management and made to work as the firm's legislative body. In order to insure a measure of countervailing power against the management, the board would be led by a strong and well-paid chairman to bring to the board greater independence and effectiveness. To Brown it is more important

> to have a vigorous and informed review of the proposals that come before the board from the point of view of both the company and the general interests than it is to have contending and specialized individuals on the board trying to represent the particular interests of limited constituencies.[4]

In effect, Brown warns management that the board is in for changes and he advances a constructive argument for such changes.

Brown believes that the board could be so structured that it would strenuously seek the relevant facts and relate them to the public as well as to the corporate interest—even if management is reluctant to disclose the full truth for self-serving reasons. While admittedly an optimistic view, Brown's conclusion flows from a cool and probing appraisal of the vital question of corporate structure in its relation to power and truth.

Christopher Stone goes further than Courtney Brown. Stone, assuming that business executives are honest until immersed in the formlessness of the modern corporation, believes that they engage in unethical conduct only after shedding their individuality.[5] Therefore, he advocates clearing the fog of the *"persona ficta"* legal status of the firm. Corporate executives are human beings who should not be granted broad disclaimers of responsibility for unethical conduct. Stone proposes two other things: (1) a law requiring written reports to superiors and making those superiors liable for their actions, and (2) strengthening the board vis-à-vis management by broadening director liability for the firm's actions.

All these recommendations assume ethical purity among directors. But a recent experience conflicts with both Brown and Stone. In the

---

[4] Courtney C. Brown, *Putting the Corporate Board to Work* (New York: Macmillan, 1976).

[5] Christopher Stone, *Where the Law Ends: The Social Control of Corporate Behavior* (New York: Harper & Row, 1975).

United Brand/Eli Black scandal of 1974-75, the cover-up for an illegal bribe to the president of Honduras was known by many directors themselves. When Board Chairman Eli Black jumped from his window in a suicide leap, no fewer than seven of the eleven members of the board were engaged in the cover-up. Lesser officials, including the controller, a vice president of finance, and the new chief operating officer finally tipped off the accounting firm and the real truth became known.

WHEN PERSUASION COMES TO FORCE

The epic history of the struggle of science against the canons of religious authority, fear of the unknown, groundless superstition, and the arrogance of intellect is so well known as to be easily forgotten. The hallmark of science is method and the method of science is profoundly "Protestant," in the general sense of the word. Science seeks revealed truth by reading the book of nature with constant awareness of the hypothetical quality of human knowledge and the requirement of *what is,* is subject to the test of the senses. The method of science is a form of persuasion. It is neither the persuasion of force, nor, in principle, the persuasion of authority. The essence of the scientific institutions of governance is truth-telling. Scientific governance is laissez faire, subject to the constraint of truth-telling. People can study what they will, write what they will, talk what they will. The only constraint is that others may test their conclusions, by appeal to evidence gathered by the senses. The process results in a fair evaluation over time. This, at least, is the scientific ideal.

A special ethical case arises because of the enormous power of television which rests in the hands of corporate executives. It will be recalled that the defect of liberalism (almost a fallacy in Frank Knight's view) is that the individual is to a great extent the creature of society. And remember, too, that the difficulty of executives is the lack of credibility with people. People simply do not believe what corporate executives say.

What is not sufficiently appreciated is that the scientific revolution has had a direct effect upon our culture and upon the way we think. The hallmark of science, commitment to the truth, implies reliance on rationality. But the hallmark of commercial television is its commitment to the manipulation of irrational hungers and desires. What makes the issue of commercial television so important to a discussion of corporate ethics is its overwhelming power as a medium of communication. It raises for the liberal ethic in the most profound way the question: when does persuasion become coercion? The cartoon "Small World" put the issue vividly when the husband looks from the television set and says to his wife: "TV brings people into my living room that I would not have in my living room." There are two sides to the issue: who *should be* in my living room?

A *Newsweek* article early in 1977 reviewed the evidence of what television is doing to the child. The view is that the intellectual growth achieved up to age five equals that of the next thirteen years. Children under five watch an average of 23.5 hours of television per week. While it is less than the average (forty-four hours) video diet of adults, its effects are potentially enormous. Over a seventeen year span, the rate of viewing means that by high school graduation, a typical teenager will have goggled at least 15,000 hours of television fare—more time than spent in any activity except sleep. This means exposure to an estimated 350,000 commercials and—at the 1977 rate—vicarious participation in 18,000 murders. George Gerbner, Dean of the University of Pennsylvania's Annenberg School of Communication is correct when he says that television has profoundly affected the way in which members of the human race learn to become human beings.

The issue of violence, sex-role stereotypes, paranoia, and advertisements for junk foods are examples of ways business shapes the social behavior of American children. Up to the present generation of children, the ethical issue of the impact of commercial messages on the formation of the individual personality has not been of great pragmatic significance. Flowing from power that science provides, technology has commandeered, on behalf of the corporation, what is potentially the greatest character-forming instrument of the century.

An overwhelming body of evidence from some 2,300 studies and reports suggests an antisocial legacy in that television violence tends to produce more aggressive behavior. The American Medical Association in 1977 asked ten major corporations to review their policies about sponsoring excessively violent shows after regional meetings by the Parent-Teachers Association protested what *Newsweek* called "TV carnage."

Studies also suggest that television programs and commercials reinforce sex-role stereotypes; by and large, men are displayed as dominant, authoritative, and the sole source of family financial support. Blacks are probably subject to even greater distortion of roles than are women. Black children watch television more than white children, and some evidence tends to suggest that blacks respond to that medium by regarding whites as more competent than themselves. A significant ethical question must be raised: do some people tend to act out and imitate the antisocial acts they witness on television? Certain studies suggest that some juvenile offenders copy television technique while others suggest that video violence increases children's tolerance for violent behavior in others. Furthermore, some researchers believe that television may instill paranoia in the young by creating an exaggerated fear of the danger of violence in their own lives.

A study cited by Columbia University psychologist Thomas Bever suggests that television advertisements may be "permanently distorting children's views of morality, society, and business." From in-depth interviews with forty-eight children, Bever concluded that by age twelve

> many find it easier to decide that all commercials lie than to try to determine which are telling the truth. . . . They become ready to believe that, like advertising, business and other institutions are riddled with hypocrisy.

As for "junk foods," millions of children watch Saturday and Sunday morning television, where more than 70 percent of the ads peddle sugar-coated cereals, candy, and chewing gum. One attorney for a San Francisco public interest group, quoted by *Newsweek,* said: "This is the most massive educational program to eat junk food in history."

It is easy to respond that freedom and free enterprise are at stake regarding television commercials; however, three points should be made. First, it is by no means clear that network companies represent competition free of genuine monopoly elements when the government limits franchises through regulatory policy and does not even auction them off to recover for the taxpayer the market value of the franchise. Second, the liberal ethic itself is defective because it fails to distinguish between persuasion and coercion in mass advertising. Third, the tools of science could be brought to bear far more effectively, as a matter of public policy, to examine conclusively the questions raised about the influence of this medium on personal development.

Finally, there is the most basic question: *why are private corporations and their executives the appropriate managers of the most powerful process ever created for mass acculturation of human beings?* It is certainly not a question that the only alternative is government. There is the free enterprise alternative of pay television; there is the public-subscription network; there is the design of advisory evaluators —equivalent to Nielson—and the requirement that program content and commercials be subject to periodic debate with equal time *on television* as to its results in affecting people's personalities. There are other alternatives.

This issue illustrates my theme. We live in a society created by science and the liberal ethic of free enterprise. The ultimate test of such a society is the quality of its individuals and this quality depends on truth. If the public seems unimpressed with the truth-telling quality of business executives, and if the public calls for a higher standard of truth-telling, what lies behind the demand? My answer is this: science itself is a major force for changing values; the ethic of the scientific enterprise is truth. Does the executive ethic conform to the enterprise of truth-seeking and truth-telling from which the executive benefits and on which the executive depends? I do not think so. We have a right to insist that the executive's large rewards require better performance. His price for failure is the loss of power.

George Cabot Lodge

2

Managerial Implications
of Ideological Change

If Professor Madden perceives ethical light in science, George Cabot Lodge finds it in the new ideology. The traditional liberal Lockean code of competition and equality of opportunity is being replaced by an ethic of cooperation and equality of results. The ideological change is coming fast, and if leaders in major corporations and labor unions are slow to interpret it correctly, the price of their tardiness will be exorbitant for all society.

Adjusting to the emerging ideology may be as painful to contemporaries as adjustment to the liberal economy was painful to committed mercantilists of the eighteenth century. But adjustments must be made because the philosophical tide is irreversible: we shall ride it out or we shall be engulfed. Since the State is destined to play a greater role, accommodation to this development may indeed be one of the most painful adjustments that corporate executives will have to make.

C. C. W.

The administration of President Carter finds the United States in the midst of one of the great transformations of Western civilization. Richard C. Gerstenberg, former chairman of General Motors ex-

---

GEORGE CABOT LODGE *is Professor of Business Administration at the Harvard Business School. Before entering federal government service, Professor Lodge was a political reporter for the* Boston Herald. *From 1958 to 1961 he was Assistant Secretary of Labor for International Affairs. A trustee of a number of public affairs organizations he has written several books and many articles on business and political science, including* Engines of Change.

pressed a common feeling when he wrote in a company statement dated February 8, 1973: "I am concerned about a society that has demonstrably lost confidence in its institutions—in the government, in the press, in the church, in the military—as well as in business."

What is happening is that old ideas and assumptions, which once made our great institutions legitimate, authoritative, and confident, are fast eroding. They are slipping away because of two sets of changes. First, the institutions, especially large publicly-held corporations, have themselves departed from the old ideas, not for ideological reasons but for solidly pragmatic motives: growth, efficiency, and return on investment. What big business really does has less and less to do with the rituals it lives by or the hymns it sings. In this sense business has been a major force in eroding these old ideas which gave it legitimacy. The second composite of changes concerning new developments relating to the institutional environment of America: demographic concentration, resource shortages, competition from other economies, ecological threats, increasing levels of education and more.

By examining institutional and other major transformations we can discern the presence of new ideas which help define values and provide new criteria for legitimacy and, thus, for authority. Because they are so recently visible, they are ill-formed and contradictory, shocking and threatening. The transition itself is neither good nor bad. The point is that it is taking place and we had better deal with it explicitly. (See Figure 1.) We cannot pass ethical judgments on individuals unless we—and they—know the criteria by which they are to be judged.

While the change has been going on for a long time, the present degree of transition is intense, the gap between institutional practice and justification is unprecedented. Much is irreversible. No matter what we do we are not going to return General Motors or New York City to what they were in 1910. *The ability to distinguish relatively quickly between what is inexorable in our institutional evolution; and where we have choice, will to a great extent determine our success at making the transition with minimum waste and maximum freedom.*

In the section that follows I shall argue that:

1. The ideology which has served us well and which owes its inspiration to the great English philosopher John Locke has been eroded by new forces, not the least of which is the larger corporation.
2. The strands of a new viewpoint are already visible and the coinage of simple words to capture the flavor of the new intellectual currents will help us better perceive the present socio-political climate.

Fig. 1. Ideologies: Bridges Connecting Values to the Real World

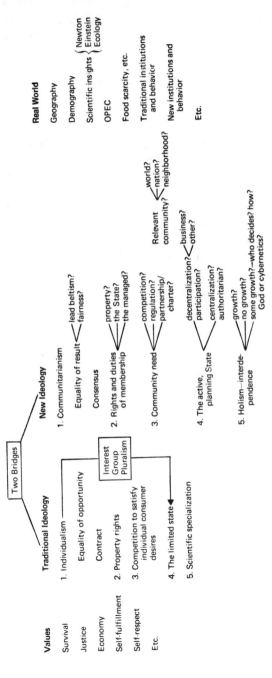

3. Various experiments in certain industries already illustrate how the new values can be absorbed into corporate policies and corporate plans for reorganization.
4. The new managerial type reflects a "gamesman" who must resolve certain tensions within himself if the corporation he leads is to adjust and grow.

The Challenge

It is hard for managers in either government or corporations to operate within an environment where old ideas no longer seem to work. If the new conceptions which are upon us were well defined, it would be difficult enough, but since they are still plastic, unfamiliar, and disruptive, we are baffled—and perhaps afraid. There is need to stand back in order to look at the whole array of problems and not merely at those dilemmas and questions which come at us one by one. In the current situation, the old "forest-from-trees" syndrome is more than a cliché. I therefore urge managers to clear their heads, to inspect all old assumptions, to identify rather precisely what is happening, to probe for the new definitions of values which are germinating, and then to look objectively at the choices that remain.

Meeting the challenge is not easy. Old ideas die hard and are harder to let go; they have glorious associations because they date from the great revolutions against hierarchical medievalism of the sixteenth and seventeenth centuries. It is difficult also because the old ideology is often used to legitimize the seats of power and justify the status quo. Nobody likes to look at the weakness beneath him.

But the stakes are high. Some institutions may adapt to the incoming ideology, and survive and prosper. Others may look outside the United States for more hospitable surroundings where the old viewpoints are still acceptable; still others will be shaken apart. And while they are beginning to know it, they are often paralyzed by unwillingness or inability to move.

Signs and Symptoms

When the Carter administration assumed power in January of 1977, the nation's economy was nearly at full throttle. Sales, profits, and production were high. But there was an unease, a certain absence of control and direction with which the economists could not reckon.

1. There was a deterioration of authority and legitimacy at the workbench as well as in the larger community: orders were not obeyed as they once

had been; quality was questioned; pride in the organization yielded to indifference.

2. Malaise on the assembly line continued to reduce productivity.

3. Opinion polls regularly revealed eroding trust in important institutions of government, business, labor, education, and religion. Even science and technology were suspect.

4. Procedures for making crucial trade-offs between energy, ecological integrity, transportation, housing, the good life, and economic growth have been disappointing and wasteful.

5. The structures of government were bloated and inefficient, manipulated by powerful interest groups whose clear-cut ends seemed to justify any means.

6. New York City, that symbol of so much that is glorious in our history, was and is a diseased shell, and other cities are in line to follow. There was a dawning realization that cities are communities and not simply mere collections of individuals to be used as long as they are useful and then scrapped like an old car.

7. Unemployment and inflation inched up together. In violation of the old rules, it may even be true that unemployment contributes to inflation. If so, the last excuse for tolerating it has been removed. The chilling question then comes: *Must* a person work in order to survive?

8. Global shortages—food and fuel, for example—have reached our shores. We are no longer a nation of surpluses. This change alone strains political and economic institutions. The pricing mechanism in the marketplace was not altogether acceptable or reliable as a means of coping with shortage. Uncertainty and catastrophe marked the delay in creating new mechanisms.

DOUBTS AND FEARS

Thus an ominous doubt prevailed: there was fear that we were moving inexorably away from old, familiar moorings and sailing off, for all we were worth, into an unknown sea of storms. We needed a chart, a plan, to find our way—but whom could we trust to draw the plan and mark the course? There is a propensity in times of stress to blame devils and praise angels. Some may even welcome the ruination of the old, blindly hoping to find the good and reliable in the purity of the ashes.

But neither praise nor blame nor ruin is the answer. Needed are new social and political constructs that clearly embrace our economic and technological activities, and allow for the development of a new sense of community. But what should these constructs be? In essence, they must weave together a new system of definitions for the ancient values —survival, justice, economy, creativity, self-respect, and the like. All communities everywhere have treasured these values; they are timeless and essentially noncontroversial. It is the definitions of such values and their applications that vary from time to time and from place to place. For example, in ancient Egypt, justice and self-respect involved lugging stones to memorialize the Pharaoh's transition to the next life; in modern China and Japan, these same values are fulfilled by service to the community and the nation.

If our own definitions are different, they are also fuzzy and contradictory. Nevertheless, urgent questions press down upon us: By what criteria shall we measure our progress? What is the "good" community? Can we agree on how many people it should have? Where should they live? What do they need? What are their rights?

There are not pragmatic answers to such questions; "ad hocery" of the kind to which we have become addicted leads to floundering from crisis to crisis. The need for broad conceptions has become essential. They may come, as they have so often in the past, with cruelty, bloodshed, repression, and waste. They may come in the exceptional way—humanely, efficiently, and with liberty. If we perceive the nature of our crisis promptly and do not shrink from its implications, the chances increase that the transition from an old to a new ideology will be relatively benign.

One great difficulty in facing up to ideological transition is that we have always thought of ourselves as a successfully pragmatic people who do what needs to be done to meet the requirements of the time. We have supposed that ideology is something left behind in Europe with our ancestors—a theoretical bag of confusion socialism, communism and other "isms," which hardheaded Americans happily reject.

This, of course, is nonsense. We are just as deeply imbued with ideology as any other community—probably more so. At times it has been called "Americanism"; at other times it has paraded under "Manifest Destiny," or the "Great Democracy." To assert that we are free of ideology is as absurd as to assert that a person exists without the subconscious mind.

The Traditional Ideology

Our traditional ideology is easy to identify. It consists of five great ideas that first came to America in the eighteenth century, having been stated in seventeenth century England as "natural laws" by John Locke and others. These ideas found fertile soil in the vast, underpopulated wilderness of America and served us well for a hundred years or so. The Lockean Five are:

Individualism—This atomistic notion holds that a community is no more than the sum of the individuals in it. Fulfillment lies in an essentially lonely struggle where the fit survive. Nonsurvival simply means unfitness. Closely tied to individualism are three other ideals: *equality,* which means "equal opportunity"; *contract,* which binds individuals together as buyers and sellers; and in the political order, *interest-group pluralism,* which became the preferred means of directing society.

Property Rights—The best guarantee of individual rights was to sanctify property rights. By virtue of his private property, the individual was assured freedom from the predatory powers of the sovereign state. "A man's home is his castle" was the homely way the English expressed their attachment to private property. It became the bulwark of individual freedom and representative government.

Competition-Consumer Desire—Adam Smith most eloquently articulated the idea that the productive uses of property are best controlled by each individual proprietor competing in an open market to satisfy individual consumer desires. It is explicit in the Sherman Antitrust Law, the Clayton Act, and in a host of Supreme Court decisions.

Limited State—In reaction to powerful divine-right monarchs, the conviction grew that the least government is the best government. It is less a question of size or "big government" and more a determination to restrict its focus, authority and scope. It leads to the cry, "Down with planning by Washington. Be responsive to interest groups. Whoever pays the price should call the tune."

Specialization and fragmentation—This is the corruption of Newtonian mechanics which says that by attending to the parts through experts and specialists, the whole will take care of itself. The experts, therefore, must ultimately run the society. Scientific specialization is tied to the notion of progress. But fragmenting knowledge has brought at least one hideous result: an amoral view of advancement so that nuclear ballistic missiles represent progress over gunpowder and cannonballs, which in turn represent progress over bows and arrows. This treacherous myth places no apparent limit on ways whereby man can gain dominion over his environment; nor does it stipulate any other ideological criteria for defining progress. In *Conversations with Henry Brandon*, Sir Isaiah Berlin made the point forcefully:

> As knowledge [becomes] more and more specialized, the fewer are the persons who know enough . . . about everything to be wholly in charge. . . . One of the paradoxical consequences is therefore the dependence of a large number of human beings upon a collection of ill coordinated experts, each of whom sooner or later becomes oppressed and irritated by being unable to step out of his box and survey the relationship of his particular activity to the whole. The experts cannot know enough. The coordinators always did move in the dark, but now they are aware of it. And the more honest and intelligent ones are rightly frightened by the fact that their responsibility increases in direct ratio to their ignorance of an ever-expanding field.

An overview of the past 5,000 years of human history dramatically reveals how this atomistic, individualistic ideology has constituted a fundamental aberration from the typical "norm," aptly called communitarianism. This radical experiment achieved its most extreme manifestation in America during the nineteenth century. Its tone gave a distinctive stamp to the culture—so much so that if one sought the heart of the American creed it would surely be located in these few tenets.

The Traditional Ideology in American History

Amherst Professor, John William Ward, pointed out that the very word *individualism* appears to have been born in America and for American usage. Alexis de Tocqueville coined the term to describe the social philosophy he had discovered in America in the 1830s. Although careful to distinguish individualism from sheer egoism, Tocqueville warned against the shattering effects of separating man from man:

> As social conditions become more equal, the number of persons increases who, although they are neither rich nor powerful enough to exercise any great influence over their fellows, have nevertheless acquired or retained sufficient education and fortune to satisfy their own wants. They owe nothing to any man, they expect nothing from any man, they acquire the habit of always considering themselves as standing alone, and they are apt to imagine that their whole destiny is in their own hands. Thus not only does democracy make every man forget his ancestors, but it hides his descendants and separates his contemporaries from him; it throws him back forever upon himself alone and threatens in the end to confine him entirely within the solitude of his own heart.

But what Tocqueville feared, Americans came to cherish. A climax seemed to be reached around 1890, and historian Frederick Jackson Turner confidently asserted that the meaning of American life is found in the movement of the individual out of society, away from others, to a new beginning along the frontier. Earlier Ralph Waldo Emerson had carried individualism to such a euphoric pitch that the state became virtually unnecessary.

> The wise man is the State. He needs no army, fort or navy—he loves men too well; no bribe, or feast, or palace, to draw friends to him; no vantage ground, no favorable circumstances. He needs no library for he has not done thinking; no church, for he is a prophet; no statute-book, for he has the lawgiver; no money for he is value; no road, for he is at home where he is; no experience, for the life of the creator shoots through him. . . . He has no personal friends.

Such ecstasy may have represented the world he knew: boundless land, limitless resources, an open and fluid society fed by streams of immigrants fleeing the oppression of Europe. But when great cities with their squalid slums and poverty tarnished the dream, the first response from those in power was simple: the plight of the poor resulted from individual failure. The Association for Improving the Condition of the Poor went about the slums of New York distributing free copies of Benjamin Franklin's "Way to Wealth." As late as the 1960s leaders of New York's Urban Coalition thought that sending mobile libraries down through Harlem would do some good. The old ideology simply could not offer any other explanation for human failure.

But even when individualism burned brightest, it was not devoid of irony. The very phrase, "the self-made man," for example, was born in an 1832 speech by Henry Clay asking the government to raise protective tariffs around Kentucky hemp manufacturers whom he described as "enterprising self-made men." Nor would this be the last time Lockean motivated businessmen would seek government intervention to help this cause.

The cult of the self-made man encountered other anomalies with the development of Big Business. It became increasingly difficult for the small businessman and entrepreneur—prototypical Lockeans—to survive in the corporate world of Andrew Carnegie, Jay Gould, and John D. Rockefeller. Antitrust laws were intended to preserve competition in the face of corporate collectivism. But even as they were enforced, Herbert Croly foresaw in *The Promise of American Life* that the nation would need big organizations to achieve the economies of scale which mass markets would require.

Large industrial enterprise also eroded the individualistic relationship between worker and employer. Unionization meant inevitably the wrapping of individualism into labor unions and the "collectivization" of the contract. To protect himself the worker had to collectivize; but to collectivize meant to diminish his individualism.

So it was that the increasing social and economic organization strained the traditional ideology. The key to industrialization was not independence but interdependence, not the individual but the group, and Frederick Winslow Taylor became honored as the father of "scientific management" because he demonstrated the fruits of this principle: "In the past the man has been first; in the future the system must be first."

In 1906 Taylor uttered a prophetic statement which had enormous import for the traditional ideology:

> Let me say that we are now but on the threshold of the coming era of true cooperation. The time is fast going by for the great personal or individual achievement of any one man standing alone and without the help of those around him. And the time is coming when all the great things will be done by the cooperation of many men in which each man performs that function for which he is best suited, each man preserves his individuality and is supreme in his particular function, and each man at the same time loses none of his originality and proper personal initiative, and yet is controlled by and must work harmoniously with many other men.

Here may be seen the coming of a radically new definition of self-fulfillment and self-respect; each person discovers his place in an organic system and finds fulfillment by participation in (and identification with) the whole.

During the past eighty years, organization, complexity, and concentration have so greatly increased that America has become a "collectivized" society. Yet there has been a singular unwillingness to face the ideological consequences. The result is a visible measure of schizophrenia, torment and agony.

The New Ideology

Although many small enterprises may remain comfortable with the Lockean Five, managers of large institutions are increasingly forced not to practice what they preach. This gap between behavior and avowed ideology causes some trauma. What, then are the contours of an ideology which could legitimize the behavior of large corporations and large government? Surely they must be different from the past. With some diffidence I will suggest that the "Lodge Five," a new ideology will come to dominate if not supplant the Lockean Five.

COMMUNITARIANISM

The community is more than the sum of the individuals in it. It has its own special and urgent needs, and individual survival and self-respect depend on the recognition of those needs. Personal fulfillment in today's society depends on a place in a community, an identity with a whole, and a participation in an organic social process. Further, if the community, the factory, or the neighborhood is well designed, its members will have a sense of identity with it; if it is poorly designed, people will be alienated, cynical, and frustrated. In America today, few can live in ways Locke or Emerson idealized.

In what might be called a classic statement, the editors of *Fortune* magazine wrote in February 1951:

> In our time, individualism has clashed with the whole industrial development, mass production and the division of labor. The key to industrialization is not independence but interdependence; no individual is self-sufficient; each is involved with others in complicated relationships. Dominating all this is the modern corporation, an organization of vast powers, which exacts of its managers purely impersonal decisions. It is little wonder that men have turned to the state to protect themselves in such a world.

Both corporations and unions have played leading roles in this evolution, but invariably they have been unmindful of the ideological significance of their actions.

A central component of the old individualism was the so-called Protestant Ethic: hard work, thrift, delayed gratification, and obedience to authority. Business extolled these virtues on the production side of things even as it systematically undercut them on the marketing side. Advertising departments spend millions to remind us that the good life is good living. Buy now and pay later; leisure and luxury are the hallmarks of happiness. Also the assembly worker has been led to believe that the old idea of individual fulfillment is valid. But he finds himself constrained by a work setting dramatically unlike anything that he has been led to expect. He may strike out, perhaps violently; he may join the absentee lists, taking Fridays and

Mondays off to eke out some spurious individualism via drugs, drink, old movies, or—if he is lucky—a walk in the hills.

Paradoxically, such behavior puzzles both management and unions. They linger with the traditional individualistic idea of the contract long after the contract has ceased being individualistic and has become "collective," unmindful of the inevitable dissonance between the idea of contract and the new forms of *consensus* toward which communitarianism is tending. When we speak of consensus as opposed to contract as the basis for relationships within an organization, we mean that those relationships are based on the continuing consent of those involved in the relationship, and we assume that the interests of the organization as a whole are or may be shared by all of its members. A contract, on the other hand, is binding over time and presumes an adversarial condition within the organization among its various members. Authority in a consensual organization springs from the consensus and depends upon there being an effective set of mechanisms for making the consensus manifest. Authority in a contractual organization is bipolar, the authority of management emanating from its inherent rights as proprietors or as agents of proprietors (shareholders), and the authority of employees deriving from rights granted to them by law to bargain collectively, to safe working conditions, to a minimum wage, and the like.

THE NEW EQUALITY

Former social policy attempted to guarantee to each worker an equal opportunity. The lawyers enforcing equal employment legislation, however, have taken quite a different tack. American Telephone and Telegraph, for example, argued that discrimination had become institutionalized; it had become so endemic to the corporation that women and minorities had been slotted into certain tasks. When this kind of argument is accepted, it is no longer necessary to prove individual discrimination in order to get redress.

The government moved to change the makeup of AT&T so as to provide, in effect, *equality of representation at all levels.* Without any specific charge having been brought, the company, in turn, agreed to upgrade 50,000 women and 6,600 minority group workers and—perhaps most significantly—to hire 4,000 men to fill traditionally female jobs such as operator and clerk. The company also agreed to pay some $15 million dollars in compensation. Thus the issue has become one of *equality of result,* not of opportunity. A communitarian idea had superseded an individualistic one. Given this definition of the issue, the company had to redesign itself according to a rather novel dictum—namely, that since individuals *are unequal in many respects,* a good organization is one which adapts itself to those inequalities to assure some measure of equality of result.

Needless to say, the union protested bitterly because the government's action was a direct threat to the labor contract which had been the regular device used to resolve inequities in seniority and promotion policies. The company itself has had commensurate difficulty in meshing its old thinking with the specific steps demanded by representatives of the new ideology. Yet the changes are being forced in one fashion or another. One of the uses of ideological analysis is that it dramatizes the range of choices and, conversely, prevents management from being a victim of intellectual arteriosclerosis.

An imprecise understanding of the ideological implications of communitarianism can lead to bizarre and even scary suggestions. In the name of self-fulfillment some have suggested, for example, that modern communications and data processing technology be used to allow persons to work at home individually—under, of course, the control network of central corporate management. This is a travesty of individualism. One of the most important aspects of work is the opportunity it affords to meet and be with other people. Individualism of this sort is an illusion.

MEMBERSHIP RIGHTS—AND DUTIES

A curious thing has happened to private property—it has ceased to be very important. What difference does it really make whether a person owns or just enjoys property? While a person may get certain psychic kicks out of owning a jewel or a car or a television set or a house, does it really make a substantive difference to own or to rent? There is a new right which clearly supersedes property rights in political and social importance. It is the right to survive—to enjoy income, health, and other rights associated with membership in the American community—or in some component of that community, including a corporation. As of January 1, 1974, for example, all United States citizens who reached age sixty-five or were blind or disabled had an absolute right to a minimum income of $140 a month. A guaranteed income and health legislation providing medical care to all is likely.

These rights derive not from an individualistic action or effort; nor do they emanate from a contract. They are, rather, communitarian rights that public opinion holds to be consistent with a good community and signal a revolutionary departure from the old Lockean conception.

Escalating rights of membership has strained the ability of government to pay. New York City hovers on bankruptcy. City mayors cry for federal dollars; state governors watch revenue-sharing carefully. There arises necessarily the question of duties of membership: who decides the duties, the individual or the state? If government is employer of last resort, does this impose an ultimate obligation to work at a job prescribed by government? The new ideology presents ominous choices.

The utility of property as a legitimizing idea has also eroded. Large public corporations are not private property in any real sense. The 1,500,000 shareholders of General Motors do not control, direct or bear responsibility for "their" company, and the vast majority have not the slightest desire to do so. They are investors, pure and simple. If they do not receive a good return on their investments, they will put their money elsewhere.

"Campaign GM," and similar attempts at stockholder agitation, represent heroic but naively conservative strategies to force shareholders to behave like owners and thus to legitimize corporations as property. But such action is clearly a losing game. It is a peculiar irony that James Roche of General Motors branded such agitation as radical machinations by "an adversary culture . . . antagonistic to our American ideas of private property and individual responsibility." In truth, of course, GM is the radical; Nader and his followers were acting as conservatives, trying to bring the corporation back into ideological line.

But if General Motors and its counterparts are not private property, what are they? The best that can be said is that they are a sort of collective, floating in philosophic limbo, dangerously vulnerable both to the charge of illegitimacy and that they are not amenable to community control.

Consider how the management of this nonproprietary institution is selected. The myth is that the stockholders select the board of directors, which in turn selects the management. This is rarely true, however. Management selects the board and the board, generally speaking, blesses management.

Managers thus become managers according to some mystical, circular process of questionable legitimacy. Under such circumstances it is not surprising that "management's rights" are fragile and its authority waning. Fifty years ago Alfred Sloan (*American Business History*) warned of this trend:

> There is a point beyond which diffusion of stock ownership must enfeeble the corporation by depriving it of virile interest in management upon the part of some one man or group of men to whom its success is a matter of personal and vital interest. And conversely at the same point the public interest becomes involved when the public can no longer locate some tangible personality within the ownership which it may hold responsible for the corporation's conduct.

This profound problem has been suppressed by the unquestioned efficiency of the corporate form *per se*. When economic growth and progress were synonymous we preferred that managers be as free as possible from stockholder interference. But today's definition of efficiency is influenced by an ideology which urges on some varieties of growth.

If efforts are taken to legitimize the large corporation and make it responsive to community demands, several suggestions might be offered:

1. Effective shareholder democracy might work in small companies.
2. More comprehensive and intelligent regulation by the state is needed, especially with respect to public utilities.
3. Self-management schemes, such as those in Europe, are being tried by some American companies.
4. Federal corporate charters which define corporate purpose, management rights, and community authority might be further "legitimizers."
5. Nationalization, perhaps the most brutish and inefficient way to legitimization, is a course that could eventually be suggested, if managers do not take leadership in rebuilding their base of legitimacy.

After all, there are only three possible sources of management authority: property rights, the managed, and the state. If property rights does not work, the other two are left.

COMMUNITY NEED

It was to the notion of community need that International Telephone and Telegraph appealed in 1971 when it sought to prevent the Justice Department from divesting it of Hartford Fire Insurance. Much in the manner of Henry Clay and the Kentucky hemp manufacturers, the company lawyers said, in effect:

Don't visit the old idea of competition on us. The public interest requires ITT to be big and strong at home so that it can withstand the blows of Allende in Chile, Castro in Cuba, and the Japanese in general. Before you apply the antitrust laws to us, the Secretary of the Treasury, the Secretary of Commerce, and the Council of Economic Advisers should meet to decide what, in the light of our balance-of-payments problems and domestic economic difficulties, the national interest is.

Note that here again it was the company arguing the ideologically radical case. The suggestion was obvious: ITT is a partner with the government—indeed with the cabinet—in defining and fulfilling the community needs of the nation. There may be some short-term doubt about who is the senior partner, but partnership it is. This concept is radically different from the traditional idea underlying the antitrust laws—namely, that the public interest emerges naturally from free and vigorous competition among numerous aggressive, individualistic, and preferably small companies attempting to satisfy consumer desires.

In the face of the serious pressures from Japanese and European business organizations (which are legitimized in ideological settings quite different from our own) there will be more and more reason to set aside the old idea of domestic competition in order to organize United States business effectively to meet world competition. Managers will probably welcome such a step; they may, however, be less willing to accept the necessary concomitant. If, in the name of efficiency, of economies of scale, and of the demands of world markets, we allow restraints on the free play of domestic market forces, then other forces will have to be used to define and preserve the public interest. These "other forces" will amount to clearer control by the political order in some form or other.

THE ACTIVE-PLANNING STATE

It follows that the role of the state is changing radically. It is becoming the setter of our sights and the arbiter of community needs. Inevitably, it will take on unprecedented tasks of coordination, priority setting, and planning in the largest sense. It will need to become far more efficient and authoritative, capable of making the difficult and subtle trade-offs which confront us—for example, between environmental purity and energy supply.

Government is already big in the United States, probably bigger in proportion to population than even in those countries called "socialist." Some 16 percent of the labor force now works for one or another governmental agency, and by 1980 it will be more. Increasingly, United States institutions live on government largess—subsidies, allowances, contracts to farmers, corporations, and universities; individuals benefit from social insurance, medical care, and housing allowances. The pretense of the limited state, however, means that these huge allocations are relatively haphazard, reflecting the crisis of the moment and the power of interest groups rather than any sort of coherent and objective plan. A glaring example is the web of interrelated factors which together constituted the energy crisis.

Significantly, political leaders, starting with Franklin Roosevelt's New Deal have found it necessary to plan. But they cloak their departures from the limited state in the language of the old ideology. Interventions are made to appear pragmatic. Ignoring the ideological implications is confusing and hypocritical and delays the time when we will recognize the planning functions of the state for what they are and must be.

If the role of government were more precisely and consciously defined, the government could be smaller in size. To a great extent, the plethora of bureaucracies results from a lack of focus and comprehension—an ironic bit of fallout from the old notion of the limited state. With greater awareness of what needs to be done it will be possible to consider more fruitfully which issues are best left to local action, to regional planning, to centralized coordination, and which transcend the nation-state to require a more global approach.

HOLISM—INTERDEPENDENCE

Finally, and perhaps most fundamentally, the old idea of scientific specialization has given way to new consciousness of the interrelatedness of all things. Spaceship earth, the limits of growth, the fragility of our life-supporting biosphere have dramatized the ecological and philosophical truth that everything is related to everything else. Harmony between the works of man and the demands of nature is no longer the romantic plea of conservationists. It is an absolute rule of survival, and thus it is of profound ideological significance, subverting in many ways all of the Lockean ideas.

The Dilemma of Protest

Introducing cohesive and organic order into our fractionated world is not painless. It is difficult (even for those most intimately involved in the process) to see clearly where the real problems lie:

contradictions are met; frustrations are induced; and anger is the residue of misguided efforts. Two examples illustrate.

THE YOUTH REBELLION

The so-called youth counterculture was rooted in an ideological contradiction which it diligently sought to minimize. It voiced a traditional (if extreme) cry for the full promises of the Enlightenment —individualistic and romantic: "Do your own thing now, no matter what." At the same time it represented a call for new communitarian norms to govern income distribution, inheritance, harmony with nature, and a new political order. Young people, not surprisingly, were unable to live with such contradiction.

Educational institutions gave them little help. Academic bureaucracies, based on the old idea of specialization, constituted a series of long dark tunnels called disciplines. The best man in each field was at the end of his tunnel, digging an ever narrowing trench of new knowledge. "If you are diligent you may find him," the student was told. "If you are persistent, you may get him to raise his head and mumble."

Whatever the ultimate value of specialized research may be, the student has come to wonder whether this kind of education is what he needs to understand the world; whether, in fact, what is truly important is not what ties the tunnels together in their cross-cutting relationships. What, for example, are the implications of genetics, biology, or psychology for political science, philosophy, and sociology? When the student tries to find out, only a few mavericks are ready to hold out a helping hand. It is no wonder that increasing numbers of college seniors have no conception of where they are going to fit. It is also no wonder that increasing numbers of students are dropping out to seek their own integration through direct experience in the world. Understandable as this reaction may be, it is woefully inefficient. Realizing this fact, the educational bureaucracies are beginning to budge—but no more than that. Hierarchies of the business world are doing somewhat better, because the threats to their survival are more dramatic.

AN AUTOPSY ON INDUSTRY

Once General Motors harmonized beautifully with the community. In 1910, what were to become GM's components, were clearly owned by entrepreneurs: Louis Chevrolet and his counterparts at Buick, Oldsmobile, Hyatt Roller Bearings, and so on. Their authority and legitimacy were clear. Young men came hungry for work in Detroit;

thousands massed outside the hiring gates. The rights of property were secure and the contract which followed from them was authoritative. Mr. Chevrolet offered the terms on a take-it or leave-it basis.

Time passed and workers demanded more power, so they submerged their individualism into an interest group called the United Automobile Workers. When management, acting out of a sense of property rights, resisted, violence ensued. The UAW finally won, and the contract became collectivized—almost a contradiction in terms, if one thinks of the contract in pure form.

At the same time property rights were being eroded through bargaining techniques animated by an adversary philosophy. These rights were further diluted by the divorce of management from ownership. Nevertheless, the structure worked efficiently, and the United States accepted it because of its respect for the automobile and for the material growth it helped to spawn.

A new evolution might be perceived in the union experiences of the 1960s. The UAW started to splinter as individual locals (and individual workers within locals) experienced needs which could not be embraced by already bloated contracts. Individual survival having been assured by the community, the workers began to demand avenues to individual fulfillment in a communitarian setting.

So the legitimacy and power of management, on the one hand, and of union and the labor contract, on the other, have deteriorated. But the hierarchies have barely budged. For a while, company management's answer was to pay workers more for their unhappiness —certainly a recourse suitable to the contractual form. The union hierarchy, on their side, had roughly the same idea—a fatter contract. Absenteeism, sabotage, and lowering productivity continued, however. Meanwhile at Toyota, when the night shift went off duty, it cheered the day shift on to harder and harder work. This whole syndrome is generic to United States industry. Its root is simply that the old ways of doing things are largely irrelevant and new ways which accord with present realities and new definitions of values must be found. And, it must be said, General Motors and other large corporations are hard at work doing so.

The Manager's Mind

Let me now consider what these five transformations imply for managers—especially those of large publicly held corporations. In simplest terms, the manager must form an attitude of mind permeated by willingness to confront openly manifold change with breadth of vision. More than ever, he must see his task as a general not a specialized one. He is not an expert; he is an integrator and synthesizer who is responsible for the whole enterprise in its internal and external relationships.

This requires courage to rinse from the mind and inspect all assumptions, especially those that underlie his power and legitimize it; to consider the interests of the whole and not merely his own momentary bureaucratic status and prerogatives; and to risk innovative organizational arrangements not necessarily tied to the old hierarchies of authority.

It also requires *hope:* hope not for return of "the good old days" and combined *ad hoc* solutions, but hope for greater potential value in man's future, the hope which supports those who, in Erich Fromm's words, "see and cherish all forms of new life and are ready at every moment to help the birth of that which is ready to be born."

SOME SPECIFICS

Having opened the mind fully, a manager can consider two sets of problems which the changing ideology raises for the large corporation. The first applies to the internal organization and concerns matters of ownership, accountability, and contract. The second concerns the relationship between the corporation and the communities which it affects: the neighborhood, the city, the state, the nation, and the world. Then he can focus on the questions that all these problems raise:

1. Which problems should the corporation resolve and which must be decided by the community?
2. How are community decisions best made—by government, by consumers, or by interest groups?
3. If by interest groups, then how—by direct (perhaps radical) action, through legislative and legal pressure, or through the ITT pattern of leverage on the executive branch?
4. To what extent is dispersion of power a desirable thing politically?
5. As managerial legitimacy has declined, the central government has moved in to control increasing segments of corporate operation. Should corporations try to regain what political edge they have lost?
6. If dispersion of power is good (I think it is), how should the corporation encourage the design of more dispersed forms of community legitimization and control—within its own framework and outside it?

This is a valuable exercise, not so much because the manager can always influence the answers directly, but because it helps them set out the possibilities. (See Figure 2).

Fig. 2. Internal and External Questions Relating to Large Public Corporations.

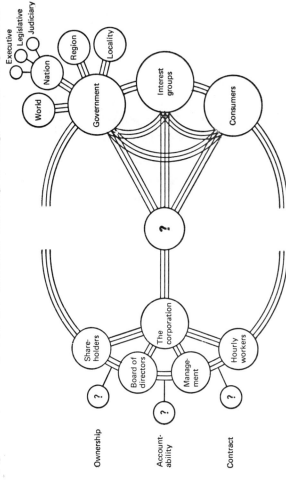

Internal

Traditional ideology has it that the corporation is property; that it is owned by its shareholders; that the owners elect the board of directors; that the board names the managers; that the managers thus have the rights associated with property by "natural" law and, therefore, the right to contract for labor. The contract between management and the union that was once individualistic is now, in general, collective. Every aspect of this sequence is vulnerable

External

Traditional ideology has it that the fundamental control on the corporation is that exerted by individual consumers in an open market. Circumstances, however, have required the intervention by government into this essential relationship. Traditional ideology, however, has fostered the development of interest groups to pressure government and, lately, as a result of declining confidence in government, to act directly on the corporate-community relationship.

Industry has taken some hesistant steps toward resolving its ideological confusions, some of which seek to minimize or eliminate the
labor contract and replace it with institutionalized consensus. Somewhat like its Japanese and certain European counterparts, the United
States corporation is moving from the adversary-contractual structure
toward a consensual form in which, to put it simply, no one feels left
out of anything. As this occurs, alternatives to property rights are
emerging as the way to provide legitimacy and thus authority to management. Here are some vignettes of the change.

FOOD PROCESSING

A Kansas plant manufacturing pet food in Topeka is organized into
self-managed work teams which are given collective responsibility for
large parts of the production process. To accommodate the capabilities
and needs of individual workers assignments of individuals to tasks
are subject to team consensus. There is a deliberate attempt to break
down division of labor and specialization: "Pay increases are geared
to an employee mastering an increasing proportion of jobs first in the
team and then in the total plant." The plant is productive and profitable.

Note the radical implications of this experiment. In a real sense,
management's legitimacy and authority come from workers and not
from an outworn conception of property rights. This fact feeds the
workers' sense of fulfillment and thus contributes to the high productivity and profits of the operation.

But top management of the company thus faces two excruciating
questions:

1. "Do we extend this idea to other plants—maybe to headquarters itself—
   to increase ROI even though it will undercut our own jobs?"
2. "If we do it anyway, what happens to the myth that we are answerable
   to the board of directors who represent the shareholders?" (The answer
   to this one is complicated by the fact that shareholders appear to be getting
   a better return on investment from Topeka. Perhaps the management
   hierarchy, or part of it, should be dispensed with.)

The threat to the idea of equality should also be noted when an
organization moves to consensus from contract. Since each team is
responsible for hiring replacements, it is likely that recruits will be
sought from those who will get along well with the group. If the group
objects to certain persons, they will not be hired. Bias of race, religion,
sex, ethnic group, could be involved. My point is this: collectivism can

be dehumanizing unless it is infused with a definite social theory or ideology. Moving from contract to consensus obviously threatens unions as well. The Topeka plant is small and new, with an innovative management and no union. To apply the same principles in the automobile or steel or utilities industries, however, raises many problems. Yet all these industries are trying, albeit in somewhat different ways to launch experimental organizational plans.

THE AUTO INDUSTRY

Detroit was introducing job enrichment and organizational development programs which some union leaders promptly criticized as elitist nonsense and as paternalistic attempts to divide the worker from the union. "The better the wage, the greater the job satisfaction," said William Winpisinger, general vice president of the International Association of Machinists (*Wall Street Journal*, February 26, 1973). He added: "There is no better cure for blue-collar blues." At the same time, company industrial relations officials joined Leonard Woodcock of the UAW in attributing "the alienation problem" to academics who do not know what they are talking about (*Newsweek*, March 26, 1973).

It is not surprising that labor relations bureaucrats on both sides eye any threat to the contract anxiously since this idea supports their bureaucracies. Their resistance testifies both to the ideological nature of the problem and to the difficulty of solving it in situations where rigid hierarchies are unwilling to inspect the assumptions beneath them.

STEEL

The steel industry is following a somewhat different route to establish a basis for consensus. Industry labor relations officials and union leaders in 1973 worked out a peace agreement involving a no-strike clause and binding arbitration in the face of the common interest— namely, making the United States goods more competitive against foreign imports. Although neither side is likely to admit it, such an arrangement is a step toward replacing the idea of contract with that of consensus.

This scheme differs from the organizational development and job enrichment schemes of the automobile industry because it protects directly all of those whose power is threatened. Its weakness is that, in itself, it does nothing to give a greater sense of participation to workers on the shop floor. But an HEW task force noted in 1972 that this may be a serious shortcoming: "What workers want most, according to more than one hundred studies made in the past twenty years, is to become masters of their immediate environments and to feel that their work and they themselves are important." The dispute for leadership within the United Steelworkers Union in 1977 reflected the tension between consensualism at the top and contractualism at the bottom.

If consensual systems are going to work, it will be necessary to educate young people according to the new ideology and to hire people who want to become part of a whole community effort. No matter how consensual a collective may get, there are going to be boring jobs, which will not provide fulfillment. Workers will have to be screened for jobs with the idea of weeding out those whose capacities are more, or less, than the work requires. This prospect raises ominous specters of Orwellianism and deserves careful watching.

ELECTRIC UTILITIES

For years, the utility companies tried—successfully—to keep government regulation diffuse. Government has responded, steadfastly failing both to manage our nation's energy needs and to plan a procedure to fulfill them. The result is that many utilities find themselves in a devilish mess: rates fixed by state agencies, taxed by the cities, partly regulated by the Federal Power Commission, and affected by nuclear energy regulatory bodies and a host of other local and national governmental entities.

At the same time, environmental interest groups are grabbing for the utility companies' throats. The scenic Hudson Preservation Society, for example, successfully kept Consolidated Edison Company of New York from building its pump-storage power station at Cornwall on the Hudson River for more than ten years, and the battle is not entirely over. Like great dinosaurs, many public utilities are being bitten to death in a swamp partly of their own making. Con Ed became notably healthier in 1974 when it became a partner with New York State rather than an adversary.

The need for federal intervention to plan the future of electric power production seems plain. Regional power production jurisdictions should be planned; research on new technologies needs to be increased; technology and site decisions must be made. The problem is far too big and too national in scope to leave to a scattering of private companies.

But this does not mean that these companies should be nationalized. That will be the inevitable result, however, unless more intelligent steps are taken soon. These companies must realize what government, and only government, can and must do: plan the allocation of resources and make the critical judgments of costs and benefits. To do this it must intervene with authority and coherence.

Summary on the Executive's Responsibility

The transition described in this chapter requires responsible managers to inspect and question all ideological assumptions. The questioning may lead to a conclusion that the organization is safely nested in Lockeanism; on the other hand, new terrain may have to be explored. In either case, it is necessary to avoid wishful thinking, the possibility of which was revealed in a pool conducted by the *Harvard Business Review* in the summer of 1975, and reported in the November/December issue. There were 1,844 respondents to the poll, and most were executives in the upper ranks of American corporations. They were asked which of the two ideologies described above they (1) preferred, (2) found dominant in the United States today, (3) expected to dominate in 1985, and (4) believed would be more effective in solving future problems. It turned out that the respondents preferred the traditional ideology 70 percent to 30 percent. Sixty-two percent thought that individualism was dominant today; 36 percent felt that communitarianism was. But by 1985, 73 percent thought that communitarianism would dominate, with 60 percent continuing to feel that the old way would be the most effective. Most readers felt that the ideology which they detested was the one that was coming—and regretted it.

Three dangers are implicit in these figures; (1) the desire to "wish" communitarianism away; (2) the sense of inevitability; and (3) the notion that "I'll be too old when it comes so let the kids take care of it."

My plea is to managers to develop a capacity to think in ideological terms and to inspect carefully the ideological assumptions which guide them. It seems clear to me that communitarianism is, in many ways, already here and that in some form or other it is inevitable. The quick and accurate perception of crisis is crucial because it is through the intelligent use of crisis that change occurs most effectively. The central managerial task of the future may well be the use of minimum crisis to cause maximum change with least waste and violence.

Ideological analysis also will allow managers to evaluate what is best in the old ideology and how it may be preserved. One ideology obviously builds on another. The glories of the old—the rights of the individual, his dignity, the beautiful efficiency of price competition, the incentives of enterprise and invention—are all in jeopardy. The best of them can be preserved only if we consciously design them into what is coming.

Why should managers bother? Because they lead powerful corporations and what managers believe affects the way they lead. The success of the great corporation will be due in no small measure to its ability to adapt consciously to communitarian norms. Several future choices can be seen most clearly in communitarian terms; it would be tragic if major policy is formed on an exclusively Lockean basis.

After six years of interviewing 250 corporate executives in twelve large high-technology companies, Michael Maccoby, director of the Harvard Project on Technology, Work and Character, concluded that a "gamesman" has come to the fore:

> A new type of man [he might have added "woman"] is taking over the leadership of the most technically advanced companies in America. In contrast to the jungle-fighter industrialists of the past, he is driven not to build or preside over empires, but to organize winning teams. Unlike the security-seeking organization man, he is excited by the chance to cut deals and to gamble. Although more cooperative and less hardened than the autocratic empire builders and less dependent than the organization man, he is more detached and emotionally inaccessible than either. And he is troubled by it: the new industrial leader can recognize that his work develops his head but not his heart.
>
> More dependent on the organization than they realize for their life's meaning, their efforts at self-development make them valuable tools for the company. Outside the company, they have little social function or individual purpose. More than anyone else, they have exploited themselves.

The new top executive, a team player whose center is the corporation, feels himself so completely responsible for the functioning of the system that his own career goals have merged with those of the corporation. And yet, as the Maccoby survey suggests, a manager is torn by separation from the romantic image of individualism associated with the traditional ideology. To an extent, he is soothed by the idea that if things get bad enough he can go out and make it on his own as an entrepreneur. In reality this is improbable. In the early nineteenth century, some 80 percent of all Americans were self-employed; by 1950 it was 18 percent, and in 1970 only 9 percent. So Maccoby said we should be learning

> how to establish the rights of managers and workers so as to develop a new basis of cooperative independence in the corporations based on mutual respect, equity, and democratic participation. Instead, we indulge in day-dreams of romantic independence, and they tend to support narcissistic fantasies, jungle-fighting careerism, and game-playing.

There is a danger and a propensity to indulge in name-calling as we move from one ideology to another. Big business is chastised for departing from the old hymns which it continues lustily to sing and for being insensitive to community needs. Government is criticized for "planning" to define those community needs because we linger with the notion that such a role is inconsistent with the Lockean ideal. Passionate interest groups are taken to task either for the corruption of their means or the narrowness of their ends. And yet the alternative to interest-group pluralism—objective definition of the public interest by a more insulated state—carries with it the menace of authoritarian unresponsiveness. But name-calling will not do: it is both paranoic and schizophrenic. Our problems will not be addressed by seeking out saints and sinners, but only by carefully examining the assumptions we make about the definition of the unchanging values of survival, justice, economy, self-fulfillment, and self-respect; ridding ourselves of old ghosts; and building explicitly a new framework of definitions for carrying those values into the real world.

Max Ways

3

A Plea for Perspective

Having observed the business scene closely for nearly fifty years, a distinguished journalist, Max Ways, takes a generally optimistic view of corporate ethical behavior. If public credibility in business has declined, it may be due largely to an intellectual community which spends more time criticizing the system than seeking to understand it.

There are, of course, real ethical problems. Tax loopholes, for example, are often viewed as evil even when they are the necessary vent through which business breathes. Yet the very existence of loopholes has encouraged some entrepreneurs to exploit them, and this has become a major source of scandal. But one should not miss the significant point, namely, that corporations have added to our wealth, increased our options, and provided thereby a greater degree of individual freedom. This century, properly viewed, is the most ethical of all centuries—not because men are better behaved but because individuals can make conscious choices of actions whose consequences are foreseeable and, hence, open to judgment for their rightness or wrongness.

C. C. W.

There are cogent reasons why United States society in general and such groups as The American Assembly in particular should

MAX WAYS *was for many years editor of* Fortune *magazine. He has been a professional journalist since beginning with the* Baltimore Sun *in 1926. Mr. Ways is the author of* Beyond Survival, *a study of foreign policy. He has written countless articles on business subjects from Antitrust to Worker Participation.*

be concerned with the ethics of business conduct. Certain heavily-traveled approaches to this subject, however, may be producing results contrary to those intended. Many recent comments and proposals in this field start from the premise, explicit and implicit, that the incidence of corporate misconduct is known, and that it has been rising in recent decades. Since neither part of this premise is evidentially solid we should not be surprised if reform programs built upon it crumble. Meanwhile, the unprovable assumptions of the premise form a noxious gas of cynicism that weakens the morale of the business community and confuses opinion in the surrounding public.

This chapter will try to sketch a better approach. But it is first necessary to deal with the rather peculiar way in which public attention to business ethics has been aroused.

What Do We Really Know?

Across a darkened stage a spotlight flits accusingly from one business scandal to another. The national audience has no clear view of what else is happening on the stage. Not surprisingly, many conclude that the tableaux of malfeasance, unveiled daily, are typical of business behavior. The Equity Funding scandal, for instance, may have suggested to some people that most or many other insurance companies increase their income by passing on forged policies to re-insurers. Few sources of public information attempt to put such scandals in a perspective with general patterns of corporate conduct.

Specific scandals foster generalized suspicion. Demands for the internal purification or external restraint of business inevitably arise. A diffuse hostility and suspicion permeates many popular attitudes toward business. On the other hand, an overwhelming majority of Americans answer *no* to the question of whether they want a very different kind of economic system. Even larger is the majority of Americans—employees, consumers, parents, bank depositors, and investors—who act as if they respected and trusted business.

This ambiguity—practical acceptance along with ethical disapproval—instills a poisonous cynicism. Indeed, many people working as part of business management have a low opinion of business morality. Sample groups of managers believe that "most businessmen" would behave worse in various situations than the surveyed respondents themselves, on average, say they would behave. This interesting discrepancy indicates that the ambiguity and its consequent cynicism have reached deep into management itself.

The ill-repute of business, whether or not justified, may actually encourage wrongdoing; people who believe their associates are immoral often succumb to a perceived contagion that might otherwise have been avoided. The effect is similar to that known in medicine as iatrogenic infection, *i.e.,* disease carried by physicians. The best-known example, of course, is childbed fever. Dr. Semmelweiss' cautionary cry to the Viennese obstetricians, "Wash your hands!" is applicable to all those who deal as diagnosticians or therapists with the ethical aspects of behavior. They may be spreading the excuse, "Everybody else does it," an excuse not used only by schoolboys and street hoodlums; it has been heard in exalted business—and other—offices.

If some well-meant exposures of business sins have spread more misconduct than they cured, we should not conclude that exposure itself was at fault. Sometimes the damage is done by the failure of corporate or government officials to take appropriate corrective action. More often, perhaps, the trouble lies in the context of the exposure. Should any particular scandal be thought of as isolated, exceptional? Or is it "the tip of the iceberg" alerting us to a concealed mass of fraud, deceit, trickery, and other illegitimate uses of economic power?

SCIENTIFIC MEASUREMENTS?

In short, the scandals raise but do not answer the key question: how widespread is corporate misconduct? At first glance, this seems to be a quantitative question, calling for the twentieth century's favorite kind of behavioral investigation: a statistical analysis. To describe such a project is to demonstrate its practical impossibility. The investigator would have to count the publicly exposed transgressions over a period. Such a review could be assembled, but by itself would tell us very little about the incidence of misconduct. The total of known misdeeds would have to be related to a base made up of the trillions and trillions of business transactions that occur each day in this economy, most of them open to some sort of cheating or other impropriety by somebody. If we assume (recklessly) that a believable estimate of total transactions could be made, then the sum of the publicly known malfeasances almost certainly would be a minute fraction of the whole. At this point the investigator would have to abandon the conclusion that the incidence of business misconduct is so low as to be insignificant.

We may fantasize a resourceful social scientist, Professor Otto

Groundglass. He starts with the commonsense assumption that the number of publicly known business misdeeds must be lower than the number of all business misdeeds. He needs a multiplier. Should it be two or twenty or two thousand or twenty million? Professor Groundglass, inhibited by scientific discipline from choosing the figure he personally favors, sets up a survey. He constructs a sample of 500 people from interested groups—businessmen, clergymen, prosecutors, editors—and asks each to estimate the ratio by which undisclosed business misdeeds exceed such misdeeds publicly known. The responses average 47,556. This becomes known as the Groundglass Coefficient, and all subsequent scandal counts are multiplied by it to yield, when compared with the estimated total of all transactions, the "real" rate of corporate misconduct. After a time nobody would remember that the Groundglass Coefficient had been calculated in a way no more authoritative than if it had been drawn out of a hat.

This fantasy is not much more fantastic than many appraisals of the American ethical condition. More than ten years ago I reviewed a book replete with statistics (or, at least, with large numbers) that purported to show that fraud was one of the major lines of United States commercial activity. At the apex of his counts and estimates the author had placed a figure that represented what he called "unreported fraud." I gently derided this concept. The nature of fraud makes instances of it hard to count. In some cases (see *The Sting*) the victim has been cheated, but does not know it. In other cases, the victim knows he has been cheated and chooses not to complain to the police. In still others, he complains vociferously; but a judge and jury may later decide that no fraud was committed. Thus an estimated figure of "unreported fraud" seemed to me nonsense. The book's author indignantly protested that he had used "the best estimate available." Knowing him to be a tireless and resourceful investigator, I did not doubt his word. I continue, however, to believe that, barring information from supernatural sources, any estimate of "unreported fraud" will be a numerical delusion.

No matter how hard we try we are not going to get a quantitative answer to the question: how good or bad is corporate conduct? Even if we had—and believed—Professor Groundglass' real rate of transgression we might not know whether that rate should be deemed high or low. Nor would we be able to track back into the economic life of other generations to determine whether business conduct had advanced or declined on an ethical scale.

PUBLIC OPINION

Some proposals for the urgent reform of business avoid the direct assertion that business conduct has deteriorated. They say reform is required because the public *believes* that business conduct has descended to an intolerable level, citing many polls and other evidence indicating loss of public confidence in business. As a political or public relations proposition it is true that business and the whole of society will suffer unless public respect for the ethics of business rises from it present level. But as an ethical proposition it is dubious at best. Should anybody change his conduct because somebody else, possibly ill-informed, disapproves of what he is believed to have been doing? Public opinion, as mediated by surveys, is a powerful force in political and economic affairs; but it is not an infallible ethical arbiter. Emphatically, American public opinion of business conduct is currently not well enough informed to give business useful guidance on specific issues of *how* it should reform.

Basic Reform Areas

CONDUCT

There are really two different, though intertwined, fields possibly in need of reform. One is business conduct itself. The other is the way in which business conduct is publicly perceived. Any useful approach will cover both. We have to back off from the daily scandals and establish a framework large enough to contain an ethical appraisal of the business evolution to its present phase. Along with this we need a way of dealing critically with the main characteristics of the public's ethical attitudes toward business. With that conceptual equipment we can return to consideration of business scandals and related issues of current concern.

COMMUNICATIONS

Early in this chapter reference was made to a "darkened stage" surrounding the spotlighted tableaux of business malfeasance. The other business activity occurring outside the illumination is seen only dimly and fitfully, if at all, by the public. Why is most of the stage obscured? Some would blame that on the guilty desire of businessmen to conceal their plots. Some would blame politically biased information media, intent on showing only the worst of business. No doubt, examples of each tendency can be found; to recite them here would only distract attention from the main point. By far the most important cause of "darkness" over the corporate scene is the inherent difficulty of communicating an activity as complex and as fast-changing as modern business.

The complexity is a product of the specialization of knowledge and work. A hundred years ago most heads of corporations could do any job in the shop—or at least understand how the job should be done. In those days a businessman who knew his own company knew also the procedures and problems of most other companies. Today's chief executive is unlikely to have a firm, detailed mental grasp of more than one or two of such specialized and disparate departments as engineering, law, accounting, marketing. In the subspecialties of any of these departments he would be quickly lost. Corporations spend millions of dollars and mobilize some of their ablest people in the effort to maintain and improve internal communication—no frill but a task necessary to the coherence and unity of the organization. Indeed, management which used to be thought of in terms of "decision-making" now tends to be seen as a communication function.

If internal communication among groups of highly motivated people, most of whom have spent years in the same company, is that difficult, then communciation with an outside public must be a more formidable task. And it would still be formidable if representatives of the media were better disposed and better qualified than they are now. Most of the media and most of academia are presenting the business scene through stereotypes that are twenty to fifty years out of date. The quality of public judgments concerning business cannot be much better than the quality of the information the public receives through the educational network, the journalistic network, and the networks of entertainment and the arts.

At this time it should be pointed out that business is not the only segment of modern society suffering under inherent communications difficulties created by complexity and rapid change. Modern government, though a somewhat more stable scene than business, is complex enough to daunt most reporters and academics. United States journalism does devote a high proportion of its coverage to activities that fall under the rubric "politics." But only a tiny fraction of this makes any serious effort to explain how bureaucracy, for instance, works or why it behaves the way it does. As in coverage of business, journalistic handling of government tends to concentrate on scandals and other forms of social and ethical pathology. An angry accusation of moral turpitude is easier to communicate than, say, a description of how any part of the Department of Health, Education, and Welfare works. Very old literary models—the prophet as scourge of the wicked, the medieval morality play—are adapted to reportage on contemporary government.

Indeed, knowledge of all the complex organizations on which modern civilization depends reaches the public mainly through old and inappropriate forms of communication that distort present reality. The lag in the communication function may be the gravest general defect in advanced societies.

One of the admirable characteristics of the United States is that almost everybody participates in significant communication. Nevertheless, some are listened to more than others, and therefore bear a larger share of responsibility for the quality of the society's communication.

THE INTELLECTUALS

Among the groups with extraordinary communicative clout are educators, politicians, journalists, clergymen, novelists, script writers, and others whose role in the social anatomy is derived from their special competence in helping its members understand themselves and one another. These groups are collectively known as "the intellectuals," a word that sometimes misleads the unwary into supposing it connotes superiority of intellect. What it indicates is professional devotion to expression—a field which may, but need not, include intellectual activity of an unusually high order. Ironically, the intellectuals, who have a heavy share of responsibility for the communications function, seldom recognize that they, as a group, are part of the problem.

A few years ago the Irish playwright, Brian Friel, wrote *The Freedom of the City;* ostensibly it was about the bloody conflict in Northern Ireland. Its deeper subject was the distortion of reality by professional communicators. In the play demonstrators and soldiers opposing them were both treated sympathetically. Less gentle handling was meted out to other characters: a ballad singer, a military public relations man, an American sociologist, a clergyman, and a metropolitan television reporter. Each was shown as interpreting the action through ill-fitting and oversimplified stereotypes that exacerbated the conflict.

The play closed after a few days in New York, where the critics simply could not understand a drama in which the bad guys were their fellow intellectuals.

Business is not being treated worse than other groups when intellectuals, having given to the public a distorted picture of the ethical situation in business, then urge that business be reformed *because the public lacks confidence in business conduct*. There is no guarantee—or even a probability—that if business conduct quickly improved the public would hear the news for many years, if ever. Some scandals will always be available to observers who will not tackle the hard task of communicating business normality. The reasons for seeking improvement in business ethics have to be established on a firmer base than the need to placate a public opinion that many, assuming no improvement in the attitudes of the intellectuals, turn out to be implacable.

The Base for Ethical Reform

In search of such a base I turn to the evolution of business itself and to the development of those societies, notably the United States, in which business has been not only the main organizer of economic life, but also the main agent of social change.

From the viewpoint of the late twentieth century the most conspicuous achievement in the history of business has been the effectiveness with which it has deployed technology and developed management to produce mass prosperity. People still alive were born in a world where the majority in every nation, without exception, lived below or at or slightly and precariously above the level of bare subsistence. Today in the United States and the other advanced countries the overwhelming majority of the inhabitants live far above the subsistence level.

Hardly anyone denies the fact that this huge change or the further fact that it occurred first and has gone farthest in countries with well-developed business systems coordinated through markets. But usually the onset of mass prosperity, one of the great advances in human history, is presented as "merely" a material gain. As such it is often despised on cultural grounds. By ethical standards mass prosperity is commonly deemed either irrelevant or corruptive. A "Faustian" view of twentieth century material progress says we have traded our spiritual and ethical estate for a mess of petrochemical pottage.

PROSPERITY AND PROBITY

Relatively ignored are the profound ethical consequences of mass prosperity. The economic activities of past centuries took up a large part of life, as they still do. But in those former centuries most people, as producers or as consumers, followed rigid tracks of prescribed routine and iron necessity. Choice rarely entered the economic side of their lives. And where choice is absent ethical distinctions are meaningless. Mass prosperity has hugely multiplied the number of situations where it is possible to act rightly or wrongly, with almost infinite gradations of better or worse. Meanwhile, our ability to help—or hurt—ourselves and others has suddenly magnified. This new power, with its accession of ethical responsibility, affects great decisions of war or peace in which all citizens of a political democracy share—indirectly but surely. The new power also gives an enlarged ethical dimension to the most commonplace decisions of family life. Should immediate pleasures, such as an expensive vacation, be foregone in favor of increased insurance premiums covering children's college education? This kind of choice, obviously, was not unknown before the twentieth century. The difference is that now almost everybody is faced almost daily with some such alternative.

When I assert that the twentieth is the most ethical of centuries I do not mean that its people are the best-behaved; whether they are we cannot know. I mean the twentieth is the century most permeated by conscious choice between actions whose consequences are more or less foreseeable and open to judgment on a scale of right and wrong. Power is morally neutral. For millions of Americans one of the opportunities of increased economic power is the chance to contribute to charitable efforts. For several hundred thousand others the prosperous society presents an opportunity to destroy themselves with narcotics. Clearly, temptation must increase as the power to do harm expands. Clearly, opportunities for benevolence also increase. All today's economically advanced democracies are teeming with public and private debates with an ethical content: whether income and wealth should be less unequal—how fast social and ethnic quality can be achieved; how much should be spent on welfare or foreign aid; what are the causes and the possible cures of violent crime.

We may be producing answers that are flawed—or dead wrong. The point is we have a flood of ethical discussion because we know that mass prosperity has thrust upon us so much power to help or hurt. Many Americans have a painful conscience arising out of our technological and managerial power to plunder the resources of the planet to an extent unjust to future generations. This was not a concern of past societies that possessed only a tiny fraction of the power we deploy. In the centuries when much of the land in Spain was eroding, nobody felt guilty about the economic practices that did the damage; nor were these practices a subject of accusation and debate on ethical grounds. In the twentieth century we have "lost our innocence"; we can foresee harmful consequences of present economic practices in such matters; we can hope to develop further technological and managerial skills that will avoid or diminish the harm done to the interests of future generations by the exercise of present power. We know we are free to handle our technological power in some ways that are ethically better or worse than others. And that consciousness is itself an ethical advance—although it by no means guarantees "good conduct."

THE NEW TRUST

Mass prosperity in the advanced countries is the most general, but far from the only, way that business has stepped up the ethical component of life. In this context, the development of credit provides an interesting area for reflection. In essence, credit is a way of organizing cooperation on the basis of trust. As the television commercial of one bank puts it, "If you have a good reason for a loan, we have a good reason to say yes."

A bank often finds overriding reasons to say no. Credit is always limited and always discriminatory. Those are the qualities that allowed credit to build its edifice of cooperation in the wide ground between total trust and total distrust. A moralist can say, "Neither a borrower nor a lender be" or "Trust everyone in all circumstances" or "Trust the trustworthy." The businessmen who developed the credit system took the last axiom and made it workable by elaborating devices of limitation and discrimination. The past performance of the borrower, his credit record, included ethical judgments on his behavior. Such judgments are now and always have been imperfect, but their development has been strong enough to support the practical extension of the credit system to most of the United States population.

That abuses and injustices appear in the operation of the credit mechanism is hardly surprising. Discrimination can be applied in an ethnically offensive manner that places women or blacks or residents of run-down neighborhoods at a disadvantage when they try to borrow. Quite justifiably, victims of this kind of unjust discrimination appeal to the moral judgment of the community seeking legal relief. A difficult, though not insoluble problem emerges: how may we outlaw certain unjust kinds of discrimination without destroying the lender's discriminatory function on which the operation of the whole system depends?

What a mass of misconduct has been brought into being by the credit system! Borrowers abscond, lenders conceal true interest rates, people are led by credit into spending beyond the level of their present income or future prospects. Yet all this ethical pathology occurs within a system that embodies, as does mass prosperity, a fundamental ethical advance. Breaches of trust—a category covering a large part of today's economic misconduct—would certainly be diminished if we trusted one another less. But is mistrustful autonomy an ethical desideratum? Or should we not, on ethical grounds, be respectful of an institution, credit, that allows us to increase our interdependence and cooperation?

In historical perspective today's use of credit appears to me as a morally edifying spectacle. Only a few generations ago buying in installments was widely regarded as a reckless innovation, too risky for all parties concerned. I can remember when only a minority of bankers thought the day would ever come when salaried people without assets to put up as collateral could walk into a bank and borrow substantial sums. Now they can. Loans are repaid, pacts are kept, and the credit system expands the area of behavior in which trust is a more and more prominent element.

DIGNIFIED WORK

Trust of a different—and more important kind—is involved in changes occurring in the relationships among people within business organizations. The intellectuals who make ethical assessments of business conduct were quick to notice the assembly line which they deemed, reasonably, to be deplorable on ethical grounds because it reduced workers to machine-like operations designed in every detail by managers; it was assumed that the assembly line was the wave of the future and that industrial man was destined to be robotized. Of the thousands of hand-wringing comments on this somber theme perhaps the most artistically brilliant was Charlie Chaplin's *Modern Times*, produced in the late 1930s—just before the tide turned and the times he depicted were about to become antique.

For reasons quite independent of the adverse criticism, the kind of job exemplified by the assembly line has been receding, relative to all jobs, for at least twenty-five years. For a generation the dominant trend in the workplace has been to give more responsibility to more people. This occurs not because bosses want to make employees "happy." (It is highly doubtful, anyway, that happiness in the sense of contentment increases with responsibility.) The evolution of business reached a level of specialization and complexity at which the old forms of direction from above were inapplicable to many work situations—hence the explosion of white-collar jobs, especially those involving professional competence. Bosses today are surrounded by people who can be "led" but not commanded. Leadership takes the form of listening, collating, moving specialized information and initiatives from this group to that, and persuading.

What has been going on inside the corporation is a tremendous distribution of power to the points where the best knowledge and competence can be brought to bear on particular actions. In present conditions this must seem the most effective way to get the work done. But what are the ethical implications of this trend? If the robotizing tendency was ethically bad, because workers were deprived of using more than a small fraction of their human potential, then the present derobotizing tendency should be deemed good. But the intellectual community neither applauds nor notices the new trend.

In fact, the new trend goes much further than a restoration of workers to some previous level of human dignity. Far from being cogs in the economic machine, millions of workers find themselves encouraged and even pressed to exercise initiative, to find better ways than the boss dreamed of for doing the work. Moreover, at many levels employees are expected to arrive at consensual decisions about the design of the work. They are, in effect, self-managers. And this is a situation that should—but apparently does not—gladden the hearts of intellectuals who include among their professional activities the task of monitoring the ethical evolution of business.

What the professional communicators do not notice the public does not know! Indeed, many businessmen in companies where the trend toward new modes of work is well advanced are hardly aware of what is happening. In the summer of 1976 I wrote an article for *Fortune* under the title "The American Kind of Worker Participation." The trend here, evolving quietly and naturally out of fundamental changes in corporate tasks, was contrasted with a wave of statutes in European countries mandating various kinds of worker participation of a very different sort. Shortly after sending the article to press I left for France to attend a conference on worker participation. Most of the conferees were executives of European companies in a single line of business. On the first day we heard reports on worker-participation laws from each country. These added up to a grim story from the viewpoint of the executives—and from my viewpoint. The second day was taken up with reports from each company on changing management practices that had, in effect, increased the authority of employees below—often far below—the top. These changes were not responsive to worker-participation laws or union demands; as was the case in the United States, power within corporations was being more widely distributed for functional reasons of improving business performance.

Perhaps clumsy statutes decreeing worker representation on boards of directors, consultation with workers on important decisions, *etc.*, would not have been passed if legislators and the public had understood the much more significant kind of participation that was already occurring. I got the impression that even the executives at the conference had not been aware of how widespread the functional distribution of authority had become in their industry—and presumably in other European industries. Nobody had told them. Professional communicators recognize the worker-participation laws as examples of a familiar—and readily tellable—story of class confrontation and struggle for political power. The other kind of participation does not fit into this dramatic matrix. So it does not get told!

Sharing Power and Prosperity

The distribution of responsibility within business, like every other great advance to a higher ethical level, may have the effect of multiplying instances of misconduct. One executive I interviewed stressed the point that responsibility cannot really be distributed unless management has also distributed the power to make mistakes. These errors may include ethical and legal transgressions for which the corporation may have to accept formal responsibility. In public opinion the perceived incidence of corporate misconduct rises. But, again, this perception fails to take into account that many more people in business are making many more decisions that have an ethical content. And it fails to notice that this broadened base of decisions is in itself a magnificent ethical advance.

THE TRAVELING ENTERPRISE

One other fundamental characteristic of modern business has important ethical implications—business moves. Moralists, however, tend to prefer static social and economic conditions where the rules, once "discovered," are clearly understood by all the actors and spectators. That kind of settled social environment brings to bear on individuals and groups potent pressures in favor of "good conduct."

Travel has always heightened moral risks. Business never ceases pushing into strange territory where the rules of behavior have not been clearly formulated by it or any other agency. The wider distribution of responsibility within business, for instance, multiplies occasions for personal conflict and misconduct. New technological power requires enactment of laws to protect the environment; some of these may be unclear or impractical in detail, facing businessmen with ethical choices between compliance that may waste resources and efficiencies that may evade the law. Ever-changing economic conditions demand new accounting rules; while these are being worked out certain ethical judgments of business conduct lack a firm factual base.

For years it was widely—and correctly—believed that many corporations overstated profits. At first glance this would appear to be a massive fraud on the investing public; but in fact the discrepancy came about because chronic inflation was raising the replacement cost of plant and equipment, a condition not adequately reflected in the accounts. This defect has now been corrected, but no decade is likely to pass without the need for other accounting changes of like magnitude. The rule book of business, in short, cannot be stabilized, because the game itself changes.

MULTINATIONALS

The plainest example of the effect of "travel" on the ethical character of business is the transnational or multinational corporation. The corporation, legally one person, may be operating simultaneously in fifty or more countries, some of them with very different legal and ethical restraints. To examine its conscience a multinational company needs a computer, but even a computer cannot deal with delicate moral distinctions of where permissible business behavior ends and misconduct begins. To say that the deciding officer has only to consult his own conscience oversimplifies the question. The decision may be processed at many levels by people from several different cultures, each using a different ethical scale. Involved in the decisions may be the jobs of thousands of workers and the property of thousands of investors. One executive of a multinational described a situation where a $70 million investment, built up over many years in a host country, was jeopardized by a new national law placing a discretionary power of effective confiscation in the hands of a few public officials. The company might be able to stave off the loss by distributing a few hundred thousand dollars in ways that were not outright bribes, but were certainly intended to influence the officials' decision. Those of his associates who were nationals of the host country favored making the payments, while some from other cultures took the opposite view.

No wonder a high proportion of the business "scandals" of recent years have involved multinationals. There is no evidence that they are less moral than other companies. Multinationals are, however, likely to run into more situations that are ethically "questionable," in the sense that clear answers have not been worked out.

This new set of ethical difficulties clustered around the multinationals occurs within a broad business change that has a strong claim to be considered, from the viewpoint of ethics, an advance. The twentieth century has suffered enough grief associated with excessive national economic autonomy. If multinational corporations provide opportunities for intense practical cooperation involving people from different cultures, that fact cannot be ethically deplorable. Probably, the multinationals have had the effect of increasing competition and stimulating innovation both abroad and in the United States. That we can learn from one another across national boundaries and become more dependent on one another's cooperation is, ethically, a plus. The new forms of misconduct—or "questionable" conduct—that attend this advance should not be regarded with complacency. But they will be more correctible if they are seen in a perspective that recognizes the dynamic character of business. Everywhere a corporation travels it raises for itself—and for others—moral problems that come with increasing freedom and responsibility.

Such a perspective will be hard to establish in the public mind against the resistance of the professional communicators. Their defenses are deeply entrenched. Antibusiness attitudes of today's intellectuals were not invented by Karl Marx. They run far back into European culture. We may be reminded of that depth by a wry passage in Paul Johnson's recent *A History of Christianity*. In summarizing the influential views of St. Ambrose, Bishop of Milan in the late fourth century, Johnson says:

> He condemned commerce: an honest trade, he thought, was a contradiction in terms. So it served a merchant right if he were shipwrecked, since he was driven to put to sea by avarice. No doubt Ambrose would have taken a different view if he had been bishop of Alexandria. As it was, being bishop of a great food-producing area, he thought the best form of property was inherited land: to cultivate, improve and extract profit from an inherited estate was not only legitimate but praiseworthy; thus he formulated one of the central religio-economic doctrines of the Middle Ages. Was not agriculture, he argued in *De Oficiis*, the only form of making money that did not give offense? Millions of Christians would agree.

Unfortunately.

The Hostile Tradition

For more than a thousand years after Ambrose (though not mainly because of his teaching), the economic base of Europe was agricultural. Commercial enclaves like Venice, Genoa, Ragusa, Amsterdam, flourished in the teeth of a general ethical disapproval of the unsettling spirit of enterprise. This opposition was expressed in many ways, including the condemnation of interest payments, an opposition that retarded, though it did not stop, the development of credit.

Today's secularized clerisy has many members who neither know nor care what Ambrose said. The antibusiness tradition, nevertheless, has been transmitted to them by all sorts of improbable carriers, including the Romantic Movement's contempt for "shopkeepers" and the many passages in Karl Marx scorched with moral indignation against business. *Profit, economic innovation, markets, credit*—all such words are likely to evoke automatic indignation or, at least, suspicion among the twentieth century's professional communicators. A few years ago a professor of ethics at an Eastern university told me he had never really given thought to the subject of business ethics because he had always assumed that the whole activity was unethical. He would have been surprised to learn he was paraphrasing St. Ambrose. The good bishop, no hermit, seems to have been a busy-man-about-Milan. He must have met at least one upright merchant and at least one avaricious peasant. Such inconvenient phenomena, however, apparently made no impression on his sweeping ethical constructs. In his day, as in this, more effective communication was achieved by dismissing the whole of commercial activity as unethical.

But facility of expression is not the same as validity and relevance in ethical guidance. Collectively, twentieth century intellectuals are "bishops of Alexandria," to adopt Johnson's phrase. They bear a measure of responsibility for developing ethical standards that are relevant to a complex commercial economy. This responsibility cannot be discharged without careful observation of the actual patterns of behavior developing in the economic system. To stand back from it, selecting for observation only those examples of behavior that seem to confirm a sweeping condemnation of the dynamic economy, may achieve a sonorous resonance with present popular prejudices transmitted from Western culture's rural past. But that rhetorically successful mode is no help in the present task of improving business ethics.

TO ACT MODERATELY

The need for improvement is urgent—and would be urgent if no recent business scandal had enlivened a newspaper page, lent color to a sermon or influenced the results of a public-opinion poll. Since business multiplies ethical problems by opening up higher levels of freedom and power, then the unprecedented business advance of the last thirty years must have brought into being a formidable ethical agenda. Nor is there any reason to suppose that the pace of business-generated change in the next thirty years is going to be markedly slower than in the past thirty; possibly it will be faster. The prospect of further change, stretching away into the next century, implies that the need for ethical improvement cannot be met by some intense spasm of reform, after which society can settle back in peace and confidence. Because ethical challenges created by business dynamism will continue to proliferate, what is needed is a strengthened ability to cope with challenges month-to-month, year-to-year, decade-to-decade.

Responsibility for this continuing process of ethical innovation and renewal must lie essentially with society as a whole. Some defenders of business, in their understandable horror of another wave of clumsy and destructive government intervention, sometimes come close to arguing that business should be considered an autonomous social segment with the right and capacity to generate all the rules needed to handle the ethical problems that business creates. The proposition that society should let business alone so long as it "delivers the goods" is not destined to prevail politically—and does not deserve to prevail.

The whole society is so dependent on business, the conduct of all of us is so pervaded by business conduct, that it is nonsense to suppose that society could give business an unlimited ethical trust to be the sole source of business rules.

Historically, business has never had ethical or legal autonomy. Looking at certain periods—one may cite the nineteenth century—the restraints seem to us relatively insignificant. But as the power of business rose, and as society became more dependent on it, restraints and interventions from outside of business became more prominent. This expectable change is not in itself "bad for business," which has in the past derived much of its progress, including ethical progress, from the tension between it and outside institutions; for example, the common law of England.

Such, however, is not the present situation. The main institution now affecting business is, of course, government. Along the immense and active front of government-business relationship the tension now appears to be having consequences that are, on balance, destructive. The deterioration occurs not only in the field of efficiency and material progress, but also in the realm of ethical development. The trouble is widely recognized in public discussion, but most efforts to understand its causes tend to get caught in commodious over-simplifications. One side says that government intervention in the economy is too great; the other side says it is too little. The United States (along with other industrialized democracies) has been spinning around in this debate for half a century. It may be the wrong debate.

WHERE THE ACTION IS

To see what is really happening, ethically, in government-business relations we have to get closer to the points of actual fact. One very large area of impact is the federal power to tax. Originally conceived as a necessary device to raise revenues for government functions, the taxing power could obviously also be used for other purposes. In the nineteenth century, at the behest of some manufacturers, it was used to encourage domestic industries to protective tariffs. The twentieth century found a more ambitious purpose for federal taxing power; "social justice" would be advanced by a tax structure that brought about a less unequal distribution of net income. The top tax bracket now stands at 70 percent. The tax schedules for forty years have seemed to promise a drastic redistribution of incomes. But they deliver much less redistribution than they promise.

Most congressmen and other elected officials are not stupid, not ignorant of economics, and not without experience in practical affairs. They know—or sense—that an income tax structure as steeply progressive as ours seems to be would soon stifle the economy, probably shrinking the aggregate income available for redistribution. Therefore, elected federal officials have been receptive over many years to demands from various interest groups that exceptions be written into tax law, some as incentives to stimulate one or another specific economic activity, some to rectify this or that perceived "injustice."

In time, these became known as "loopholes." The economy breathes through the loopholes. Great Britain's income tax structure, which has higher rates and fewer loopholes, has been stifling that country's economy for decades, diminishing incentive, innovation and the ability to form new capital. In this country, thanks to more and wider loopholes, the economic harm done by the tax structure has been less grievous; but the effect of the system on social morale and on ethics has been worse. Exploitation of the loopholes becomes a major breeding ground of scandal. Stories purporting to be examples of how "the rich," as a group, evade taxes keep alive obsolescent ideas of class conflict. Armies of tax accountants—able people who could otherwise be contributing their skills to the nation's progress—are busy finding and enlarging loopholes. The loopholes are now so numerous and in some cases so ill-defined that ambiguity breeds inconsistency of enforcement. This in turn breeds widespread suspicion that apparently unequal treatment is the result of corruption or political favoritism.

In short, what began as an effort to achieve a higher level of social justice than the income distribution produced by the economic system itself has degenerated into a tax structure that is not more just but is itself a major source of public disgust with both government and business. Many practical people, including Citibank's Walter B. Wriston, have suggested that the way out of the tax mess is a drastic lowering of the top rates—say 30 percent—along with an equally drastic closing of loopholes. The government might get the same revenues without generating all the cynicism and sharp practice attending the present set-up. Congress apparently prefers to continue the massive hypocrisy and deceit of a rate schedule that, in its actual effect, is not so high as it looks.

Some critics say that the root error was enactment of a progressive income tax. Others choose a broader target; they argue that any governmental effort to change whatever distribution of incomes is shaped by "the market" is an impermissible violation of business autonomy.

I reject these views believing that government has a right to try to modify the market's income distribution and has a right to try to do so by a progressive tax. But no right, by itself, necessarily produces sound policy. The root trouble with the tax structure is the failure of legislators to examine its "real world" consequences, including its ethical consequences.

Practical Ethics

This line of thought, which seems to call for pragmatic tests of ethical rules, will give offense in some quarters. Idealists sometimes use "pragmatic" as the opposite of "ethical." This habit can be misleading. While ethical standards should be derived ultimately from principle—and not from behavior—they are, nevertheless, intended to affect behavior. Considered ethically, laws and business policies are intermediate institutions connecting the broad principles of right and wrong with actual human conduct. Some of these institutions work well and some work badly. That the tax structure was intended to serve a legitimate ethical purpose should not override the pragmatic conclusion that, ethically, it has been doing more harm than good.

Government, as it tries in one way or another, to improve business conduct could well take a leaf from the history of business itself. Business has had a huge and generally positive influence on ethical development not because its leaders had larger or stronger ethical vision but because their system was and is subject to pragmatic tests. Every part of the credit structure, for instance, has been tested and retested in action. Every present practice would be rejected if a superior substitute appeared.

Business should not ask for the absolute trust of government. It should recognize the right of society to invade the autonomy of business by government regulation or intervention. But business should insist that the *quality* of government action become less economically and ethically destructive than it has been. The debate over aggregate government interference needs to be replaced by many discussions appraising government policies and agencies. From such discussion the public might learn that government intervention is neither too much nor too little. Rather, it is too bad.

That brings us back to the intellectuals whose indispensable communicating function gives them so much influence on the public agenda and the framework of discussion. They will be reluctant to abandon their exciting game of exposure and accusation, reluctant to give up ancient concepts and prejudices. Such a shift in the attention of the communicators is perhaps the key move in getting the American society in position to tackle more vigorously the new ethical challenges encountered as the society, with business dynamism as its main thrust, enlarges the scope of individual and societal freedom.

4   *Ronald D. Rotunda*

Law, Lawyers, and Managers

Few laymen understand how the lawyer's obligation (prescribed in his professional code) toward the entity—as distinct from stockholder, director, officer, employee, or representative—adds to the difficulty of resolving conflict-of-interest problems. Fewer still understand the ethical implications of so-called derivative suits, and the entity theory may be gravely deficient when questions of corporate takeovers arise.

In the following essay Professor Rotunda raises—and answers—a series of fascinating questions. In malodorous corporate situations, who should blow the whistle? And when? Is the legal code of ethics deficient in not drawing sharper distinctions between obligations imposed on inside and outside counsel? How should a corporation protect itself when a lawyer resigns from the board or refuses to handle a case? If the board demands to know why, does this demand violate the sacrosanct lawyer-client privilege? Finally, should lawyers encourage, join, or resist corporate delaying tactics in cases before courts and regulatory agencies? The ranging complexities of the questions suggest that corporations have much more cut out for them to do.

C. C. W.

Before joining the faculty of the College of Law of the University of Illinois, RONALD D. ROTUNDA *practiced law in Washington, D.C. and then served as Majority Counsel to the U.S. Senate Select Committee on Presidential Campaign Activities. Professor Rotunda has written a number of articles on ethics and reform and a legal ethics coursebook entitled* Problems and Materials on Professional Responsibility. *A volume on constitutional law is in preparation.*

Cartoonist Garry Trudeau, in one of his Doonesbury strips, turned to the teaching of legal ethics in law school. Particularly in this strip I have in mind, the professor is addressing Joanne Caucus and her fellow students. In the first frame the Professor asks his students to hear him out as he offers, in pompous terms, his "brief rationale" for the course:

> Ambrose Bierce once defined a lawyer as "one skilled in circumventing the law." It was a devil's definition, of course, but the events of recent years have more than once lent it truth. It is not sufficient for a lawyer to simply *know* the law. Law Schools today have a far more fundamental obligation to insure that their graduates have an understanding of its *spirit*, its *moral essence.* (Emphasis in original)

The professor adjusts his glasses, places his left hand in his pocket, and in the final frame of the cartoon strip he grandly concludes: "[This course,] 'Right and Wrong 10-A' is one such stab in the dark."

The learning and practice of legal ethics should be more than a stab in the dark. This is not to say that the area of black and white is greater than the area of murky gray; but it does assert that the tools of legal analysis, which seek to bring some order to areas of corporate law, apply equally well to legal ethics and to the law of professional responsibility for corporate lawyers and managers. Since ethical issues always arise in a context, abstract discussion of them without reference to that context is unproductive. I would therefore like to identify several complex areas of corporate legal ethics (focusing in particular on some conflicts-of-interest issues within the corporate entity) in order to determine how corporate managers and lawyers may help one another to fulfill their ethical and professional obligations.

By way of caveat to the layman it should be noted that the following examples represent complex issues of law. Yet in every case, the relationship to corporate ethical behavior is important, and the mode and resolution of the technical legal problem has a bearing on the style and substance of corporate ethics.

First I will consider some examples of corporate lawyers and managers trying to represent the diverse interests within a corporation. Then I shall turn to some of the lawyer's and manager's duties to interests outside the corporate entity; duties of loyalty to the public, and how these duties place limits on one's loyalty to the corporation.

Conflicts of Interests within the Corporate Entity

We all know that the corporation is considered a legal "entity" and that, much like our own souls, it has no body. While it cannot be seen, it exists legally apart from its constituencies of officers, board, stockholders, creditors, and so on. Such a multifaceted client creates special problems of conflicts of interest for the corporate manager and lawyer.

To deal with such problems for lawyers the American Bar Association has promulgated a Code of Professional Responsibility, which most states have adopted as law with varying modifications. This code is divided into Canons (axiomatic norms and disciplinary rules which are mandatory in character) and Ethical Considerations which suggest the aspirations that properly motivate the ethical lawyer. Canon 5 of this code deals primarily with the lawyer who confronts conflicts-of-interest situations. Recognizing the special problem of the *corporate entity* in its Ethical Consideration 5-18, the code announces that a corporation lawyer "owes his allegiance to the entity and not to a stockholder, director, officer, employee, representative, or other persons connected with the entity."

It is the entity's interests which the code insists must be kept "paramount." While the code applies only to lawyers, its entity theory is not a novel one. Corporate managers as well owe their legal duty to the corporation and not to themselves or to certain factions.

Sometimes (perhaps too rarely) the law offers mechanical tests to solve legal problems. There are, of course, a few problematic issues where the entity theory is useful in solving corporate ethical problems, but such problems are not the difficult ones. For example, if a competitor sues a corporate client alleging an antitrust violation, it is easy to conclude that the corporate lawyer does not represent a shareholder of defendant who is also a shareholder of plaintiff; rather, the lawyer represents the corporation as an entity. Similarly the corporate manager owes no duty of loyalty to another corporation simply because one of its shareholders is also a shareholder of the manager's corporation.

DERIVATIVE SUITS

Aside from such rather simple problems, the entity theory proves less helpful. A good example occurs with the problem of so-called "derivative" suits. When a shareholder sues his corporation, the action may be classified as either an individual or a derivative action. If the complaint is that the corporation has individually injured him as a stockholder—by unlawfully refusing to pay mandatory dividends or by not allowing him his right to inspect corporate books—the action is called an individual action. Its characteristics are those of an ordinary lawsuit, and we expect corporate counsel to defend the corporation in the action. If the corporation loses, it must pay money or give some right to the plaintiff-shareholder.

The situation is more complex in a derivative action. In such cases the shareholder is suing because he claims that the corporation is injured. The shareholder may believe the directors have breached their duty to the corporation by mismanagement or by theft of corporate assets. If a third party stole from the corporation we could expect it to sue to recover the proceeds. But if insiders stole, the corporation may be reluctant to sue since these insiders are in control. The law thus allows the shareholders to sue on behalf of the corporation. If a money recovery is sought and recovered, the insider-defendants must normally pay that judgment to the corporation, not to the plaintiff-shareholder. To motivate shareholders to become, in effect, private attorneys-general, the courts will grant attorney fees to the plaintiff's lawyer if the suit is successful. And, as we might surmise, the expectation of attorney fees encourages frivolous lawsuits.

ROLE OF COUNSEL

If the corporate directors are sued derivatively, what is the proper role of the law firm which is counsel to the corporation? Which issues may the corporation raise in defense of the derivative suit and which issues may it not? Is the lawyer in an impossible conflict-of-interest situation if he represents both the corporate insiders as well as the entity? If he represents only the corporate entity, what is his proper role?

Some court decisions and bar association ethical opinions have tried to decide these issues, supposedly by using the test of the entity theory of a corporation. But the proper resolution of most questions is still very much open. The corporation counsel's role in cases where insiders are sued derivatively—insiders who have been advised in their actions by the same counsel representing the corporation—is a particularly awkward one. In the case law we can find examples of the corporation in some instances aiding the plaintiffs suing derivatively; in other instances, the corporation has resisted the action and aided the real defendants by raising procedural defenses, such as a lack of proper service or misjoinder of causes of action, or moving to require security for costs. If these procedural hurdles have been passed, and settlement is being discussed, how does the corporate attorney advise the entity to bargain in a settlement conference of a derivative suit when some, or all, of the defendants are also insiders of the corporation? After all, if the derivative plaintiff bargains successfully, the reluctant corporation, aligned as a defendant, may find more money added to its coffers.

In all aspects of the derivative litigation the corporate lawyer's ethical response is complicated by the fact that he may represent, or appear to be controlled by, the alleged inside wrongdoers. This appearance is fortified by the lawyer's natural incentive to favor the corporate officers and directors with whom he has dealt and advised. A lawyer who ignores this fact by trying to represent only the incorporeal entity may find himself dismissed by the flesh-and-blood insiders who actually hired him.

THE LEWIS CASE

In one leading federal case, *Lewis v. Shaffer Stores Co.* (1963), where the regular corporate counsel was also defending the officers and directors, the district judge ordered the entity "to retain independent counsel, who have no previous connection with the corporation, to advise it as to the position which it should take" in the derivative suit. But these new lawyers, selected pursuant to court order, are not in an enviable position. The same insiders who are being sued may be influential in selecting new counsel. This same court voiced no concern that "the selection of such independent counsel will necessarily be made by officers and directors who are defendants." And if the newly selected counsel for the corporation becomes too independent-minded, he may then be dismissed by the interested insiders. Such insiders need not be corrupt or evil men. From their perspective—a self-interested perspective to be sure—they may view the particular derivative suit against them as a frivolous one.

In those cases where the corporation is aligned as a defendant with its insiders, a rule could require the corporation to raise no defenses or otherwise participate. It would be passive though, in theory, a defendant. In such cases, the law might instead, allow the real defendants having their own counsel to assert the corporate and individual defenses. But this rule would completely deprive the shareholders of their corporation's participation in important litigation that could significantly affect it.

To expect the court to allow the insider-defendants initially to choose counsel (with the court subsequently engaging in constant monitoring of the representation process) is not realistic. It may cause excessive entanglement between one of the litigants and the impartial judge. The directors who are not being sued derivatively could choose counsel, but all directors might be sued. Or the court might find that they are influenced by the other directors who actually are defendants. The judge could choose independent counsel for the corporation only in those cases where he thinks the suit is not frivolous, but the question of frivolity really goes to the merits of the case and ought not be decided by the court in a preliminary hearing.

A POSSIBLE APPROACH

All of these alternatives have unsatisfactory consequences. But the problems of the court itself choosing independent counsel to represent the corporation in the derivative suit (in those cases where there are an insufficient number of independent directors who have not been sued by the plaintiffs) may be less serious than other alternatives. Court imposition of its own choice of counsel on the corporation reduces the later need for monitoring. Arguably, it does deprive the corporation of its normal right to choose its own legal representative. But in such circumstances, this normal right should not apply since there are no impartial insiders who can choose counsel on behalf of the corporation. We should not expect the defendant managers to act without regard to their self-interest.

The court should then choose independent outside counsel to represent the corporation, to examine the suit, and to determine the positions the corporate entity should take. The role of the corporation and its appointed counsel in such derivative litigation need not be entirely passive, but it should not be completely active either. That is, corporate counsel's main concern should be to protect those rights peculiar to the corporation which neither the derivative plaintiff nor the other defendants have any real incentive to protect. For example, corporate counsel should assure that discovery of corporate papers does not violate trade secrets, but the appointed lawyers should not seek to use the special court-appointed position merely to aid one or the other side in the lawsuit.

To insure that the corporate lawyers' independence is not short-lived, the appointed counsel should be prohibited from later being retained by the corporation. Otherwise, the new lawyers may seek to please the allegedly wrongdoing directors in order to secure more permanent employment later on. The court will probably also have to approve counsel's fees to verify that the new lawyers have not overbilled their involuntary client.

Corporate Takeovers

The entity theory is perhaps even less helpful in a takeover situation. Assume that a larger corporation plans a takeover attempt of a carefully selected target. Corporate counsel for the target must represent it as an entity. Therefore the attorney does not represent the significant number of minority shareholders of the target which now controls the corporate offeror or "raider" and approve of the takeover. Nor does the lawyer represent the board or officers of the target who are expected to fight the takeover.

What is the lawyer's role in such a case? What if the lawyer thinks that a takeover would probably be better for the corporation's stockholders? Perhaps he is persuaded that the raider can run the target better than the mismanagement revealed by the present board. Recall that the lawyer for the corporation is to keep that entity's interest "paramount." The board of the target, by way of defense, may suggest a charter amendment which would make it very difficult for any takeover attempt to succeed. How does the lawyer's loyalty to the "entity" resolve his possible conflicts between the interests of the present management and the present or future stockholders? Is it ethical for management to propose and urge adoption of such a charter amendment? Does duty or loyalty to the corporation require them to resist a takeover attempt? Or is their judgment to fight obviously clouded by their own self-interest?

One lawyer who specializes in defending targets of takeover attempts told me that he resolves his dilemma in defending targets by delaying tactics. He has opposed charter amendments which make takeovers virtually impossible because he believes they pave the way for less favorable legislation. But the delay, he feels, is beneficial to the shareholders of the target because it allows other offerors time to come in and bid up the offer. If a corporation is really ripe for a takeover, these other offerors will assure stockholders a better price. Perhaps the managers' role should be similarly limited to the blitzkreig situation—simply to assure that, procedurally, the takeover attempt is not so sudden that all sides cannot present their best case to the shareholders. This proposal, while it may solve one problem, raises another—the ethical issue of delay, particularly the calculated use of tactics for delay. This area will be considered toward the end of this essay.

These examples have considered the problem of an attorney for a public corporation, but the issue of representing a corporate entity may not be lessened in the closely held, family corporation situation. If there are various, fighting factions of a closely held corporation, the lawyer for the "entity" can have his hands full. Does he primarily represent the faction that controls? The faction that is more interested in corporate officers or jobs? Or the faction that is more interested in dividends?

Blowing the Whistle

In the good old days, when it was thought that the sole purpose of a corporation was to make money lawfully, the entity theory was probably a useful tool to analyze the ethical aspects of corporations. But that era ended with the emergence of a belief in corporate responsibility which created a different role for corporations. This problem may be illustrated particularly well by the issues of whistle-blowing on the entity or on constituencies of the entity: board members, officers, and others. How must the corporate lawyer or manager blow the whistle? To the Board of Directors; to the Securities and Exchange Commission; to the Antitrust Division of the Department of Justice; to the Food and Drug Administration; to a state blue-sky commissioner; or to others?

The problem has been considered in detail by many commentators and no Rosetta Stone exists to offer a creative solution. From the way the law is developing, I think that lawyers should withdraw from employment rather than aid, in any way, in the preparation of a materially misleading registration statement filed with the Securities and Exchange Commission or, for that matter, in any other similar situation. Once having withdrawn, the attorney's duty of confidentiality would probably prohibit whistle-blowing to the government in all except the most unusual cases. If the corporate lawyer is willing to withdraw, the prudent manager should quickly desist from pursuing the challenged action.

A COROLLARY ISSUE

Before continuing with this problem of the corporate counsel who withdraws, I should like to focus on a corollary issue. In such situations of withdrawal should the posture of in-house counsel be the same as his counterpart working for the outside law firm? The Code of Professional Responsibility draws no such distinction. It draws no distinction either between the duties of partners versus associates or between large-firm practice and the one-man enterprise. Perhaps it should recognize some differences. *Can we realistically expect the same responses from in-house and outside counsel in a whistle-blowing situation?*

If a corporate lawyer comes upon illegal conduct by high corporate officials, his first whistle-blowing would probably be to the Board of Directors. But in some corporations it may be harder for the inside counsel to secure an audience with the board. Outside counsel, on the other hand, may have a seat on the board. Or his presence may be more or less expected. More importantly, the inside counsel may find it inordinately difficult to go over the head of the officers to the board. As inside counsel he is part of the organization.

If a corporation persists in certain improper conduct, the lawyer may have a duty to withdraw from representation rather than risk aiding and abetting an improper activity. When push comes to shove, the outside counsel can reluctantly withdraw by "firing the client." The parting of the ways may not be easy. No one likes to turn down business, particularly when there has existed a mutual and rewarding ongoing relationship. Difficult as it is for a law firm to drop one client, it is even more difficult for in-house counsel to, in effect, quit the job. This means giving up *all* of the employment, not one client. Also surrendered normally are pension rights and other forms of re-numeration tied specifically to particular employees: stock options, phantom stock, and so on.

INSIDE COUNSEL—A HEAVY BURDEN

Do we ask too much of inside counsel? Should the Code of Professional Responsibility draw distinctions between the independence of judgment expected of outside counsel and the independence expected of inside counsel? Presently it does draw distinctions between the zealousness *expected* of private counsel *vis-à-vis* a government prosecutor. For example, the law could require that the responsibility of inside counsel be normally satisfied by reporting to outside counsel and accepting his judgment as to the proper course of action in close cases and ambiguous situations. By expecting too much of inside counsel we may receive nothing. By requiring less we are more likely to obtain all that we can realistically require. Yet we ought not, by relaxing rules, to encourage wrong behavior. We should continue to require in-house counsel to be responsible for the exercicse of independent judgment. However, in close or ambiguous situations, in-house counsel ought not to be satisfied with relying solely on its own judgments. In-house counsel should be required in these close cases particularly to inform outside counsel which is subject to different pressures, and then rely on the latter's advice.

The corporate manager's position is analogous to that of in-house counsel. Just as in-house counsel ought to seek and abide by the judgment of outside counsel, so also should the corporate manager, in fulfilling his ethical responsibilities to the corporation, be under a similar obligation: he should make full disclosure to, and seek the advice of outside counsel, particularly in close or ambiguous cases.

One should not overdraw the differences between outside and inside counsel. The associate of a law firm is also subject to similar pressures because disagreement with the ethical judgment of his partners means he must withdraw from the firm. The code does not provide in such instances for a discreet withdrawal from a particular matter anymore than it provides for discreet withdrawal on the part of in-house counsel. Even a large firm may be under economic pressures because a large percentage of its business may come from a very few corporate clients. Although this line, which distinguishes the differing pressures on in-house and outside counsel may not be a bright one, it still provides a useful starting point.

If we place a larger whistle-blowing burden on outside counsel by encouraging in-house counsel and corporate managers to confer with him we do, of course, add even more to his ethical burden. To expect independence of judgment other methods of furthering that goal should be considered. For example, if we require outside counsel to report to the board, then guaranteed access to the board becomes very important. Some outside counsel have such access as a matter of course; others are not similarly circumstanced. All should be guaranteed access. Managers are not fulfilling their duties to the corporation when they seek to preclude either in-house or outside counsel from addressing the board, even if these legal messengers carry bad tidings.

THE SHAREHOLDER'S ROLE?

It has been suggested that the shareholders ought to approve outside counsel in the same way that shareholders approve directors or auditors. But this proposal may be more cosmetic than substantive for, in reality, it would simply shift the choice in appearance only. The board which votes for counsel directly will be the very same board that controls the proxies for choice of outside counsel. It is more realistic to require management to report to directors whenever a lawyer withdraws. The directors should then demand to know, directly from the lawyer involved, why any in-house or outside corporate attorney has resigned. The ethical ball would then be in the directors' court. They have both the information and the legal incentive to take action.

A rule might also be fashioned to require the corporation to explain to shareholders why it is changing outside counsel or why outside counsel is quitting. Such a proposal, finding some kinship to the Securities and Exchange Commission requirement regarding a change of outside auditors, necessitates infringements on the attorney-client privilege because shareholders are not the client. Further, such disclosure would be tantamount to public disclosure to the world at large. Guidelines could, however, be drawn to limit this infringement. And in any event, it should be realized that *neither the ethical nor evidentiary attorney-client privilege is sacrosanct.* For example, Disciplinary Rule 4-101(C)(4) provides that a lawyer may reveal "confidences or secrets necessary to establish or collect his fee. . . ."

Given the many inroads on the lawyer-client privilege, the advantages of one more modification may outweigh the losses in two ways: (1) the resulting "tenure" process could go a long way toward guaranteeing independence and (2) it provides more logical and moral justification for the burden that the law places on outside counsel. It may also justify managers' greater reliance on outside counsel's ethical judgments in close cases. However, in my judgment, this important limitation on the privilege of confidentiality will not be needed if managers and lawyers are required to report candidly to the board all reasons for an attorney's resignation.

Lawyers as Directors

Related to this issue of true independence of outside counsel is the problem of lawyers who also serve as board members of their corporate clients. While I believe that corporate lawyers should be guaranteed an audience with the directors, it does not follow that the corporation's attorney should also be a member of the board. Lawyers who are directors of their clients justify this role by insisting that they are more carefully listened to in this capacity than in the capacity of an outside counsel invited to speak to the board or who insists on speaking to the board. They often feel that not only are they less likely to lose the client to another firm, but that, as lawyers, they bring an added dimension of expertise and a broader perspective to board decisions.

But there is a deficit side to this ledger. From the perspective of his own self-interest, the lawyer had better be right because he will be judged as a director with legal expertise. More importantly, from an ethical standpoint there are other difficulties. The lawyer may be motivated to serve as a director because the position allows him to attract new clients more readily and to hold old ones. Such an individual has subordinated his duty to the corporate entity to a greater loyalty to his own firm.

TIGHTENING THE RULES

The attorney's independence may also be compromised by becoming a member of the client. One distinguished New York attorney, Paul Cravath, believes that "in most cases the client is best advised by a lawyer who maintains an objective point of view and such objectivity may be impeded by a financial interest in the client's business or any participation in its management." His partner, Robert T. Swaine, wrote in the *American Bar Association Journal* of 1949 "most of us would be greatly relieved if a canon of ethics were adopted forbidding a lawyer in substance to become his own client through acting as a director or officer of a client." But he resignedly lamented that "the practice is too widespread to permit any such expectation."

In spite of Cravath's personal beliefs he himself served as chairman of Westinghouse and, at the insistence of clients, other "Cravath" partners wound up on important corporate boards. Perhaps the ultimate solution will be these prophylactic rules: *Lawyers should not be on the boards of their clients. Nor should corporate clients employ, as their outside counsel, a law firm that has one of its partners on the Corporate Board.* Corporate managers should consider the advantages of implementing such a rule. Attorneys could continue to serve on boards so long as they are not also counsel to the client.

Conflicts of Interest as Weapons

Some corporate law firms, by specializing in an extremely narrow range of legal problems, develop a national reputation which enables them to attract corporate clients from around the country. Some corporate clients, in an unusual behavioral twist are now using as a weapon against these firms the professional rules relating to conflicts of interest. One example suffices. Let us imagine a firm which specializes in representing target companies or raiders in takeover attempts. A prospective raider-client—through one of its corporate officers—*deliberately* telephones this law firm and talks to a partner about possible representation on a takeover fight. He discusses possible theories of action, discloses some facts, and so on. But the prospective client never follows through by retaining the firm. Now the raider telephones other law firms similarly situated, proceeds in the same fashion, and does not hire any of them either. By this technique the ruthless raider can keep its regular firm as counsel. Yet, it has also been able to disqualify other firms from representing the target company since disqualification of one partner or associate is imputed to the entire firm. The Code of Professional Responsibility creates the "conflicts" rules but does not reckon with their use as a weapon. There is not merely economic harm to law firms in lost business; more importantly, a sophisticated and ingenious lay person can use such rules to limit his opponent's choice of attorneys.

It would not be sufficient for the code to explicitly prohibit the practice because the code applies only to lawyers. Certainly the ethical manager would not seek to abuse the attorneys' professional code in such a manner. But if the opponent is not ethical and does not use them, how can the ethical manager fight back? Should the Code of Professional Responsibility create a defense to such activity? If so, how would that defense work? The client will not be happy with a rule of law which requires a lawyer to spend a half year or more making preliminary motions just to establish his defense to a conflicts-of-interest charge. After all, the legal time meter keeps running throughout the entire period.

The legal conflicts problem could be significantly reduced if we allowed the presently "disqualified" law firm to take the case on the proviso that it would insulate its disqualified member. Under such a role we would not impute to the entire firm the conflict of one of its partners or associates. But this "walling-off" technique would not be satisfactory to the opponents who may always suspect leaks from a poorly insulated wall.

The Corporate Lawyer and the Public

CORPORATE LAWYERS IN PUBLIC CAPACITIES

The expertise of corporate lawyers often leads to their involvement in special bar association projects or other public service activities. A city or state bar association may wish to invite a particular corporate lawyer to sit on one of its major committees in order to bring to it a special knowledge. In such situations, lawyers often confuse their roles by acting as advocates rather than as advisers.

The Code of Professional Responsibility does not forbid lawyers to shed their client's interests in such "nonrepresentational" situations. Its Ethical Consideration (8-1) specifically encourages lawyers to propose and support legislative programs "to improve the system, without regard to the general interests or desires of clients or former clients." The code further states:

> The obligation of loyalty to his client applies only to a lawyer in the discharge of his professional duties and implies no obligation to adopt a personal viewpoint favorable to the interests or desires of his clients. While a lawyer must act always with circumspection in order that his conduct will not adversely affect the rights of a client in a matter he is then handling, he may take positions on public issues and *espouse legal reforms he favors without regard to the individual views of any client.* (Ethical Consideration 7-17; emphasis added)

Later the code states:

> When a lawyer purports to act on behalf of the public he should espouse those changes which he conscientiously believes to be in the public interests. (Ethical Consideration 8-4)

But lawyers, in fact, do often try to "sell" their clients' positions in such situations. Sometimes this selling flows naturally from their coming to identify with client needs, but realism requires recognition of the fact that, at other times, it may be due to fear of losing clients with whom they actually disagree.

In language relating to a lawyer who "purports to act on the basis of the public . . ." the code suggests that disclosure of the lawyer's interests may be all that is required. But disclosure is not an adequate remedy in all such situations for two reasons: (1) a lawyer is not appointed to a bar committee or to any other professional group in order to represent his clients but is expected to share his professional experiences and to bring his technical knowledge to help solve various legal problems. To exploit his position, to promote client interests at the expense of his own convictions is to breach faith with those who brought him to the committee in the first place. (2) Committee members themselves are not privileged to allow use of public-service membership as a forum to lobby for a particular client or group. When committee members assent to partisan advocacy, they too are behaving unethically. They are also suggesting that in future assignments of a similar nature they too should be allowed to act as advocates of their clients.

The lawyer should divorce personal and professional beliefs from clients' interests. Yet some do treat such appointments to professional or public service committees as another advocacy opportunity. And, *a fortiori*, the attorney ought not to bill the private clients for professional time; nor should a lawyer use client resources to support public-service functions. Separation of these public and private capacities is a basic ethical necessity. Mere disclosure is not enough. Ethical corporate managers, should in turn, expect such separation of roles and never pressure an attorney in these situations.

THE PRO-BONO CLIENT

Private law firms often commit time to *pro-bono* practice—and for a variety of reasons. When they do, a desire not to displease the "establishment" client often infects a decision whether or not to accept a nonpaying client F. Raymond Marks (in the American Bar Foundation study of *The Lawyer, The Public, and Professional Responsibility*) has charged:

> When a firm decides whether or not to accept employment from a paying client, only narrow and immediate conflict of interest is considered. . . . [But] the law firms scrutinize the public interest client in a more searching manner. Threats are seen; conflicts are imagined or manufactured. . . . The public interest client who poses the least threat to the firm's economic stability and the least threat to the interest of the regular clients can be accepted. (pp. 260–61).

Marks' point may be illustrated by Ralph Nader's associate, Mark Green. In his study of Washington law firms (*The Other Government*), Green noted that when the National Legal Services Program asked a Washington firm to defend "some truck drivers fired in a labor dispute with the department store Woodward and Lothrop," the firm refused, "not because it represents Woodward—it doesn't—but," the firm told NLSP, "it *could* in the future." There are contrary examples, of course, but the prevalence of evidence to support Marks' conclusions is disturbing. The solution is not simple. It is difficult to legislate independence of judgment. The Code of Professional Responsibility should be amended to make explicit what is probably already the law: conflict-of-interest rules do not change for *pro-bono* clients.

Sometimes an attorney will seek a waiver from the corporate client in such pseudo conflict situations. This "waiver" is not properly labeled since there really are no conflict-of-interest situations; here there is nothing to waive. A lawyer may ethically take a legal position in one case involving one set of clients and take a contrary approach in a similar matter, but involving different clients. In fact, a lawyer may take inconsistent legal positions in the same case.

Since the lawyer is not really asking for a waiver—there being nothing to waive—he really is seeking corporate permission to accept a *pro-bono* case. Managers should generously exercise this power of waiver, if requested, because these are usually artificial conflicts. To do otherwise is to use their economic strength to foreclose legal representation of poorer clients. If no conflict exists and no waiver is asked, the corporation should *not* express its displeasure. Even if a given conflcit exists, the corporate manager may properly waive conflicts if no real injury and no confidential information occurs to the enterprise because of a waiver.

THE PROBLEM OF DELAY

Corporate lawyers are often accused of unnecessary delaying tactics before courts and agencies. A *Wall Street Journal* reporter noted in May of 1976:

> A water-pollution suit against Reserve Mining Co. is in its fifth year. . . . An antitrust suit against U.S. Steel Corp. filed fourteen years ago, has gone to the Supreme Court again—for the third time.
>
> These instances of drawn-out business litigation aren't flukes. They are typical, according to legal experts, of what happens when big companies go to court.

Some lawyers have bragged of the practice:

> Now I was born, I think, to be a protractor. . . . I quickly realized in my early days at the bar that I could take the simplest antitrust case that the Department of Justice Antitrust Chief could think of and protract it for the defense almost to infinity. . . . If you will look at the record [*in United States v. Bethlehem Steel* 315 U.S. 289] you will see immediately the Bromley protractor touch in the third line. Promptly after the answer was filed I served quite a comprehensive set of interrogatories on the Government. I said to myself, "That'll tie up brother Hansen [*the Antitrust Chief*] for a while," and I went about other business. BROMLEY, JUDICIAL CONTROL OF ANTITRUST CASES, 23 Federal Rules Decisions 417 & 420 (1958).

But delay is a knife that cuts both ways. Some corporate lawyers have charged that environmentalists and other public-interest litigants have used delay to bog down the regulatory system, to prevent needed rate increases, to prohibit or delay power plant expansion, to obstruct programs for highway construction, and to delay or modify housing developments.

Sometimes corporations benefit from delay. Sometimes their opponents, who may also be corporations, benefit. And sometimes only the lawyers, who have too many irons in the fire at one time, benefit. But the public interest, properly concerned, only fortuitously benefits, if at all, by calculated delays for the sake of delay. Efficient judicial administration and prompt decisions are normally in the public interest.

The Code of Professional Responsibility, frankly, is not very effective in preventing delay. One of its relevant provisions [Disciplinary Rule 7-102(A)(1)] forbids filing a suit, asserting a position, conducting a defense, delaying a trial, or taking other action on behalf of a client "when it is obvious that such action would serve merely to harrass or maliciously injure another." Striking the word *obviously* and replacing *merely* with *primarily* might mark an appropriate change of emphasis; it would probably cause little substantive difference because of the absence of clear guides in this area. For the same reason, little would be gained by exhorting managers to exercise self-restraint. Unnecessary delay will not be significantly reduced by exhortations either to lawyers or managers: those who act in good faith do not now engage in such tactics; those who act in bad faith will not be moved by such pleas.

POSSIBLE REFORMS

Perhaps a more significant reform would occur if we work to remove some structures in the legal system which reward delay. Delay is in part a function of a complex (I think *overly* complex) legal system. Law reform requires law simplification. Much of the delay in trial work, for example, is caused by expansive use of the discovery rules. A government attorney echoed a typical complaint, "Business lawyers will paper a little guy to death. . . . The first thing they'll do is give him a 10,000 page set of interrogatories. There's no way he can answer that." The discovery rules should be tightened and the scope of relevant material narrowed for both sides to a dispute. The justice we may achieve by drawing unnecessarily fine distinctions—particularly the distinctions that are the products of lengthy litigation—are often outweighed by the injustice of time lost.

There is a second point. When government creates a regulatory agency it should insist on means which require the least number of lawyers. The present system operates like a public works program for attorneys. If the government seeks to control corporate conduct, it should first try to use market mechanisms. Only when these fail visibly should government create a ponderous bureaucracy to administer a complicated set of tedious regulations. Let me illustrate. If society wants safer plants for workers through accident reductions by X percent, the most efficient system is not to (1) set up a safety board, (2) promulgate several feet of regulations, (3) litigate their meaning with an army of government lawyers, and (4) permit *post facto* application of reinterpretations. We could, instead, decide that those plants having an accident rate above a certain norm must pay a fine or a tax proportional to the number of above-average accidents for that industry. Companies with a better-than-average record might be given a proportional award or tax credit. Business managers, without need of any other instruction, will, themselves, find the most efficient means to reduce accidents because it will be profitable to do so. And the "thickness" of regulations requiring—or prohibiting—various activities can be reduced from seven feet to one quarter of an inch.

Within administrative agencies reform could also take the form of changing agency structures to punish delay and reward prompt action by administrators. This can best be illustrated by reference to changes in the federal system in the Southern District of New York. Delay in criminal cases was reduced when the judges changed from a central calendar system to an individual calendar system. Under the central calendar system all criminal pretrial motions were decided by one judge on a rotating basis. If a judge continued (that is, postponed) a motion he would not have to decide it; it would merely be sent to the next judge who would, in turn, either decide it or continue it and thereby pass it to another judge. A judge was, in effect, rewarded for delay because the more he granted postponements, the less was his work load.

Under the individual calendar system, criminal cases are assigned almost immediately to a given judge for *all* purposes. No longer does a jurist benefit from granting a requested continuance; he keeps the case until it is finally disposed of. Under the individual calendar system unnecessary delay has been significantly reduced.

While there is no single solution to the problem of delay, these proposals may help. Corporations can support such structural and attitudinal changes and thereby refute a *Wall Street Journal* headline, "use of stalling tactics by corporate lawyers appears to be growing." Lawyers have a responsibility to promote such reform. Unless such reform is supported and enacted, it is unfair to place primary blame for delay on lawyers or managers. In using delay they are not guilty of poor ethics; rather they are merely responding to incentives that the present system has established.

While much of the responsibility for a corporation to behave ethically rests with corporate lawyers, managers can help lawyers do their job. Since the ethically correct or professionally responsible alternative is not always clear—so that reasonable people may differ—the job involves more than coming up with the "solution" to an open-and-shut issue. Sometimes difficult ethical issues may have no solution. Nonetheless, analyzing ethical problems serves to sensitize both lawyers and managers to the issues at hand. Ethical analysis makes people aware that there are choices.

Developing sensitivity to ethical ambiguity in apparently unambiguous situations is another important objective. The unsophisticated public may demand solutions to problems for which there are no clear solutions. To respond to such clamor is itself unethical. To encourage it is, if possible, even worse. But we can always seek to prove Garry Trudeau wrong: ethical responsibility is more than just a stab in the dark.

Clifford E. Graese

5

Accounting, Accountants, and Managers

Accountants feel keenly the winds of changing ethical values, and three possible responses by auditors to "improper payments" demonstrate how accountants might react and how the public might perceive such reactions. Whatever the professional response and whatever the public reaction, the fact remains that the public is more assertive that corporations be "clean" and that the accounting profession has a special role to play in the clean-up process.

If reform is in the air, who are the reformers and what are the results? Clifford Graese draws on his vast experience to pinpoint the roles played today by the Securities and Exchange Commission, the Internal Revenue Service, and by Congress. Yet the net results are sometimes ominous. Withholding of a corporation's Registration Statement by the SEC, demands by the IRS for information that violates the client's relationship with the accountant, and congressional expectations for unrealistic modes of internal control are the result of overzealous reform activities.

Mr. Graese reminds us that auditors do not manage the industry and that primary responsibility for ethical improvement rests on corporate management and on corporate boards.

C. C. W.

A partner of Peat, Marwick, Mitchell and Company, CLIFFORD E. GRAESE *is in charge of accounting and auditing activities. From 1972 to 1975 he was chairman of the Ethics Division of the American Institute of Certified Public Accountants.*

America is undergoing a serious and somewhat painful reexamination of its standards of ethical conduct. The public is unhappy with what it sees in corporate business, in government, in education, in the professions, and indeed in every walk of life. But although the public knows it is not happy, it has not yet concluded what to do about the situation or where it should start to bring about a change. Indeed it is not at all convinced that there has been an accurate diagnosis. Is it an intestinal tumor or just plain food poisoning? But everyone agrees that, left untreated, the aches and pain are not likely to be gone the next morning.

Nor is it clear what triggered this reexamination. Certainly Watergate and the political payoffs, bribery, cover-up and other improper actions which that investigation disclosed outraged a major part of our citizenry. Certainly also the public disclosure that major corporations were involved in exerting influence on the affairs and decisions of government through payments of large sums of money to government officials was a major scandal in the eyes of most Americans. I suspect that there were few so naive as to not be aware that influence peddling, payoffs, and similar actions were going on throughout the society. But I believe most were surprised by the extent to which the practice had permeated the business community, the amounts involved, and the apparent loss of corporate conscience or corporate morality it seemed to signal.

However, I believe the present serious reexamination of our ethical standards was going to happen with or without the revelations of Watergate. These events merely served to accelerate and focus the process. Scandals had been uncovered before, but this time America seemed to have had a heightened sensitivity to human and ethical values. The past decade has been marked by significant advances in public awareness of, and response to, social problems: witness the battle against discrimination and the concern for protection of the environment. These issues, and the trade-offs involved, have caused all of us to look behind our production and consumption practices to some of their broader social consequences, and to make new value judgments. Thus we now find ourselves uncertain about the key question: just what kind of standards of corporate behavior should prevail? What are the value trade-offs? Who makes the decisions? What are the probable results?

Let me be quick to add that although it is totally appropriate to focus on corporate behavior and business practices, we must recognize that the basic issues are equally applicable to all other walks of life. It will be more difficult to bring about solutions if we single out only one segment of society for the entire blame.

The Accountant's Vantage Point

My particular vantage point is that of a CPA, a partner in an accounting firm that audits thousands of corporate business entities. From this perspective, it has been possible to gain some fairly deep insights into corporate behavior because I have been invited inside to review their business transactions. Many people believe that accountants are, or can be (or should be) in a unique position to deal with matters of corporate conduct. Just how do accountants and auditors fit into the picture? Are they part of the problem? Or are they part of the solution? Or both? And to what degree? Perhaps the answer is "all of the above." But that begs the question.

The reexamination of the effects of our production and consumption practices on the environment has generated widespread interest. In many ways, the value judgments involved are similar to those inherent in the general standards of corporate conduct. However, there is a significant difference in the diagnostic process. There is little disagreement over whether pollution exists; indeed we can use highly objective scientific measurements to establish its existence, the quantity, and its sources. Our judgment problem basically relates only to how much pollution to accept as the by-product of some other benefit. Unfortunately, we have no similar objective standards to determine when corporate conduct or behavior goes beyond public tolerance; nor have we any particularly scientific or definitive evidence as to its source or its consequences. This adds to our frustration and, at times, leads to inadequate or even counter-productive attempts to solve the problems. Let me try to illustrate the difficulty of pinning down the problems by relating several alternative scenarios of the same situation—the revelations of corporate "improper payments."

"IMPROPER PAYMENTS": THREE SCENARIOS

Almost everyone is basically familiar with the so-called "improper payments" problems. Our major corporations are disclosing to their stockholders and to the public that they have made payments to agents, or were giving kickbacks or making political contributions—all in order to obtain more business or to get equal or preferred treatment. These disclosures have, for the most part, been forced by the Securities and Exchange Commision and have raised serious questions, not only about the standards of ethical behavior of corporate executives, but also about the standards of the accounting and auditing profession in permitting such transactions to occur without "blowing the whistle." But opinions as to the answer differ significantly.

In the first scenario, the public reasons that both the company officials and the auditors must have known what was happening and that the transactions should have been stopped or, in any event, fully disclosed promptly to the stockholders and to the public. Yet since they were neither stopped nor disclosed, both the company officials and the auditors must have conspired to hide them. Presumably the motive was that it would make the company look better and therefore both the company executives and the auditors could collect higher salaries and fees. This scenario suggests a fundamental loss of integrity and a deliberate attempt to deceive for selfish reasons.

In the second scenario we find that the same transactions in question were not discovered by the auditor during the course of his examination and he was thus in no position to take any kind of action concerning them; but the public reasons that he *should have* both discovered the transactions and taken steps to have them disclosed. However, the auditor did not undertake any special procedures solely to seek out these transactions since he felt it was not part of his responsibility. The auditor felt his obligation was to pass judgment on the fairness of the financial statements, not to report what some persons might consider to be unethical acts. Indeed, he had concluded that if he became aware of such acts and disclosed such information on his own, he would violate the confidential relationship between him and his client. By so acting, not only would he impede his ability to fulfill the main auditing responsibility in the future, but he might also subject himself to legal liability for improper professional conduct. Moreover, the auditor felt it would be impossible to do enough work to be sure that he had found all such types of transactions. Even worse, since there were really no specific standards he could go by as to what was, and what was not an improper item, any judgments would be personal rather than professional, and therefore, of little value. This scenario suggests a difference between what the auditor and the public perceive to be the auditor's role and his responsibilities to the stockholders and the public.

On the other hand, some segments of the public do not directly blame the auditor for not stopping or disclosing the so-called "improper acts."

Perhaps they agree that was not really why the auditor was there. But after reflection, they conclude that the auditor is probably in the best position to keep tabs on corporate management and to introduce a higher level of discipline to prevent or, at least, disclose such incidents. Therefore they apply pressure to auditors to take on an added responsibility not only to prevent, or disclose, improper payments but also to establish (as in the case of financial statements) some guidelines for distinguishing between proper and improper practices and disclosure.

In the third scenario the public again reasons that both the company officials and the auditors knew what was going on and should have disclosed the transactions and taken steps to prevent similar occurrences. However, company management and the auditors did not do so because the transactions were entirely legal and, moreover, commonplace; therefore neither considered the actions improper. Nor did they feel the items needed to be disclosed any more than any other business development or sales technique. This scenario might suggest that the corporate executive's and auditor's perception of proper ethical conduct had become so blurred and indistinct that they no longer had a proper perspective. Although the failure may not have been willful, the consequences are the same.

Yet may it not also be suggested that the public's perception is unrealistic or, at a minimum, has changed too quickly to permit the corporate system to respond? The evidences of current responsiveness by corporate officials hardly indicate either permanent blindness or hardened arteries. As a matter of fact, in some cases, the pendulum seems to have swung far past the balance point to another extreme.

BASIC CONCLUSIONS

Which of the foregoing scenarios is most realistic or illustrative of the improper payments problem? No doubt each applies to some degree, but whichever scenario is most applicable, all point to three basic conclusions:

1. The public is demanding an end to, or at least a reduction in, what it considers to be improper corporate behavior.
2. Corporate management and personnel need a sharpened consciousness of ethics in making their business judgments and in carrying out their business responsibilities.
3. The public is looking to the auditing profession to help develop and enforce a stronger discipline in preventing and in disclosing improper activity.

The "Reformers"

SECURITIES AND EXCHANGE COMMISSION

Although there have been numerous forces at work seeking to bring about a change—for example, stockholder groups and various church and other moralist groups—undoubtedly the most significant and effective pressure to date has come from the Securities and Exchange Commission and other government agencies and bodies. Unfortunately their approach inevitably seems to be based on the conclusion that business is inherently and incorrigibly corrupt and that nothing short of strict legislation and regulation will solve the problem. Considering their vantage point and the nature of the background and experience of most of the personnel involved, perhaps this approach is to be expected. Perhaps it is also inevitable that in trying to stomp out one abuse, other important rights are trampled. Indeed some of the actions to date to solve the "improper payments" problem seem to involve a "cure" that is as bad, if not worse, than the disease. Let me cite some specifics.

There are relatively few controls which the government exerts over the actions of our corporate business community other than policing violations of law. If the corporate activity takes place outside the borders of the United States, even that control may be limited. However, the Securities Act of 1933 and the Securities and Exchange Act of 1934 impose on virtually all companies selling their securities in interstate commerce a requirement to file with the SEC, and distribute to the public, prospectuses and annual reports which must disclose material facts about their business and financial condition. The SEC is empowered to determine what facts are considered material and therefore require disclosure. It was through this vehicle that the Securities and Exchange Commission chose to require all public corporations to disclose "improper payments." It was the position of the SEC that such information was material information which each stockholder, or potential stockholder, should have prior to making a decision concerning ownership of stock in the company and voting on the election of directors. It further suggested that companies which participate in a "voluntary disclosure plan" would be given easier treatment than those who did not comply voluntarily, and encouraged all companies to confer with the SEC about their situation to determine whether or not specific disclosures would be required concerning past activities.

There is still considerable question as to the disclosure that is in fact required by statute or regulations. The SEC has not established definitive guidelines; indeed much of the guidance on the subject comes from speeches made by various members of the staff or commissioners, all of which are technically *personal* rather than *official* opinions. In these speeches, as well as in other unofficial pronouncements, the SEC has been vague. It suggests, on the one hand, that certain kinds of improper payments, such as payments to customs officials to expedite clearance, are not required to be disclosed and, on the other hand, refers corporations to the Ten Commandments as the only guide necessary in other instances.

The SEC has let it be known to public accounting firms that it is looking to them to take a leadership role in bringing about compliance with the voluntary disclosure program. By actions it has suggested to the public that such is indeed the CPA firms' responsibility. In the absence of specific statutory requirements or definition of improper payments, the difficulty is obvious. In several cases we auditors have identified transactions which, although they had no impact on the fairness of the financial statements, we believed might be the type the SEC desires to have disclosed. However, legal counsel advised the client such disclosure was not required by the Securities Acts or SEC Regulations. Thus in the absence of definitive—or even general official requirements—professionals are pitted against professionals. Corporate executives are unsure of what to do or what the consequences may be. The attitude of the SEC in such cases appears to be this: "Perhaps we can't require you to disclose such items but we can certainly make you wish you had."

It has not been uncommon for the SEC to withhold clearance of a company's Registration Statement until such time as full disclosure was made of so-called improper payment activity. More specifically, the SEC had originally said to companies: "Come down to talk and we'll decide jointly whether disclosure must be made." But more than one company has discovered that, even after the commission itself has ruled that the matters did not need to be disclosed, some of the SEC staff, who did not like the commission's decision, turned the data over to a congressional committee where it was disclosed without regard to the basis on which the information had been obtained. The motivations of the SEC in attempting to bring about what they consider to be a higher level of corporate ethical behavior are not in question. But whether in doing so, they have not resorted to—and condoned—techniques which leave much to be desired is very much in question.

INTERNAL REVENUE SERVICE

Even more serious is an action of the Internal Revenue Service where it concluded that it would require some 1,200 of the largest corporate taxpayers to submit, in addition to their regular tax returns, affidavits from one or more corporate officers in response to eleven questions concerning improper payments. Although there was some question about the propriety of this procedure and its method of adoption, there was little formal challenge to the IRS's authority to obtain such statements inasmuch as they were requested from the officials of the taxpayer.

The IRS did not stop there, however. It requested, under threat of criminal penalties for incorrect answers, similar statements of information from third parties, in this case the companies' auditors. Although the IRS has always had authority to obtain information from third parties through due legal process if such information was not provided on a voluntary basis, it was necessary for them to follow that prescribed procedure and to show due cause and need. In this case the IRS chose a different approach; it employed the tactic of refusing to finalize the examination of the corporations' outstanding tax returns until all the statements requested from third parties were obtained. The corporations thus applied added pressure to the auditors to comply.

OMINOUS IMPLICATIONS

At first glance you may well wonder what is bad about such a procedure. Let me ask you to look a little deeper. First of all, remember that the auditors in this case had a professional relationship with their client that did not involve any responsibilities to the IRS for the client's tax return. Also keep in mind that these requests were not limited to companies where there was a specific reason to suspect they had filed an improper tax return. The companies were selected solely on the basis of size. Consider your reaction if, because your income or your deductions fell above or below a particular standard, the IRS approached your neighbor to ask him, under penalty of perjury, to advise the IRS of anything he might know about you which might indicate that your income was more than reported, or that your deductions were too high. Suppose the line of interrogation was this: Did he take long trips? Did he eat out frequently? Had he ever talked about investments, stocks. and bonds, etc.? Assume further that the

IRS would not close up your tax return investigation until your neighbor provided a signed response. Shades of Gestapo or Orwell's *1984*.

What is more, the IRS did not limit its concern with the propriety of the taxpayer's income tax return; rather it developed general information about improper payments which it then turned over, or threatened to turn over, to other agencies, including the SEC. I submit emphatically there is no need to bypass the judicial process regardless of the economic pressure which can be brought to bear. Nor is it in the public interest. One court has already declared a similar approach of the IRS to be unconstitutional. A similar test may be, and should be, in the making on this specific issue.

Unfortunately, the approach of both the SEC and the IRS tend to impinge upon the confidential relationship which exists between auditors and clients. This confidential relationship facilitates access to corporate information by the auditor and enables him to reach his conclusions as to the fairness of financial statements at a minimum cost. If any governmental agency can, without due judicial process, use pressure tactics to call on third parties, including the company's auditors, to disclose anything and everything they might know about that company's operation, such third parties are literally turned into an investigative arm of the government. Imposing such a role is completely inconsistent with a free democratic society.

This does not mean that the company's auditors should, or do, condone filing of improper tax returns or misleading financial statements. Actually, uneasy truce has been worked out in both situations through a high degree of initiative by the CPA profession in an effort to get at underlying concerns of both agencies while, at the same time, retaining some semblance of constitutional privilege—all done with the hope that the situation is an overreaction. However, the use of improper investigative force to uncover improper payments raises a question as to which evil represents the greatest danger to ethical standards and to society at large.

LEGISLATIVE MANEUVERS

Congress also has seen auditors as being deeply involved in the improper payment problem. Unfortunately, here again the problem has been approached in a reactionary manner. One Senate Committee (Proxmire) seems to feel that a major factor in correcting the problem would be to make it a federal offense for any corporate entity to fail to have a so-called "adequate system" of internal accounting controls.

Second, it would be made a crime for any person to lie to, or otherwise mislead, an auditor even when there was no intent to deceive. Actually most, if not all, of the large corporate entities disclosing improper payments had what would be considered good systems of internal controls. These systems were either bypassed by top management override, which is possible with any system, or the transactions were not considered improper at the time and therefore not rejected by the system.

The second suggestion was intended to facilitate detection of improper transactions by the auditor. I believe it would have the opposite effect because making it a crime to mislead an auditor, regardless of intent, would merely serve to cut off the many voluntary responses for information which the auditor needs to collect during the course of his examination. It seems to me that what is far more crucial is a relatively clear-cut definition of what is considered to be improper. Only then can the responsibility be put squarely on the shoulders of those who cross the line.

Another Senate Committee (Metcalf) has recently released a staff report (staff reports do not require committee votes or provide for publishing minority opinions) which views the accounting profession in such a negative light that it concludes the only course left is for the government to take over the design of accounting principles. According to the report, the large accounting firms neither serve the public nor are they independent. Therefore they do not merit being called by their usual generic designation in the report: independent public accounting firms. It is hard to believe that the accounting profession has sunk so low that there is not one scintilla of goodness left in its soul; it is even more disconcerting that this perception is so clear to staff representing a body whose perception of its own ethical conduct has frequently suffered from acute astigmatism. Perhaps improper acts and ethical practices legislation should embrace congressional committee reporting as well as corporate business reporting. But my point is not to suggest that only the blameless are qualified to cast stones. It is, rather, that if this report were to be accepted at face value, there could be no constructive role for the accounting profession in enhancing corporate ethical behavior. That conclusion, like the report from which it derives, is unwarranted and unacceptable.

But perhaps I am suffering from the same malady I am attributing to the governmental agencies. Perhaps I, too, am striking out at those who are not the root cause. For while I deplore some of the tactics and the proposed solutions, I do not basically disagree with the objectives. Our regulatory agencies are not responsible for the improper payments and should not be blamed for them. I must be somewhat less charitable of Congress because they indeed, in my opinion, have had a role in fostering improper payments, particularly political contributions. In any event, I believe it is fair to say that without the kind of pressure that only government can apply and has applied, the corrective action to date by corporate executives would have been far less. The application of pressure is never comfortable, but if an artery is cut, the bleeding will not likely stop in time unless a tourniquet is applied. It just needs to be applied in the right place and in such a way as not to stop circulation altogether.

A Working Agenda

THE AUDITOR

What then is the role of the auditor? What can he do in this area? First, it is important to recognize that, with very few exceptions, none of the cases of improper payments has involved direct participation or professional advice by the independent auditors. The independence rules of the accounting profession, and similarly the independence requirements of the SEC, have served to keep the public accountant out of direct involvement in the conduct of business of the corporate entity being audited. Obviously where accountants have stepped over this line, their behavior cannot be condoned. Such instances are very rare exceptions and therefore not the problem. Secondly, it is important to recognize that the alleged acts of improper corporate behavior, also with very rare exceptions, have not involved dissemination of misleading financial statements to the public. It is also my understanding that, by and large, the so-called improper payments have been treated properly by the corporations for United States income tax purposes. Thirdly, for the most part, whatever benefits have been derived from the improper payments have not accrued to individual corporate executives who authorized such actions, but rather to the corporation as a whole. In short, these actions are not basically involved with (a) misleading accounting, (b) misleading financial statements, (c) accounting judgments or advice, or (d) misappropriation of corporate assets for personal use. Their only direct relationship to accounting and auditors is that they involve the expenditure of money generally recorded in the books, though not always clearly identified as to their true nature. So while it may not be unnatural to look to the auditors for help and control, the issues are not fundamentally accounting oriented.

Company officials must constantly make business decisions which involve value judgments, many of which, because of the amount of money involved, boggle the minds of the average person. While the ordinary citizen may find it acceptable to slip a little extra to the head-waiter to shorten his wait in line or to get a better table, that same person may find it totally unacceptable if a company gives $100,000 to an agent in order to get preferred treatment on a multimillion dollar sales order. Yet the principle is the same; only the amounts are different. In ethical terms the latter amount may be less significant than the former because, in the former case, the benefit goes to the individual making the payment whereas in the latter, the benefit generally goes to the company or, more specifically, to the stockholders and employees. If failure to get a major order means closing a plant and a loss of jobs, a real value judgment must be made by an executive to decide how far the company should go in order to remain competitive.

I believe most people would totally rule out an action that is clearly illegal. But the bulk of so-called improper payments and other criticized corporate behaviors are not illegal. In fact they may be recognized as totally proper in some jurisdictions. For example, corporate contributions to United States federal election campaigns are clearly illegal, but contributions are legal in some state election campaigns; and in Canada they are legal, are recognized as significant factors in campaign financing, and indeed, are considered a sign of good corporate citizenship.

The accountant has no unique philosophical training which enables him to make value judgments such as these or to draw lines of ethical standards any more clearly than any other intelligent individual. To be sure, his independent status and attitude in rendering professional services is unique. Many other professions typically practice as an advocate of their clients and thus become more deeply involved in their clients' activities. In this respect, the accountant is in a unique position to give independent advice and counsel to corporate executives; he can, and does, raise questions from time to time with his corporate client executives as to some of their actions. However, this is hardly considered a professional responsibility.

THE EXECUTIVE

The principal burden and responsibility for upgrading the standards of corporate behavior must lie with those who make the decisions involved, namely, the corporate executives. To the extent that some laws embrace ethical values, corporate executives are subject to relatively clear-cut standards which establish minimum levels of performance. I believe it is fair to say that corporate executives are not inclined to break laws. Unfortunately, at this time there is no clear-cut, generally accepted standard of ethical corporate behavior beyond such laws. Many trade associations, professions, and business groups are currently drafting general codes of conduct which address some of the ethical issues they are concerned with. Unfortunately, in the past, too many codes have been concerned with keeping competition within some reasonable bounds, rather than with being concerned with broader ethical values. Thus codes of conduct are too frequently viewed with an attitude of cynicism.

THE BOARD

Boards of directors of corporate enterprises in my judgment should make corporate behavior a matter of primary concern in exercising their fiduciary responsibility. Each board should establish a code for their organization which sets forth clearly the standards of conduct which they wish to embrace and to have carried out by their corporate executives and by all other personnel. It is my experience that corporate employees generally follow the example set by corporate executives and the leadership which they perceive on matters of this sort. Unless the company's behavioral principles are clearly stated and communicated, a great many improper acts may take place solely because employees believe that they are doing what their superiors want or expect of them.

Secondly, the board of directors must make it clear that it simply will not tolerate departures from its code. All too frequently, codes are considered to be pious statements of motherhood for public show. "Does anyone really expect they will be followed if business requires otherwise?" It is up to the board of directors to ensure that this attitude does not prevail.

Thirdly, the board must set up machinery to facilitate compliance and to check that compliance. This may entail periodic reviews by internal audit departments, by external auditors, periodic questionnaires to executives, and by a variety of other techniques as appropriate. The key is to establish a policy that is clear and to take the necessary steps to communicate and enforce it.

Conclusion

Obviously, a basic difficulty is that there is no universal agreement on what is proper and what is improper. Quite clearly, therefore, what has been suggested here will not achieve the great millenium. Our religious institutions have been preaching against sin from time immemorial; yet they have by no means reached agreement on what constitutes a sin or even eradicated those sins that have been agreed upon. Corporate misbehavior will also not disappear solely because we wish it to. On the other hand, a concerted dedication on the part of the board of directors and key executives can and will improve corporate behavior at all levels. The accounting profession can be of help. But most certainly, if the public is looking to the accounting profession as the primary force in correcting ills of the corporate world through policing action, it has failed to recognize the true nature of the problem.

It is my sincere belief, confirmed by my personal associations, that business executives generally want to do what they believe to be beneficial to their employees, their stockholders, and the public. When problems do arise it is seldom because of a basic lack of integrity or moral character on the part of business executives; rather it is because they see the issues in a different, wider or narrower, perspective from other segments of society. Businessmen are no more dishonest than other citizens by virtue of being businessmen, nor are they any less so. But because they are privileged to control greater amounts of our resources we can and should expect their leadership to bring us to a higher level of corporate morality and ethical conduct. All of us, however, need to help in making more clear the standards we consider proper. Only then can we expect decisions which will please a higher percentage of our population.

David Finn

6

Dilemmas in Corporate Communications

"Madison Avenue," "hidden persuaders," "image-builders"—these are among the common epithets used to describe public relations. Consequently the PR executive begins his work with an overload of pejoratives that makes his own assignment difficult to explain. Yet, as David Finn insists, professionals in this field are not concerned with manipulation or image but with the truthful telling of reality.

In carrying out his work for a corporation, a public relations officer seeks to discern the basic character of the company, the willingness or unwillingness of a corporate executive to advance his ideas publicly, and the special headaches caused for those corporations whose products have environmental impact. Drawing on his own experience Mr. Finn shows how these various dilemmas influence—and are influenced by—the public relations firm.

While future problems will be concerned with full disclosure and truthful advertising, a greater problem may emerge when two valid social ideals are in head-on conflict. In a society which often asserts such contradictory goals, the problems for corporations and for public relations ventures will become more acute.

C. C. W.

Author of The Corporate Oligarch *and other books and articles on business subjects,* DAVID FINN *is a co-founder of the public relations firm of Ruder & Finn, Inc. He is an adjunct professor of business at New York University and serves on the advisory board of the Management Program of Baruch College and of the International Business Institute. Mr. Finn is also a painter and sculptor and has written books on the fine arts.*

In the past several decades, the growth of the communications industry has more than kept pace with the rate of growth of the general economy. Advertising agencies have become multinational, and at least one has reached the one-billion dollar annual sales category. The resulting noise level in the public media has understandably affected the mental outlook of our time. It has also brought about some qualitative changes in the conduct of the corporations.

Bigger communications budgets do not of themselves produce new ways of thinking on the part of management. If anything, they lead to greater reliance on the experts and respect for promotion as a technical specialty. The day when the chief executive officer considers himself the best advertising copywriter in the business is, at least in large corporations, drawing to a close. The role of a sophisticated manager is primarily to make sure that a convincing measure of effectiveness is provided for every substantial marketing expenditure, and that the investment seems to be paying off in sales.

Perhaps the most unexpected aspect of the expansion of communications and marketing budgets is the discovery that public tastes and attitudes are as unpredictable and uncontrollable as ever. A generation ago it was thought that new methods of persuasion would soon put unprecedented power in the hands of those who would manipulate the public mind. In the post-World War II era the fuss over subliminal messages and other ideas borrowed from psychoanalysis gave rise to what became known popularly as *hidden persuasion*. It was generally thought that corporations would soon be able to employ in a more scientific way what war time propagandists (particularly in the totalitarian states) had developed for their own purposes. The new communications would, of course, have the relatively benign objective of selling automobiles, detergents, breakfast cereals, and the like, but fears of thought control by potentially unscrupulous manipulators were still rampant.

There is no doubt that people in the communications business helped foster the impression that they were acquiring extraordinary powers through the new techniques of persuasion. I remember sharing a platform in the mid-1950s with one of the first commercial depth psychologists and being embarrassed by his extravagant claims. It was now possible, he stated, to identify the unconscious appetites behind all forms of human behavior. By devising ingenious ways to feed those appetites, virtually anything could be sold to anybody. Given enough funds, he believed he could even persuade mankind to live by the Ten Command-

ments, an objective which the most gifted teachers and preachers had
failed to achieve for over 3,000 years.

It was awkward for me to disagree with the good doctor since many
of his studies ended with the recommendation that a public relations
program was the best solution to the problems he was studying. This
was the case, for instance, when his organization made a study of a
fashion product that had suffered a major decline in sales over the years.
His report was filled with a variety of sexual and erotic references ex-
plaining the deeper lure of the product, and analyzing why it had
become popular in the first place. On the basis of the report's recommendation, the industry association gave Ruder & Finn the assignment
to reverse the downward trend. We did not disclaim the conclusion of
the study that public relations could make a significant contribution
to the success of the product, but as it turned out, our program had
literally nothing to do with the psychological aspects of the report. Instead of feeding the sexual appetites of customers (which of course we
had no idea how to do), we simply conducted the educational, promotion, and publicity program which this particular segment of the fashion industry had long needed. That turned out to be a useful—though
hardly manipulative—thing.

In time the claims of the researchers and communicators who thought
they might learn to mold public opinion were abandoned. The public
was clearly a more complicated animal than the "persuaders" had
thought. And so the public mind of America was providentially no
closer to being manipulatable in the 1970s than it was in the 1950s.

However, something else did take place during this period which was
disturbing. As corporations spent more and more money proclaiming
the virtue of their products and policies, public skepticism about the
legitimacy of corporate interests became widespread. Many marketing
campaigns were successful in selling more goods and services, but the
cumulative effect of all this expensive communication, especially when
challenged by newsmaking critics, made corporate credibility a major
issue of public concern. The problem was aggravated in the mid-1970s
as the bribery scandals spread throughout the corporate world, and
doubts about executive morality were added to the general uneasiness
about product values.

During the course of this development, executives began to look for
new ways to speak out about the contributions which their companies
—and indeed the entire free enterprise system—were making to the
health of society. Some of these efforts were devoted to general economic education to make clear that profits were not what made rich

men richer but were what made rising standards of living possible. This did not improve the credibility of business as much as was hoped, largely because profits were not precisely what worried the critics; it was the emphasis on material values and the assumption that convenience and pleasure were more important than honesty, natural beauty, good health, and other fundamental qualities of life. These critics seemed to believe that corporations were managed by executives who felt free to deceive the public, who promoted artificial values in our society, and who were not in the least concerned with the potential damage their products might do to the well-being of their customers, the maintenance of a viable environment, or indeed, to the survival of life on earth.

A number of corporate communications programs were based on a comparatively new idea of how to be responsive to this broader concern about the business ethic. Top executives and their communications counselors attempted to examine the most thoughtful aspects of their business and to identify long-range company goals with the highest ideals of our culture. These efforts were—and are—among the most promising approaches to dealing positively and constructively with the serious questions being raised about an economic and social sytem.

Because the conduct of these broad-based programs may have a major bearing on the future role of corporations in our society, some of the ethical dilemmas involved merit serious examination. It may well be that these are the most serious ethical considerations in corporate communications activities.

The Image Dilemma

It has become an axiom of broad corporate communications programs that the character of a company is an important asset in the effort to sell its products, establish a fair price for its stock, build employee morale, and work toward other corporate objectives. While some of the classic corporate programs which have attempted to highlight the company character date back to the 1950s (General Electric's "Progress" and IBM's "Think"), there certainly was a stepped-up interest in this approach during the late 1960s and 1970s. The role of Xerox, Exxon, Mobil, and others in public television; the sponsorship of art exhibitions by Philip Morris, SCM, S. C. Johnson Company; the commissioning of nationwide surveys of public attitudes by General Mills and Virginia Slims—all these nonbusiness activities have been inspired by a desire to win recognition for the sponsoring company as an imaginative and creative enterprise with a definable personality and a laudable purpose.

Most responsible communications specialists who work on programs of this sort prefer not to use the word *image* to describe what they seek to accomplish because, to improve one's image, the implication is that one is concerned more with appearance than reality. "Care more for the truth than what people think," was Aristotle's counsel, and this is much better advice than what seems to be implied in a *corporate image* program.

The question is, can the true character of a company rather than an artificially contrived image be the basis for major communications programs? Indeed, is there such a thing as *character* of a company? "It is truly enough said," wrote Thoreau, "that a corporation has no conscience; but a corporation of conscientious men is a corporation with a conscience." Perhaps the same might be said about the character of a company, namely that character of those executives who make major policy decisions determines the character of the company. If this is so, communications programs of a broad nature can be meaningful—or valid—only if they have a genuine relationship to the sentiments and perceptions of a company's top management. This could give substance to the effort and make it more than a clever device to catch public attention. Programs undertaken in this spirit are likely to be sustained over a long period of time and become an integral part of the company's way of doing business.

To discover the kind of executive interests or points of view which could become the basis for an imaginative communications program requires sensitivity on the part of the communicator and respect for the personalities of the people who head the company. One of the most satisfying and effective programs our firm was involved in was for the Puerto Rico Development Bank. When we started working for the bank, we conducted a study of attitudes in the financial community toward Puerto Rican bonds and found that, although the fiscal soundness of the bonds was generally accepted, there was substantial uneasiness about the cultural and social stability of the Puerto Rican people. This was in large measure due to the well-known problems of the Puerto Rican population in East Harlem and other major cities. In exploring possible directions for an effective communications program, we discovered that the bank's chairman was a fine calligrapher who had also personally commissioned manuscripts from outstanding calligraphers around the world. Although on the face of it, there appeared to be little connection between calligraphy, bonds, and ghettos, we recommended the publication by the bank of a series of portfolios containing silk screen prints of pages from an especially beautiful manuscript commissioned by the chairman from the Queen's calligrapher in England. A brief text explained that the program grew out of the interests of the bank's chairman who valued the art of calligraphy as much as the art of banking and who wanted to make this limited edition available as gifts to those who had shown such great confidence in Puerto Rican bonds. The portfolio proved to be extremely effective in communicating the intellectual and cultural richness—and hence credibility and stability—of those who were guiding the destiny of the bank.

On the other hand, we once worked for an insurance company whose president wanted to get publicity on the occasion of a move to new offices. He thought the facilities were handsomely designed and therefore worthy of editorial attention, but actually they were merely expensive, and no reporter could possibly have been interested in writing an article about them. Under pressure to produce results, we suggested that an art program be developed for his company, beginning with an art exhibition in the new premises and followed by a conference among executives and artists about the whole idea of art in corporate offices. The president agreed and the project was successful in producing publicity. However, most of the company's employees and customers recognized the effort for what it was—just a publicity stunt. No lasting impression of sensitivity or good taste was created. Instead the general reputation of the president as a man without real convictions was confirmed, and the whole program, with all its attendant publicity, may well have done the company more harm than good.

The practical risk of being dishonest or deceptive in such programs can be considerable. A customer advocate who believes that nonreturnable containers should be banned for environmental reasons is not likely to change his mind because a major company in one of these industries subsidizes a series of marvelous films on the history of civilization. If the advocate believes that such an expenditure is made in the hope of changing his mind, he is likely to be more vigorous than ever in his attack on the company. The public service being rendered will appear to him as an attempted sleight-of-hand to cover up the real harm the company is doing to society. If, however, the public service is a genuine reflection of management's approach to policy-making, the customer advocate may come to recognize that there are reasonable and civilized men at the head of the corporation. Instead of developing an adversary relationship with management, he may consider the possibility of joining the best thinkers in the corporation in the search for solutions which would be most acceptable from all points of view.

The Ego Dilemma

If the character of management determines the public character of the company, top executives must be willing to project their personal ideas on a variety of subjects. This can be embarrassing—and even seem unethical—to executives who have been trained to think of themselves as instruments of corporate profitability rather than public figures with leadership ambitions. The striking anonymity of contemporary businessmen is a measure of their reluctance to assume this role. The captains of industry in the early days of American history may have had mixed reputations, but there is no doubt that they became public figures. Today the chief executive officers of the ten or twenty largest corporations in the country—to say nothing of the rest of the business community—are virtually unknown.

The problem is not that successful executives are excessively modest. Their photographs appear regularly in company annual reports and other official literature. Every promotion they enjoy is appropriately reported in the business and trade press. Their names are repeated endlessly in major corporate announcements. They speak before important forums around the country. Articles appear over their bylines in major publications. They are even featured in television commercials as spokesmen for their companies and promoters of their products.

The reason why all this visibility does not become memorable is probably that the true personality of these executives as human beings rarely has a chance to be seen. What is shown to the public instead is a comparatively dull portrait created by staff writers who prepare letters to stockholders from the chief executive officers, write speeches and articles, and make up attributions in advertisements and press releases. Even his official photograph may be retouched by studio artists whose job it is to produce the stereotype picture of a successful executive. All this may be good for the company in terms of practical day-to-day operations, but one cannot have it both ways. While anonymous administrators can get the company's work done profitably, they cannot establish the corporation as a responsible—or credible—institution which deserves public confidence.

Genuine leadership requires the ability to articulate ideas effectively.

True, men in public life have long had professional assistance in preparing their public remarks, but Thomas Jefferson, Abraham Lincoln, Winston Churchill, and probably most of the great men in history had the courage to speak in their own words at critical moments. Perhaps it is unfair to compare business executives to such historic figures, but it is worth recalling that Andrew Carnegie, Chester I. Barnard, and Clarence Randall were businessmen who wrote memorable prose and contributed significantly to the history of business literature. Not so with many of today's business executives. There can be little doubt that one needs a strong ego to be a good leader, and that the pleasure an ambitious man may have by standing in front of the crowd helps. The public relations man who tells a chief executive officer that only he can personalize the corporation and what it stands for is speaking truthfully. It is a serious mistake for an executive who believes in the basic validity of his role in society to consider his time too valuable to decide for himself how he feels about subjects of general interest or to learn how to use the language effectively. It is not a mark of efficiency to delegate this tiresome chore to some lower paid specialists on his staff.

If business leaders are to be effective in articulating meaningful ideas which have some lasting value, they will have to take greater responsibility for what they say and make a determined effort to project their true personalities in a meaningful way to their audiences.

The Dilemma of Rationalized Values

Perhaps of all the dilemmas in today's corporate communications programs the most difficult to resolve is the problem of maintaining one's own integrity when commercial interests appear to run counter to one's personal convictions.

As corporations interact with an increasing number of broad social concerns the possibility of conflict becomes greater. There was a time when selling one automobile or another was not a matter of consequence; each had its own features which could be highlighted in a promotion campaign. Now it is different. Some automobiles are safer than others, some use less fuel, some produce less pollution. These are not simply sales features; they are factors which affect society as a whole. It is extremely difficult for the public to make a reliable judgment about these matters, and yet as citizens of a democracy all individuals are obliged to have some opinions on issues affecting the public good. A dilemma arises when corporate management decides on an official position in regard to such an issue and those who are paid to communicate that position are not sure that they agree with it.

An effective communicator tries his best to present the company's point of view as being in the best interests of society. After all, the corporate decision-makers consider themselves to be men of goodwill; they want to feel they are making a contribution to their fellow man; and they also know more about their enterprise than the critics. But a sensitive communicator who listens to the many opposing arguments on these complex issues cannot help but recognize that their proponents are equally high-minded and that there is some legitimacy to their points of view as well. Rather than be a salesman for his company's policy, he would much prefer to be a catalyst to bring all sides together in the search for a solution acceptable to all.

In a recent talk before the annual convention of the American Public Health Association, I remarked that my firm had been involved in public relations efforts on behalf of such controversial products as breakfast foods, sugar, chocolate, chemicals, oil, cigarettes, liquor, hobby products, toys, pharmaceuticals and nuclear power plants. Although I would be hard put to single out any client in these fields whom I would consider insensitive to the public interest I know how difficult it is for an executive employed in one of these industries to deal with the possibility that his product may be harmful.

It is interesting that the contemporary art world as well as the corporate world is presently in the midst of a major debate on the problem of *relativism*. Some feel that we are living in a time when all schools of art must be recognized as equally good, and when virtually any new direction in which an artist moves is valid so long as his intention is serious. Others warn that evaluating works of art on the basis of the worthy intentions of the artist can destroy our ability to have meaningful aesthetic experiences. The world of corporate communications seems to be facing a similar dilemma. The ethical approach to arriving at value judgments about products should not be to prove that the company is right because the motives of management are high-minded. Somehow arguments must be weighed on the basis of worth. The communicator must maintain his integrity by trying to make sure that all sides get a fair hearing—his client's critics as well as his client—in order for the public to make a responsible decision.

To perform this function corporate communicators need to do more than transmit messages from the company to its audiences. Public concern must also be communicated to company management. This may generate pressure to change company policies, even to the detriment of the company's economic interests. But unless this role can be performed effectively, corporate communications programs may well fail to achieve their goal of winning broad public confidence in the free enterprise system.

The Dilemma of a Critical Press

Those who believe in free enterprise presumably should have a special reason to appreciate the virtues of a free press. Just as any entrepreneur is entitled to try to sell whatever safe product the public might like to buy, so any journalist ought to be able to write what he thinks his audiences will want to read.

Unhappily, top executives of large corporations who have been spending large sums of money on advertising campaigns are not universally sympathetic to this point of view. The purpose of advertising messages is to convey a positive impression about the company and its products, and the words are written by skillful specialists who spend a considerable amount of time studying the relevant facts and distilling the essence of what is to be communicated into effective words and graphics. Top corporate executives are suspicious of newspaper reporters who, spending an hour or two to learn facts that take others weeks to absorb, then write articles which are, at best, superficial descriptions of reality. This is especially so when the reporters are inexperienced in the affairs of business, and either make serious mistakes in their copy or do their best to make these stories sensational rather than accurate.

Executives are grateful when public relations specialists can play a role in seeing to it that company operations are reported accurately. Virtually all sophisticated communications programs conducted on behalf of major corporations include a substantial effort to achieve positive editorial coverage of the company's achievements. Often a good story in the news columns about a product or a corporate activity is considered more valuable than a costly advertisement on the same subject since the editorial coverage has greater credibility.

But the desire for a favorable press has led to some unfortunate abuses. In a review of a book written by a former public relations executive for United Fruit, Kenneth Galbraith deplored "what so disingenuous and agreeable a man says about his depraved job." The author had clearly been highly successful in misleading the press. "But even he," thought Galbraith, "might agree that there are things and people—biological warfare, Ron Ziegler, swine flu, and possibly now Nelson Rockefeller—which simply do not lend themselves to effective public relations."

Unfortunately, the role played by even the most responsible public relations specialists in obtaining favorable coverage in the press has not always helped management's capacity to deal constructively with public criticism. An alert press can expose faults which should be corrected. Sometimes it is wiser and more productive to admit one has been wrong than to defend corporate dogma to the end.

In this respect business has much to learn from the professions. Barry Commoner wrote recently:

> Science has a well justified reputation for approaching the truth, not because we are any more truthful than anyone else, but because we have a tradition of making our mistakes in public. . . . What stands in the way of a scientist faking his results is the certain knowledge that he's going to be checked.

Is it an ethical posture for an enterprise to act as though it were infallible? Or to attempt to camouflage when the company has erred? Yet both are not uncommon experiences in the corporate world.

Some business executives behave as if they would like to ban reporters from their premises or establish a controlled press which only prints the truth as they see it. The danger is not that they will get their way but, that in their desire for favorable press coverage, they will lose their ability to take legitimate criticism in stride.

Dilemmas of this sort transcend the more traditional moral issues in communications—truth-in-advertising, full disclosure, and avoiding conflicts of interest. To conduct oneself ethically in regard to these considerations requires a degree of personal integrity and an ability to see beyond self-gain. No one is immune to pressures which drive one to overstep the boundaries of prudence in such matters, but these problems have more to do with ordinary human relationships than the dilemmas of far-reaching corporate communications programs aimed at building credibility in our doubt-ridden area.

A genuine ethical dilemma is one which involves a conflict of two valid ideals. This is what seems to be emerging in the broader communications programs now being conceived as a means of establishing the legitimacy of the corporate system. Should a corporate image program reflect the true character of a corporation or can it be based on what communicators think will have the greatest effect on key audiences? Should an executive personalize the corporate point of view by articulating his ideas about social and cultural values or should he be a selfless spokesman who lends his name to official corporate policies? Should the policies which serve the economic interests of the company always be promoted in corporate communications programs or should other points of view which may be detrimental to profit goals influence management's policies? Should critics who do not know "all the facts" be attacked for their shortcomings, or should their insights and sentiments be respected precisely because they are not subject to pressures from the corporate community?

There are no simple formulas for resolving these dilemmas. Yet the way they are resolved could have serious consequences for the future shape of our society.

PART THREE:
PRACTICAL PROBLEMS,
SPECIFIC SUGGESTIONS

7

Clarence C. Walton

The Executive Ethic:

View from the Top

*The concluding essay is concerned with the way top manage-
ment perceives its major ethical problems and how it seeks to respond
to them. Relying on interview results from five executives of large
representative corporations and on material produced in the 1975
Business Roundtable Report, a vignette is drawn of the major moral
issues. Recommendations (some highly unorthodox and in the form
of "savouries") are offered, more to stimulate further analysis and discussion than to provide definitive responses.*

C. C. W.

In trying to get a handle on the much discussed and less understood issue of corporate ethical conduct it seems important to try to
understand the realities as perceived by the leading actors in the corporate drama and the range of possibilities where innovative action
might bring salutary gains. To achieve these goals, I propose to raise
—and answer—three basic questions:

1. What significant ethical problems are perceived by top managements of
   big corporations?
2. How may the corporate ethic be understood?
3. How can corporate ethical conduct be sustained—and improved?

By so questioning, one begins to discern the "gut" moral issues
which haunt both friends and foes of the corporate system, how such
seemingly disparate concerns may be fitted into a unified conceptual
framework and, finally, how the problems might be handled through

new institutional practices. In no case is it presumed that all the burning moral issues have been unearthed, that agreement will be accorded to the theoretical framework herein presented, or that the suggested mechanisms will actually work. But the effort must be initiated with awareness that false starts will be corrected and right ones pursued.

View from the Top

Although the literature on corporate ethical problems was fairly well sifted it seemed necessary—for the first question—to take two additional steps: (1) talk to a few top-level executives whose judgments I respected [1] and (2) supplement their assessments with experiences reported by the Business Roundtable on corporate responses to moral issues. What follows, of course, does not represent "scientific" findings but rather an impressionistic composite which contains much of what is familiar—plus a few surprises.

By way of preface it should be noted that there was a reluctance among the interviewees to point the finger at other businessmen whose misadventures have given an ethical black eye to all business. An even greater reluctance to praise their own enterprises too fulsomely was probably explained by a comment one made regarding Emerson's remark after a distinguished visitor had left a dinner given in his behalf: "The more he spoke of his honor, the faster we counted our spoons."

THE STARTING POINT

The following questions provided the background

1. What are the three most ethical issues your corporation has faced during the past ten years?
2. What steps were taken to meet each of the ethical problems? How effective?
3. What are the most difficult ethical issues your company now faces?
4. What is being done to meet these issues?
5. What major obstacles have you encountered in trying to solve the issues?
6. Does society need new mechanisms to help encourage ethical behavior?

[1] Those interviewed included: Ralph Pfeiffer, Chairman and Chief Executive Officer of IBM Americas/Far East Corporation; Robert Stuart, Board Chairman and Chief Executive Officer of the Quaker Oats Company; Milton Perlmutter, President and Chief Executive Officer of Supermarkets General; Frederick Collins, President and Chief Operating Officer of Sperry and Hutchinson; and Robert Fegley, Staff Executive to the Chairman of General Electric.

7. What do you consider to be the most serious ethical questions facing America?
8. What do you believe is the greatest incentive to high ethical behavior in corporations?
9. What do you believe is the major cause for ethical lapses?
10. What other comments would you care to make?

It is helpful to divide the ethical problem areas identified by these executives into *internal* and *external* categories and to comment on what appeared to be some interesting omissions.

Internal Ethical Problems

In the interviews, as executives began to review the history of their own organizations, their involvement with them, and their perceptions of the general business community, seven issues emerged which were expressed with varying degrees of intensity. Several observed initially that many problems currently described as ethical in nature are really organizational issues where common-sense awareness of business realities prompt appropriate responses. It turns out that the comment is not too wide of the mark. Presented in truncated form are issues and the commentaries.

EMPLOYEE INCENTIVES

Robert Stuart of Quaker Oats recalled that during the 1975 recession the value of his company's stock shared the common adverse impacts. When certain others, aware that management's stock options were not serving as incentives, recalled their employees' certificates and reissued new ones at better terms in order to hold ambitious young executives, Quaker Oats was confronted with a similar challenge. Stuart rejected the suggestion as unethical on two grounds: (1) management itself must be held ultimately responsible for performance and to reward for nonperformance was wrong, and (2) the ordinary stockholder had no similar options even though he bore no responsibility for declining corporate results. Robert Fegley of General Electric agreed by saying that "to give executives special advantages when a company is doing poorly is bad ethics and bad business."

A contrary view was expressed by Fred Collins of Sperry and Hutchinson who reasoned that the whole purpose of stock options was to provide incentives for better performance. If, in fact, the arrangement

had become a disincentive, "you had better change—and change fast."
If stockholders were disadvantaged in the short run they would ultimately benefit because of the more effective performance by highly
motivated executives. Among the respondents, Collins' was a minority
voice, but the observations illustrate the contrary paths that bright and
well-intentioned executives could take.

THE "PEAKED" PERFORMER

How to deal with managers who have given fully and generously of
their talents over a number of years and who have suddenly "run out
of steam" is another sensitive ethical issue. For one executive this was
truly the area of "anguished ethics." He described a vice president
who had worked effectively for the company for over twenty-five years
and who, in his mid-fifties, suddenly "went dead." Lateral job transfers were tried; a special vacation was provided on his birthday; counseling was suggested and rejected. Approached about early retirement,
the vice president responded angrily and negatively; he began to question the ethics of a corporation which would treat a loyal and devoted
worker like "a used dish-rag." Clearly, he wanted to continue employment. Clearly, his superiors found his presence not only nonproductive
but counterproductive. In the circumstances he was "retired" at full
pay until his pension rights would become available.

The single incident raises, of course, the specter of countless similar
problems. Some corporations—including large insurance companies—
who feel that the best ethical posture is one of retention because the
enterprise, having received much owes much. To this ethic is added
the argument that the price of retention of a few is small compared to
the vast unease which would permeate executive corridors if a more
vigorous forced retirement policy were pursued. As a general rule,
company policies are ambiguous or discreetly silent on this issue—yet
it rises in sufficient numbers and with sufficient force to constitute an
ethical dilemma for management. Most respondents were of the opinion
that large organizations could, as a general rule, find some niche in
the corporate structure for the square peg and that smaller companies
are the ones which find the peaked performer hard to deal with.

PRIVACY

There was unanimity that any employee who flagrantly violated
company policy should be disciplined. If the misbehavior provided
"learning opportunities for others," observed one commentator, "it

probably should be discussed as an example." How to do this while protecting the individual's privacy and good name is not always possible because the thickest corporate wall is often porous. Handling obligations toward the individual and for the totality creates, at times, a subtle ethical challenge.

In a world of changing life styles this issue promised to become more highly charged in 1977—especially if the Koch-Goldwater Bill were to become law. Labeled HR 1984 (from the title of George Orwell's famous novel) the bill extended privacy regulations in state and local governments to business organizations; it would apply not only to computerized systems but also to manual files and record-keeping accounts. Among the provisions of HR 1984 were prohibitions against any information system whose existence is secret, prohibitions against collecting information unless the need has been clearly established *in advance,* and prohibitions against dissemination of data to another system or to another individual other than the person himself unless certain tight conditions are met.

Corporate executives agree that the privacy of an individual is a prized right and must be respected. But the right of corporations and potential employers to information is also important. Easy recourse to the courts, if the individual feels aggrieved, introduces the specter of bad publicity, endless litigation, and escalating costs. One item of particular concern was the bill's prohibition of transfer of personnel information beyond the jurisdiction of the United States without specific authorization by the person or unless done in accordance with treaty or Executive Agreements. To multinationals especially, individual privacy and the company's right to know pose highly difficult legal and ethical issues.

DISCLOSURE

So far as any impropriety is concerned, corporate executives agree that if materiality is involved it should be reported. But what if the amounts involved bear no significant relationship to the volume of business and the level of profits—should management still release the data? Robert Stuart outlined the experiences of Quaker Oats which launched an intensive internal audit and concluded that, over the entire past decade, approximately $100,000 may have been spent in debatable ways; the lawyers and accountants concluded that the amount was not material since the corporation had sales approximating $10 billion over the same period. Discarding the "10-K route" to

the Securities and Exchange Commission, the company had to wrestle
with the problem: if the sums paid are not material should they be
disclosed at all? If yes, to whom? "There was fear," in Stuart's words,

> that because the company's ethical performance had been so outstanding
> in the past, any disclosure, however miniscule, might hurt employee morale
> and raise the vexatious question: "Is this simply the tip of an unethical
> iceberg?"

Robert Fegley of General Elecrtic recalled that long after the public's
clamor had subsided over the electrical conspiracy cases the "internal
pain and anguish" at GE continued. Said Fegley,

> Indeed, that memory has induced a restraining influence on corporate
> spokesmen to go public on questions of corporate ethics even though
> General Electric's enforcement activities have prevented a recurrence of
> the problem.

In its situation Quaker Oats concluded that silence was wrong and
that disclosure, though risky, must be made. Thus Stuart released the
information at a stockholder meeting on December 17, 1976. Stockholder reaction was practically nil; employee reactions were less clear.
This issue obviously goes beyond the legal or accounting definitions
of materiality because it relates to the stockholders' right to know.

ETHICS OF DECISION-MAKING

While there was appreciation by these corporate executives of the
individuals' right to share in decisions *directly* affecting them, there
was equal awareness that a corporation is not likely to become a
twentieth-century replica of the Athenian democracy. Representative
government is not judged by efficiency; corporations are. How policy
decisions are arrived at and formed have, of course, ethical consequences. But who should be involved when sensitive matters are reviewed: corporate counsel? The Executive Committee? The Audit
Committee of the board? All directors? Employee groups?

At the moment, it appears that, when critical issues surface, the
Executive Committee and/or Audit Committees are most frequently
used to provide direction and ways to monitor performance. Yet awareness exists that the process will have to be reexamined. The memory
of blue-collar rebellion against hidden television cameras is a reminder
that the white-collar worker is equally sensitive to those procedures
established to assure performance and to detect malfeasance.

THE "BALANCING ACT"

To S & H's Fred Collins, balancing the rights of various claimants in the corporation is by far the most difficult ethical assignment. He also recalled the 1973 recession and the painful situation it created for the company when, in the face of depressed profits, there was obvious need to respond with greater efficiency. But efficiency meant cost reduction—and one clear area for cost-saving was to cut the labor force or to announce layoffs. The larger question became this: faced with a sure prospect of reduced dividends to stockholders, should a corporation retain workers if this inevitably means a further decline in shareholder earnings? Under traditional law and under traditional ethics the priority in such trade-offs goes to stockholders, but Collins wondered whether or not certain new institutional mechanisms—such as the guaranteed annual wage—might now be needed if the future good of society was to be served.

"INVERTED JUSTICE"

Executives are experiencing the same ethical conflicts over affirmative action as are educators, and they expect the 1977 Supreme Court decision in the California "Bakke" Case to have far-reaching consequences. The question for the court was whether one of the University's medical schools discriminated against a rejected white applicant who had better scores than some black students admitted under the University's affirmative action plan. The larger issue is this: in efforts to recruit and promote individuals from minority groups, are others treated unjustly? Ralph Pfeiffer noted that IBM has not, despite efforts to be scrupulously fair, escaped some tensions because "favoritism" is perceived. Pfeiffer stated:

> It is true that IBM recruiting has increased its focus on minorities and this has brought a cadre of employees who are now ready for advancement. The presence of this group in readiness for further recognition alone is enough to create restiveness among some of the others.

IBM has never practiced racial discrimination. Some corporations have. One may recall the old so-called "Pittsburgh Syndrome" where certain heavy industries simply shied away from recruitment of blacks and even made promotion for "ethnics" a rather difficult enterprise. Interesting to track will be IBM's promotion policy for its Japanese employees where women are promoted on the same criteria as males and where it is highly unusual to find women in management positions.

Seniority—So far as seniority is concerned, alleged discrimination— or reverse discrimination—is particularly sensitive. The Supreme Court ruled, in 1976, that a Georgia trucking firm which had discriminated against black applicants would have to grant them employment dates from the time of their initial applications rather than from the date of actual hiring. While an important clarification had been achieved, problems remain because in times of recession, affirmative action and "last-hired-first-fired" union ethic comes into direct conflict. It is germane to note that the AFL-CIO Executive Council at its February 1977 meeting, vigorously attacked the notion advanced by the U.S. Commission on Civil Rights that bargained seniority systems must be upset to assure that layoffs do not have a disproportionately negative effect on minorities and women. The labor group stated:

> We consider these proposals repugnant to every notion of justice and fair play. The view that job opportunities should be parceled out by race and sex is blind to the basic concept of equal justice embodied in the civil rights laws.
>
> For generations, workers and their unions have sought job security agreements precisely in order to protect workers—all workers—from discrimination, favoritism and caprice on the part of employers.
>
> The schemes proposed in the report in the name of "affirmative action," add up merely to negative action and institutionalized discrimination against workers who have by long and faithful service earned the right to job security and who would be unfairly and arbitrarily deprived of that earned right.

The nagging question can be stated in these terms: is it ethical to lay off white men in favor of women or blacks with less seniority even though these white men had nothing to do with the company's discriminatory practices?

In the Georgia trucking case three justices found it impossible to reconcile this question and balked at a principle which asserted certain employees' "preferential rights at the expense of other employees." Recession, slow economic growth or a national policy of zero-growth will likely exacerbate the issue. The 1977 evidence suggested that executives are waiting for guidance from judges, legislators and regulators. But the issue worries them because of the ethical dilemma it poses as much as for the legal and economic ramifications it creates. Perlmutter of Supermarkets General has prophesied that this will become increasingly controversial:

> Management is put under the gun by the Equal Employment Opportunity Commission and by other pressure groups to play the numbers game. Not infrequently persons wind up assigned to jobs for which they are ill prepared and the damage to the individual's self-image is irreversible. We like to hire for ability and without any discrimination and the "quota ethic" deeply concerns me—especially for companies like ours which have never indulged in discriminatory hiring practices.

External Ethical Problems

Because the executives interviewed represented enterprises in sharply different industries, it is not surprising that their comments revealed ever sharper nuances over "external" ethical concerns. This caveat must be borne in mind in what follows. Certain response patterns, however, indicated that the problems most frequently mentioned tended to cluster around four major issues: (1) payouts, (2) market power, (3) government intervention, and (4) production-marketing conflicts.

PAYOUTS

To Robert Stuart "payouts" in other countries is the "most complicated practical issue Quaker Oats has ever faced. We have had cases where price-control officials have threatened to shut down an entire operation if demands were not met." Several respondents expressed frustration over the unwillingness of critics to make appropriate distinctions in "payout" situations. Not all payouts are "payoffs" and, as Michigan's Paul McCracken noted, those countries where governments manage the details of economic life tend to be corrupt societies where there is a price for a favorable decision. The executives themselves drew distinctions among *extortions, "grease"* or *"speed" money, gifts,* and *bribes.*

Extortion—What should a company do when an operation abroad is threatened with destruction if a substantial payment is not made to a colonel of the local security force? Or when the life of a plant manager is threatened unless money is paid? These questions were raised and from the guarded answers given it was reasonable to infer that the demands, when made abroad, might well be met but that, having been victimized once, counterstrategies would be developed. In no case were such payments "approved" in domestic situations because American justice and American police could be relied upon to provide protection. To act otherwise at home was to join forces in an unholy alliance with venal officials.

"Grease" Money—In a statement to Quaker stockholders on November 10, 1976, Mr. Stuart said that

> there had been numerous requests for payoffs to minor government officials in order to obtain action to which we were legally entitled anyway and had been refused, resulting in one instance in physical abuse of a plant manager and, in several instances, in arbitrary delays in the processing of paper work necessary to clear already justified governmental approvals. During the same ten years of frequently refusing to be blackmailed, we did find a handful of payments of borderline propriety.
>
> Just to show you how frustrating a problem this really is, . . . One of the demands refused was from a customs official in connection with the movement of an employee's furniture. As a consequence of our manager's refusal to pay, the furniture was stored in the open in a rainy climate and was ruined. When it became apparent that no grease money would be forthcoming, the furniture, though now ruined, was taxed at its original high value.

Mr. Stuart noted that over the last decade there were a number of "small gratuity-type payments" (primarily in one country), but on balance, "it has been Quaker's position to encourage resistance all along the line."

Some companies call this the problem of "speed" money and do permit payment abroad when there is a recognized expediter, when the amount is insignificant, and when it is an accepted local practice. In all such instances the amount, the payee, and the recipient are recorded.

Gifts—In Japan, for example, it is a time-honored tradition to offer small gifts when a person retires (to show gratitude for the relationship), or when an individual is promoted (to demonstrate respect), or when an employee has played a significant role in completing a major event (to express joy). IBM and GE view all such giving as ethically appropriate within the Japanese culture. Further, the common Japanese practice of an end-of-the-year gift to a businessman from another company who has worked with an employee in a mutually advantageous relationship is also viewed as no violation of company guidelines. Here are situations where a company may take a "permissive" attitude on the foreign activity but will exercise an absolute veto in the United States where it is viewed as "payola."

Bribery—Bribery, defined as a payout to get something done to which the company is not entitled, was universally condemned and the common view was this: bribery is wrong and stupid; to condone it is to do a disservice to the entire community. *Apropos* this comment are the remarks of John de Butts, Board Chairman of American Telephone and Telegraph:

> The reputation of our business has been seriously damaged by the widely publicized allegations originating in Texas and North Carolina, allegations to the effect that the Southwestern and Southern companies sponsored political slush funds to influence the outcome of activity in those states and that "fake vouchering" was systematically employed to feed those slush funds. *The net result for A.T. & T. was that doubts now cast on our integrity are, at least, as great a challenge as that we confronted a half dozen years ago when our service capability was in question and at least as great a challenge as we face today—the anti-trust suit and the recession notwithstanding.*

On the other hand, bribery was distinguished from political contributions. No executive felt that political contributions were intrinsically unethical. If, however, American public opinion and law frowned on such practices, then contributions must be scrupulously avoided. For multinationals there are added problems. The federal government strictly forbids political contributions by corporations; many states allow such political contributions; and some countries, like Canada and France, believe that contributions are good for the public weal. Thomas Murphy, General Motors chairman and chief executive officer, noted that his company contributed equally to the support of both major political parties in Canada because this action was "not only legal but expected—both looked for and looked upon as a responsible act by a responsible corporate citizen."

When a corporation decides not to make political contributions abroad, it faces difficulties in monitoring the efforts. Shortly after Frank Cary, Board Chairman of IBM, announced that no political contributions were being made anywhere by the company he discovered, much to his embarrassment, that IBM Canada had engaged legally in political contributions for a long time. After a meeting the Canadian managers decided to discontinue the practice in order to maintain world-wide behavioral consistency for a world-wide enterprise. But a question remains: Should the parent company impose an

American political standard on a subsidiary or affiliate whose management feels that, by doing certain things, it is being ethically responsive to local norms?

By way of summary—it is a fair inference that what most troubles executives is the ambiguity which veils definitions of various "payout" practices and the inconsistencies revealed by responsible public officials. Walter E. Hanson, Senior Partner of Peat, Marwick and Mitchell, voluntarily imposed upon himself the task of bird-dogging speeches by key SEC executives. His conclusion is illuminating:

> Suppose an auditor, following the suggestions made in SEC members' speeches, tells his client that if he has made illegal overseas payments, he had better disclose the fact. By that time the client has had his legal staff research the problem and he tells the auditor that he can find nothing in the Securities' laws or releases that tells him how to go about this disclosure. The auditor says: "Look at the speeches." The client, quite rightly, says: "Speeches don't count. Accounting series releases count. And besides," he adds, "I can find no consistency in the speeches." The SEC Commissioners themselves admit that they are in disarray over the issues and there is no single SEC position.
>
> But the real facts are these. The SEC building in Washington is eight stories high. On the eighth floor sits the Chairman and the Commissioners. And down on the fourth floor, the enforcement division works. Let me assure you, there is no disarray on the fourth floor. The uncertainty on the eighth floor has not sifted down very far in the building.

And so confusion continues.

MARKET POWER

As might be expected the ethical use of market power is of concern. IBM is not atypical. Ever since the 1952 antitrust suit (alleging that IBM had monopolized domestic and foreign commerce in the tabulating-machine business and which resulted in a consent decree in 1956) that corporation has followed a very austere mode of market behavior —a mode which might be called the "ethic of restraint." One executive reported that his company had decided to make a $5 million purchase of new computer equipment. IBM took no steps to rebid in order to become competitive—even though it became aware that the differential between its price and another was rather small. When presented with this situation, Ralph Pfeiffer observed that IBM responds only if the customer voluntarily changes specifications. This is scarcely the kind of aggressive market behavior characterized as the dog-eat-dog ethic or even that associated with Adam Smith's hallowed precepts. Whether such comportment is of higher or lower ethical dimensions will largely be determined by law and by public expectations. Meanwhile, corporate executives see market power as constituting a sensitive ethical and legal terrain where they tread carefully. No executive suggested that antitrust laws be changed or that antitrust action be pursued with less vigor. This was somewhat surprising—especially in the case of Quaker Oats which has been undergoing nearly a year of "prosecution" by the Federal Trade Commission seeking to break up the four breakfast cereal firms—Kellogg, General Mills, General Foods, and Quaker. The facts in this case are so complicated that Harry Hinkes, the FTC administrative law judge hearing the case said he may have to delay his scheduled retirement for three years as he wrestles with the FTC's novel theory of "shared monopoly," namely, that a handful of companies can have a stranglehold over markets without any overt conspiracy. Gary Kostley of Kellogg calls this "simply absurd."

The specter of antitrust causes executives to feel that their ethical image is often prejudged before the facts are in, that excessive "reinterpretation" of the ground rules by government lawyers makes it almost impossible to know what the guidelines are, and that this lack of any sanction over free-wheeling regulators may itself be a major problem for overall social morality.

A related issue involved the ethical use of advertising and public relations especially as these relate to a television industry that is gigantic in its operations, powerful in its effects on viewers, and run in ways somewhat different from other businesses. It was to be expected that none of the companies represented in the sampling felt it was culpable of immoral persuasion tactics; and some, like IBM, even refuse to engage in comparative advertising. Nonetheless, the comments suggested that this area needs monitoring. The concerns expressed proved modestly prophetic because in March 1977, Leonard Wood, executive vice president of Gallup, told a Bentley College audience that whereas a 1968 poll showed 12 percent expressing the opinion that big business was a major threat in the future, the January 1977 poll produced a 23 percent negative vote. According to Wood the respondents were most disturbed by misleading advertising and other practices they consider cheat the customer. Mercedes Bates, consumer vice president of General Mills, was quoted as saying that honesty should compel business executives to agree that the consumer movement could not have grown to its size today without mistakes and, in some instances, really unethical practices on the part of business. Perhaps the most comforting—and most chilling—message from the Gallup Poll was that 36 percent thought business ethical standards were higher than general standards and 49 percent thought they were lower.

Now a new problem is surfacing. If past use or abuse of advertising and other marketing practices has cost big business a loss of confidence, how will the public react if corporations answer affirmatively the question raised by one respondent: When social and moral values are up for grabs do we have an ethical right, or even an ethical obligation, to use advertising and public relations for advocacy purposes? How far should a company go in promoting its ideas, through paid advertising or public relations, for a good society? At the moment, there is growing evidence that companies are taking stands on critical issues—Mobil Oil's advertising compaign on energy and Chase Manhattan's advertisements on capital investment requirements being good examples.

But advocacy is a two-edged sword. Suppose, for example, the automobile industry takes a strong position on the pollution laws and suppose that one of its executives (or its corporate counsel) feels that the company is so wrong that Congress should be urged to disregard the company position. What rights accrue to the corporation to protect its self-interest? What rights accrue to the individual? This new "balancing act" in ethical decision-making has not fully been pursued and certainly is not readily resolved. But if the new thrust toward corporate advocacy and the new emphasis on individual claims continue, collisions are promised.

The foregoing implies problems associated with market problems. Related to market power is also market weakness in terms of ethical response to boycott and threats of boycott. Perlmutter related two incidents which caused Supermarkets General some anguished moments. One was an effort by Chavez sympathizers to have the supermarkets refuse to sell lettuce, and the second was pressure by some Israeli sympathizers who sought to prevent the company from selling French wines because France was selling military equipment to Arab countries. In both instances management felt considerable sympathy for the causes, but it refused to go along on grounds that its customers might entertain other perceptions of realities and cherish other values. Therefore, the company should not use its "moral preferences" to erode the principle of consumer sovereignty on behalf of some political goal and should not "cave in" under threat.

GOVERNMENT "MEDDLING" AND THE PASSIVE ETHIC

Some executives expressed the feeling that the government has become unnecessarily and unfairly meddlesome in corporate affairs and that silence in the presence of such intrusions was a growing problem for the conscience. A grim illustration of what could come to others was the September 1976 *Fortune* story of one Thomas Phillips' jousting with the SEC. Phillips was the young publisher of a newsletter for investors. While the SEC had no complaint regarding the quality of his advice, it was concerned that if Phillips went out of business he might not be able to refund to all subscribers their full twelve dollar subscription price. In a remarkably generous reading of the rules, the SEC concluded that Phillips had defrauded his readers by failing to disclose that he did not have sufficient assets to refund all subscriptions. The SEC has no authority over advisers' professional advice but it does police their advertising. Phillips' omission was particularly deceitful, the SEC said, because he promised a full refund to any dissatisfied reader at any time during the initial one-year subscription period.

The SEC also found that Phillips was insolvent. It made that determination by adding the cost of all of his unfulfilled subscriptions to current liabilities, even though accepted accounting principles in the publishing business hold that they can be treated as deferred liabilities. The Commission said Phillips could correct the fraud by informing all of his subscribers that he was insolvent and by putting all new subscription revenue in an escrow account so that he could make refunds if the company folded.

Unlike many defendants in SEC actions, Phillips refused to comply and the Commission took him to court. But it could not get Judge Edward S. Northrop to go along with its redefinition of publishing accounting principles and he dismissed the case. While Phillips viewed himself as a winner, the $25,000 legal fee was a stiff price for principle. Obviously costs escalate with size, and executives often must contrast the pragmatic results gained through *nolo contendere* actions to their ethical obligation to fight unfair intrusions.

Indirect assaults on corporate integrity also raise questions on how best to respond. Such indirect assaults are discerned in the government practice of releasing damaging staff reports without affording business an opportunity to refute in proper time. The Metcalf Report on the "Big Eight" accounting firms is apposite. The report noted that although the public believes that independent auditors have a reputation for impartiality and objectivity because of the special role assigned to them by Congress, auditors have, in fact, become advocates of the self-interest of their corporate clients.

Specifically, the report charged that accounting firms have often served different clients within the same industry with little regard for the possible anticompetitive effects, that the "Big Eight" firms have seriously impaired their independence by providing clients with such services as executive recruitment and consulting, that these same firms have joined "recognized business lobbies" to advance the partisan interest of their corporate clients both for a fee and as a public service. The ethical issue raised is a serious one. To the accountants government recommendations that the federal authorities establish auditing standards not only impugns the ethical integrity of accountants, but creates the specter of escalating government intervention. Who participates in preparing government reports, how they are prepared, when they are released—or leaked—raise moral issues for both corporate and public officials. In the end the questions get down to the accuracy or inaccuracy of the report and what sanctions are to be applied to those who distort on either the private or public side.

If government reports by special staffs the ethical profile of corporations, so too do the media. Although one corporation, after an intensive internal review, found no slush funds, no fudging of the accounts, no involvement by any top executive, no violation of corporate policies or public law, it said nothing publicly because of fear that the media, with its new bent for investigative reporting, stood ready to pounce upon any slip, however trivial.

At the risk of considerable oversimplification, the message seemed to be this: government and media handling of the peculations of the few has damaged the good name of business; yet few executives publicly express moral indignation over these "unethical" actions. There is an understandable tendency to play it safe—and this position, according to Robert Fegley of General Electric, can be the most disastrous ethic in the long run: "One sure way, so it is sometimes stated, to avoid criticism is to say and do nothing, but to many people silence means consent—surely not the message business should convey."

Yet what is moral cowardice to some is often practical prudence to another, and an example of a dilemma in handling the issue of the passive ethic is occurring in health care. Discussions invariably have run along a triangular course that involve government, doctors, and hospitals. Perhaps the triangle should be a square by including insurance companies so that we might ask these questions: Why don't insurance companies exert a discipline to cut medical costs as they do in other industries? Is it an example of a passive ethic? Or is it because their strategies would make no difference anyway? Blue Cross and Blue Shield are the largest insurance companies and they are run by the hospital establishment—largely on behalf of doctors. Hospitals do not so much have patients as they have doctors who have patients. Doctors run the hospital, not the other way around. Insurance companies have not figured ways to deal with doctors. This small example dramatizes the larger problem: When *ought* a corporation "fight"?

PRODUCTION-MARKETING CONFLICTS

In a milieu marked by deepened awareness of environmental-ecological balances the moral problem is shifting, according to my samplings, from concern for product quality to interest in product misuse and product users. For enterprises manufacturing chemicals or sophisticated instruments this problem becomes especially thorny. It tends to take two directions. If a company exhibits concern to produce good products which are needed and are of high quality, has it fulfilled its moral duty? It would normally seem so but now questions are asked of side effects. Joel Primack and Frank von Hippel (in their book *Advise and Dissent: Scientists in the Political Arena*) have insisted that industrial scientists and engineers are best situated to see the potential and real hazards of products but that few speak. Advancement comes to those whose work pays off in increased corporate profit while career stagnation or termination is the usual reward for troublemakers.

To this criticism Dr. Arthur Bueche, Vice President for Research and Development at General Electric, replied tartly: "Now I don't know what evidence the authors have to support these statements. All I can say is that they are not describing the world that I have lived in for the last twenty-five years." Yet Bueche raised another ethical issue by noting that the methodology for certifying noneffects is not a field of technical endeavor which has received much attention: "Personal and professional rewards for demonstrating adequately that something won't happen are nebulous at best." In corporate society, this is clearly an area of growing ethical interest.

An equally important issue relates to distinctions between legitimate and illegitimate customers. Occasionally production and top management clash with one another when the latter decides not to sell the product to certain potential customers because it is believed not to be ethical or in the public interest. Practically all major corporations have agonized over decisions to carry on work within areas of the globe where racial or other forms of injustice are espoused as government policy, or to sell to certain buyers when boycotts are threatened. In a statement before a congressional committee (September 29, 1976), Gilbert E. Jones, IBM's Vice Chairman, analyzed that corporation's oft-criticized operations and sales in South Africa and concluded that American business should stay because it has a vital role to play in providing jobs, products and an enlightened policy of fair employment. IBM handles its policy in a practical way: sell only to customers with whom the United States has diplomatic relations. Yet church groups and others find this posture morally defective.

Concerns do not stop here. In the face of rumors that the Mafia is buying into legitimate businesses, it is extremely difficult for corporations to be certain that the sale of their products is truly going to "legitimate" customers. And where the products are of such sophistication that the users' capabilities for unlawful interventions or for evasion from detection are enhanced in quantum leaps, the concerns deepen.

Some Omissions

Having recorded impressions of some ethical problems with which top executives wrestle it remains now to report certain omissions in the testimonies of these business leaders. A decade ago the hot issue was price collusion. During my interviews no one mentioned it, thus confirming assessments made in the *Harvard Business Review* of January/February 1977. Nor did anyone talk of subordinates' unwillingness to comply fully with corporate codes. Given the job level of the representatives interviewed, it was not surprising that no mention was made of complaints (noted by the Harvard authors) by mid-managers of "superiors' pressures to support incorrect viewpoints, sign false documents, overlook superiors' wrongdoing, and do business with superiors' friends."

Surprisingly minor mention was given to conflict-of-interest problems but there was no doubt that companies maintain constant surveillance. A possible inference is that executives have become so aware of ethical difficulties in this particular area and have responded so vigorously with detailed guidelines, that they are less worried over this issue than are board members. And in view of widespread discussions on workers participation through the much publicized "co-determination" procedures of Europe, and more recently the Bullock Report in England, no executive mentioned this as a major organizational or ethical problem. Silence on the matter of alleged outside intervention in the Steel Union election of 1977—an issue which had enraged George Meany and his colleagues—was equally interesting and is probably explained by a feeling that unions leadership was well able to take care of itself.

One might have thought that the popularity of Mark Lipman's book *Stealing*, would lead to comments on employee thievery. Lipman, it may be recalled, was a private investigator who detailed his frustrating experiences in trying to ferret out cases of massive stealing by workers and his conclusion that, for some inexplicable reason, management was reluctant to push prosecutions and courts were more reluctant to imprison.

What most intrigued me was silence over "corporate legitimacy," an issue that Irving Kristol, George Cabot Lodge, Kenneth Boulding, and other thoughtful writers insist is *the* ethical issue for American business. If true, executives are curiously indifferent. Yet the significance of this omission is subject to misintepretation.

Failure to address the issue in terms employed by Lodge or Kristol does not mean indifference to the question of "justification." Perlmutter of Supermarkets General is typical. He justified his work in terms of good products, good prices and good services, in good working conditions and good salaries for employees, and by a commitment to corporate social responsibilities. These are all forms for self-justification. Do they, then, answer the issue of legitimacy? Not if by legitimacy we mean the corporation's right to use private property legally for productive purposes under terms determined exclusively by management, to employ contract under constitutional protections, to determine alone the composition of the board, and even the right to become or remain big. It is in these latter terms that some critics are mounting a challenge to corporate legitimacy.

The Business Roundtable

The best teacher—urged by moralists, analyzed by consultants, recorded by observers, and confirmed by executives—is example. This is the primary statement of the Roundtable Report. Exhortation is useless if leadership is phony. But often personal example cannot be viewed first-hand by the thousands who work for the large organization. So the question of codes arises. A minority view should be initially recorded. Fred Collins voiced the opinion that codes are invariably pietistic, ambiguous, and rhetorical—more honored in public relations offices than in executive suites: "The real job is setting the right example by top management; if it performs in an above-board way in everything, others will follow. When others follow, an ethical company is the end result."

While differences exist over their value, majority opinion supports the conclusion of the Roundtable Report (prepared by Frank Cary of IBM, Brooks McCormack of International Harvester and Ralph Lazarus of Federated Department Stores): "While the growth and diversity of companies make it difficult, if not impossible, to develop a universal code for all business," the best approach is "to encourage individual companies to develop their own guidelines."

Reasons for support of codes come down to the view expressed by Wallace Booth, President of the United Brands Company—a company, incidentally, whose reputation was tarnished (before Booth's coming to the enterprise) by payoffs to Honduran officials: "If you have a formal code," said Booth, "you have less chance of getting into trouble unknowingly."

CONFLICTS OF INTEREST

Over one hundred companies responded to the Business Round-table Survey. Two-thirds reported that conflicts of interest was a major issue, something not emphasized by the samplings I have reported. As a result of experiences companies outlawed speculation on company stock, use of inside information, gifts and favors to any degree which might influence decisions or are not a part of accepted business practices. All gift-giving and gift-taking had to be limited in value, not contravene the law, and be susceptible to public disclosure without embarrassment to the company.

To control relationships to suppliers executives are not permitted to make kickbacks, provide lavish entertainment, engage in competitive bidding, and the like. Antitrust laws were consistently mentioned in the survey and managers were enjoined to consult counsel where necessary and to stay clear of price-fixing, exclusive agreements, tie-in sales, and deliberate disparagement of competition. Product quality, truthful advertising, a hands-off stance regarding acquisition of competitive information were spelled out. Concerning "proprietary information," new employees were barred from providing information from old jobs while, at the same time, they could not divulge to others privileged company data.

SPECIAL PROBLEMS

As might be expected "special concerns" reflected the kind of industry within which the company operated. Three examples will be given. The first is California Edison which stressed the ethical importance of working to reduce demand for electric energy. Customer information to assist in making more efficient use of power is provided through consulting services to commercial, industrial, and agricultural customers, and by encouraging trade associations and builder-development groups to improve the efficiency of electrical equipment. In the commercial world where, in Peter Drucker's terms, the function of business is to "create customers," it seems strange to find a company insisting on minimizing the use of the product it sells for profit. Yet this "ethic of restraint," expressed by many enterprises today, is premised on the unorthodox notion that management, not customer, knows best.

A second example involved multinational corporations which generally addressed themselves to such special problems as the obligation to follow investment policies that are, in Caterpillar Tractor's words, "compatible with social and economic priorities of most countries and with local customs, tradition and sovereignty." Acknowledging the validity of arguments for joint venture, this company nevertheless indicated its belief in full ownership by the parent company.

Kennecott Copper Corporation is the third example. It announced that mining companies had to be particularly sensitive to public opinion because (1) extraction of natural resources draws special attention to matters of environmental quality and (2) the increasing gap between mineral supply and the total needs imposes an obligation to husband scarce resources. Mining companies, said Kennecott, must always operate with "meticulous attention to public disclosure" and the company pledged to go beyond minimum legal requirements toward a policy of "general disclosure of all information that relates to the company's impact on society, the economy, and the environment." So much for the areas of special interest.

MAKING THE ETHIC KNOWN

General preoccupation was with the mode of promulgation. Indeed this was a weightier problem than the form of a code formation itself. Most commonly used for promulgation purposes were executive letters or corporate instructions and, in almost every instance, a forceful statement by the chief executive himself. Quite regularly, each major operating unit was directed to establish internal controls and operating procedures necessary to implement the guidelines, and staffs were designated to conduct periodic audits to ensure compliance.

Employees were required to certify compliance to the rules on conflict of interest, antitrust concerns and the like, and periodic management meetings were arranged to cover business conduct guidelines. Disciplinary action could run from an oral or written reprimand to suspension and termination. The last item mentioned in the Roundtable Survey was the belief that top-management committees on business ethics must be established to oversee and audit the entire operation. *In all such discussion little mention was made of board responsibilities.*

All reform efforts reflected in the Roundtable survey accord with the "spirit-of-the-law" emphasis expressed by *Business Week* on February 9, 1976:

> What business must understand today is that the public has a right to demand much more. If an executive sitting at the summit of some of the nation's most prestigious and powerful companies fails an elementary moral test, shareholders, workers, and customers legitimately wonder what else is going on in the executive suite—whether antitrust laws are being violated, or whether American business is consorting with organized crime. As companies probe their ethical standards, they must understand that the question of illegal political handouts should not be the end of it, but just the beginning.

The Corporate Ethics

My second question—how may the corporate ethic be understood —was stimulated by a comment, made by one executive to the effect that some corporations are still addicted to a jungle ethic. For such enterprise the guiding precept seems to be this: get what you can, when you can, and by any means available under the law. Business is a competitive game not to be played according to the Marquess of

Queensbury rules. While this ethical precept of the "robber baron" days may be sustained by some enterprises in some industries, it tends to be less evident in more mature organizations. Yet differences persist in how executives are expected to perform on behalf of their enterprise when they are in competition with others. It is to these differences that the following comments are addressed.

The nation is made up of thousands of firms each struggling for a place in the economic sun of profitability. To assure profits it must compete successfully, but new management views firms' obligation to other competitors, including labor unions, as critical to the moral tone of the company and the society. How should an enterprise interpret the fiduciary role to its employees? Basically, two quasi-philosophic answers can be given. Either the fiduciary role is to be informed by a *representationalist* ethic or it is to be informed by a *stewardship* ethic. Under the representationalist ethic, the executive operates under a clear guideline: get the best possible result for the constituency you represent. If, in the process of bargaining, your adversary or competitor makes a mistake, take enough advantage of the error to avoid risk to your own position. Next time around your adversary will have learned to behave more wisely and act more firmly on behalf of the constituency he represents.

Opposed to this is a *stewardship* ethic based on the postulate that managers have an obligation to guard, preserve and enhance the value of the enterprise *for the good of all touched by it.* When Reginald Jones took over the top job at General Electric he convened a conference of 300 top executives in January of 1973 to outline the corporation's and his own philosophy. He called it stewardship, by which he meant that executives are responsible for the assets of others, the economic well-being of employees, precious resources of the nation, and obligations to a world in need.

How is a stewardship ethic revealed? Not long ago, one corporate executive faced a dramatic issue whose resolution depended on how the fiduciary role was to be interpreted. A decision had been made at headquarters to close an obsolete nineteenth-century mill in New England, and the job of resolving termination issues was left to local management and to local labor leaders. When the final signed agreement reached by these two parties was forwarded to corporate headquarters there was, in the words of the president, a sense of being "appalled at the gross injustice that had been done to the workers." Under a representationalist ethic the company would have quietly bemoaned the injustice, pocketed the gains, and hoped that in future negotiations the asking price by labor would not be too high. But the ethical failure was clearly the union's.

What actually happened was the reverse. Taking careful steps not to embarrass either local management or local union leaders, the president arranged an ingenious and circuitous device which permitted the unions to reappeal the issue. Immediately upon the appeal, headquarters became directly involved in providing counsel and advice so that a far more equitable termination arrangement was arrived at. A stewardship ethic brought results that were unlikely of attainment under a representationalist moral code.

PROMULGATION

Once the basic philosophy for the fiduciary role has been determined, the task of promulgation, education, overseeing, and sanctioning becomes critical. In this, the example of IBM provides useful perspectives. T. J. Watson, who started the enterprise on the high road of success, had come to run the Computer Tabulating Recording Company when he was fired, at age forty, by John Patterson of National Cash Register. What the elder Watson expressed as a business philosophy strikes many as a simple re-statement of the Puritan ethic. His son, Thomas Watson, Jr., continued the tradition by saying—aloud and often—that the company's philosophy contained three simple beliefs: respect for the individual, producing the best customer service in the world, and product excellence.

As a result of these oft-stated beliefs, there developed not only a moral *tone* for the organization but mechanisms for translating the concepts into operational realities. Job security, good wages, retirement benefits, educational opportunities, growth through advancement, the famous open-door policy for handling grievances—all were practical steps taken to demonstrate that the individual was respected. And despite a reputation for sober-sidedness, IBM deliberately sought out the "wild ducks." The words were drawn from Soren Kierkegaard's story of a man on the New Zealand coast who spent hours watching wild ducks fly south in great flocks. Out of compassion, he took to feeding them in a nearby pond. Soon some of the ducks no longer bothered to fly south and wintered on what he fed. Kierkegaard's moral: you can make wild ducks tame but you can never make tame ducks wild. Said Mr. Watson: "We are convinced that every business needs its wild ducks and in IBM we try not to tame them."

What is true for Watson's company is true for Stuart and Quaker

Oats. Personal development and advancement, quality products, the highest ethical and moral standards are among the stated first principles. Perlmutter put it simply for Supermarkets General: "I believe firmly that my job is to make work satisfying, rewarding, challenging—and yes, enjoyable." And the list could be extended. The point is that formation of a corporate philosophy and its clear articulation by top management are essential in promoting the moral tone.

Professional Ethics

One cannot leave the terrain of corporate ethics without a brief comment on professional codes for management. It will be recalled that the three corporate officers who prepared the Business Roundtable Survey felt that a universal code for all business is impracticable. This conclusion could lead to an inference that concern for the creation of professional management codes might be dispensed with. The inference could be misleading. It should be observed that professional codes may be developed by groups independent from—and outside of—the enterprise itself. Already internal auditors, electrical engineers, research scientists, managers of corporate property, and security personnel have taken steps to establish their own codes which, in turn, affect management.

Possibly the most ambitious attempt to develop professional codes has been undertaken by the International Congress of Management (CIOS). In its Venezuela meeting in 1975, this international group accepted the premise that the same basic ethical code applies both to public administrators and to corporate managers. The premise should be analyzed by private corporations—especially by the multinationals which will be most directly influenced if this new trend is successful. This is not to say that the premise is wrong but it does raise—starkly and dramatically—prospects for fulfillment of the Janeway-Heilbroner prophecy that corporate managers will be seen in the future as highly paid civil servants. One quick way to fulfill the prophecy is to act on a premise that there is no difference between the two.

A second difficulty in developing a professional code of ethics for managers is a well-nigh irreconcilable conflict when attempts are made to conceptualize management as a profession. Repeated as ritual are the criteria set out by Abraham Flexner in 1912: the requirement of a sophisticated body of knowledge, its application to practice, *and a form of altruism which motivates practitioners to place client interest above self-interest.* Today's public is properly cynical of the professions so far as the practice of altruism is involved, but Flexner's formulation is, for business, inadequate for another and more substantial reason. While Flexner's definition reckons with the knowledge explosion and subsequent specialization, *such specialization runs contrary to the manager's role which is a generalist one;* the top executive must know how to coordinate and administer, inspire and lead, reward and chastise. These activities defy the easy circumference of specialization which has been at the heart of traditional definitions of a profession. It is time to redefine.

What, then, might be the new dimension in the profession of management if altruism and specialization do not fit current realities? A hint comes from a 1977 poll of six eminently successful men from six different fields of endeavor. "Colonel" Harland Sanders of Kentucky Fried Chicken fame expressed one view: "I only wanted to make a good living and to serve the best chicken in the country." Only one, Kingman Brewster, Yale President, said something different and important: "There is a tremendous satisfaction in losing your own identity in something that is much more important than you are." One might ask whether this sense of dedication, more even than specialization and altruism, provides the ultimate key to understanding professionalism in today's world. It expresses an ethic of extreme importance —an ethic which promises even as it threatens.

Some Savouries

The survey is now complete. Remaining is an assignment to raise new and possibly controversial suggestions. In times past it was fashionable among British upper classes to climax a formal dinner by serving a small and highly seasoned portion of food called the savoury. Most frequently the savoury delighted the palate but there were occasions when it proved well-nigh indigestible. At this point some savouries for the mind are called for but, in serving them, it is recognized that a few may prove less than tasty. Because corporate payments at home and abroad, conflicts of interests, market power, and the like constitute the main fare for ethical improvements other things might go neglected. The following savouries include some of "those other things."

Flavoring each tidbit is a presumption that certain improvements in corporate behavior, which are expected by the general public, must come from top management. Whether the presumption is justified depends on which of the following questions is judged to be the correct one: "Have I any right to try to make persons in my organization different from what they are?" or "Have I any right to withhold myself and my beliefs in a changing value climate from helping that change take place in directions consistent with—and supportive of— my ethical beliefs?" By the very nature of their assignments, managers should favor, circumspectly, the second question because they know instinctively that top executives are renewal-stimulators. When they cease to renew and when they cease to stimulate they forfeit leadership. Janus-like, managers look *inward* to the moral fiber of those who make up the organization and *outward* to the marketplace—and beyond.

The Inward Look

THE INDIVIDUAL

Because nothing is more precious than the individual personality, nothing is more presumptious than a business organization behaving like a "mother" corporation. Yet there are instances when the enterprise exercises such pressure on the individual that indifference to personal problems so engendered is itself ethically dubious. One issue comes immediately to mind as an example where concern for privacy and concern for the individual might clash—alcohol.

It has been asserted that ours is a "cocktail culture" and that alcoholism affects male and female, black and white, old and young. Research indicates rather strongly that whereas chemical, physiological, and genetic factors are unimportant in causing alcoholism, sociological factors (ethnicity, educational levels, social groupings, and income) are highly significant. A 1976 study of alcoholism among the elderly by David Guttman of Catholic University revealed an interesting correlation: the higher the income the more frequent was the use of alcohol; individuals invariably started to walk the dangerous road long before old age.

Because executives are in high income brackets and because they are subject to enormous pressure, it is not unreasonable to infer that the executive is especially vulnerable. Some companies follow the IBM practice of prohibiting liquor on company premises; other forms of response (counseling, medical care, job transfers, and furloughs) may be required. In my view, corporations who follow a stewardship phi-

losophy of management are more ethically sensitive than those who
follow a representative ethic, and stewardship proscribes indifference
to the plight of individuals within the company.

There are, too, frequent comments on the price paid by executives
in terms of family relationships. Yet relatively few corporations sponsor
seminars for husbands and wives which seek to probe, in an ethically
and psychologically sophisticated way, that delicate family-company
interlock. It was once said of one large corporation that its procedure
of personnel transfers made stable family life almost an impossibility.
A third possibility for exploration by the ethical corporation might
be the whole issue of value formation. Karl Jung reported that in
psychoanalyzing American and European patients, he was constantly
amazed by the differences between the two and concluded that Americans suffer from a particular type of alienation not found on the
Continent. That alienation, concluded Jung, was due to the fact that
Americans are a hyphenated people—white men living in a land with
an "Indian soul." Jung's conclusion, lacking definitive proof, nevertheless provides interesting insights for introspections of ourselves. Are
we aware of the rich diversity of our own value systems? Does that
diversity enrich or enfeeble the individual psyche? Should companies
care?

My point is not that the business enterprise should serve as psycho-
logist-psychoanalyst-confessor-doctor-teacher but, rather, that in the
present context, an ethical enterprise is drawn into areas heretofore untouched and should form its ethical policy or guidelines only after exploring a large range of possibilities that seem currently of little
interest.

THE ETHICAL PROCESS

If the foregoing represent areas where the corporation will move
gingerly, there are others where ethical demands for accountability may
be met more effectively. And accountability attaches itself to the non-
skilled worker, to top management and to the board itself.

While enterprises are moving rapidly to establish ethical guidelines
or codes of conduct for their own firms, such guidelines appear to have
been established without much input from the worker who is directly
affected. Management has operated on the old Weberian theory of
"pyramid authority" where critical decisions are made by the top and
imposed upon subordinates. Given the present *consensual* climate,
noted by Lodge, one has to consider methods whereby middle man-

agement and other employees can be involved in formulating such codes—especially as these relate directly to the individual's special area of responsibility. The process could be long and expensive; it could also be rich and rewarding.

The process could take various forms and the following is merely suggestive. Sensitive issues which affect substantially certain kinds of work could be discussed by groups of managers engaged in that work and their conclusions sent to top management for review. It would be salutary if, then, top management returned the proposed guidelines with its observations to the lower organizational level for further critique and comment. In all cases final authority would rest with top management and/or the board. But process itself is part of the ethical content, and an individual feels more accountable when there has been opportunity to participate in stipulating the rules which determine his or her behavior.

One other area teases the imagination with new possibilities, and that is a further use of the open-door policy. Companies which employ this technique allow a subordinate who has a grievance to go over the head of his immediate superior—and to the very top, if necessary. Why restrict the open-door policy exclusively to grievances? Might not the same technique be extended to include cases where a subordinate knows he has done something unethical and simply wishes to get it off his chest? In present circumstances he simply watches, waits and hopes. There is no incentive to clear the ethical deck and considerable incentive to play it safe. But, absent serious crime, the open door could be used to encourage employees to unload some of their problems, under assurances that the penalty would not be dismissal. A totally different ethical climate could evolve. Top management would have to concede greater powers of discretion to mid-managers and they, in turn, would carry a heavier burden to determine the sanction, to protect the individual's confidence, and to decide how much ought to be reported.

THE BOARD

While management is responsible for performance the board is ultimately responsible for policy. The present spate of criticisms tends, strangely enough, to ignore the boards themselves. Three questions are germane: (1) How should the board operate? (2) Who should sit on the board? (3) What restraints should the board put upon itself?

To the first question, the former Columbia dean, Courtney Brown, has written persuasively that corporations are not simply economic organizations but quasi-polities as well and, therefore, require some checks and balances. Drawing on his rich experiences on many important boards, Brown concluded that the functions of the chief executive officer and the board chairman should be separated and that each should report directly to the board.

While each might entertain, at times, different views of appropriate policy responses, the board would be better informed and better able to perform its essential functions when major policy questions arise.

The second question touches on the *composition of a modern board.* Various suggestions for a "public" representative, when related to widespread interest in more cosmopolitan memberships, signify a new force in public values. A corporation can wait—and be acted upon. Or it can act—and act upon itself and the society. It should act.

The first criterion for choice obviously must be competence. But beyond competence (and this term itself is subject to diverse meanings) are other needs. A good board should enlist individuals of rich experiences in business and in unions, in government and in education, in the performing-literary arts and the media. But no one should go on a board without rigorous indoctrination and education by other board members and by top management. The new board member must have a genuine understanding of the enterprise for which he is asked to assume so much responsibility. One may truly question the ethics of a corporation which recruits to the board persons of high intelligence and integrity but with indifferent knowledge of the characteristics of the industry, and make no effort to correct their deficiency.

In carrying out board duties corporations might profitably watch a trend in university governance whereby board members are regularly assigned to a different school within the institution. The presumption is that each board member would learn more through a special assignment and that the dean of a given school would, in turn, have ready access to one seat of authority. There are problems, of course. Communication channels could become clogged by biased information, innuendo, and rumor. But here again the good judgment of the board would have to be relied upon to sift truth from fiction.

In more direct relationship to ethical behavior, Theodore Purcell, citing the examples set by General Mills, General Electric, and Pitney-Bowes, has suggested, in the May 1975 *Management Review,* the appointment of corporate-ethics specialists to identify generic questions of an ethical nature that should be asked routinely along with the usual legal, financial, and marketing questions. A strategic planner asks what would the firm's market share be if certain actions are taken.

Will it run afoul of antitrust laws? The ethics advocate might want to know how a given decision will affect the right of employees, or the long-run general welfare of the cities or countries where plants are located? He might develop the company ethical code and encourage ethics seminars for managers. All this calls for an ethics director who is a strong and able manager and who has the backing of his chief executive officer. The CEO will be a prime force in the success or failure of the ethical advocacy idea.

Taking on a larger array of duties raises a significantly new question, namely, the number of boards upon which any individual can efficiently serve. Corporations might wish to examine two things: (1) the practicability of limiting the number of directorates held, and (2) the establishment of regular annual review processes of the director's activities elsewhere to preclude conflict-of-interest problems and any slippage in the performance of duties.

THE PROFESSIONALS

The liberal sprinkling of accountants and lawyers on boards can create especially sensitive moral problems. Take the case of the lawyer. Not so long ago it was discovered that some Philadelphia law firms had developed a practice of permitting personal injury lawyers to acquire interest in their client's causes by providing monthly support for the injured plaintiff and by paying doctor bills. Such lawyers resisted any settlement that did not handsomely repay their interest in the outcome of the case. A clamor for change produced reforms. But the problem caused when a lawyer acquires an interest in the securities of a corporate client has rarely come to public notice. The insider position gives the attorney special opportunities for special gains. While suggestions have been made that law firms should not permit a member to invest in a client's securities except with the approval of the firm's executive committee, this is only one side of the coin. The corporation has an obligation to protect itself and may actually disagree sharply with the decision of the law firm's executive committee. Furthermore, it is not uncommon for a big law firm to have two partners giving advice to clients who oppose one another in litigation. While the corporate client has a moral stake in procedures—even when approved by the lawyer's code—one rarely hears the issue discussed publicly.

Another question has been raised regarding the rights of an attorney to represent a client when, in his own conscience, he is strongly opposed to the position espoused by the corporation he is called upon to represent. In most cases the lawyer and the corporation seem to want it both ways, that is, to retain the association and to mute the differences through subtle compromises. One might ask whether a more honest policy would call for the corporation not to employ lawyers who do not really share their views; at a minimum, might not corporations ask aloud whether the law firm is honest with itself and with its client when it elects to represent a corporation with which it has substantial differences. A good rule might simply be this: no outside accountants and no lawyers with their own practice on the board. When the enterprise needs professional advice let it pay for it. Yet the proposal may represent overkill. If, therefore, accountants and lawyers stay on boards they surely must be aware that public opinion finds it hard to understand how, in the bribery cases, management could disburse sums reaching seven or eight figures without the professionals' knowledge—and possibly help. It is not hyperbole to state that a regular reading of the *United States Law Week* brings up enough incidents to warrant concern by corporations that client-professional relationships also need monitoring. Are the fees regularly analyzed for fairness and accuracy? Are the communications channels between enterprise and law firm understood?

Astronomical legal fees are ultimately paid by customers or stockholders; inordinately long periods of time given to a case by government lawyers are paid by taxpayers. Always there is the excuse that justice cannot be hurried. True enough. But the other side of the coin is that justice can be deliberately delayed by a calculated strategy on either side. One wonders what total figure would be unearthed by researchers who could report the cost to the American people of needless delays. That the sum would be staggering few deny; that neither corporations nor lawyers show a strong inclination to tackle the problem is equally undeniable.

There are other concerns. Enterprises having large defense contracts with government have to be very careful in using lawyers who have come from recent government employment. The law profession shows a strange ineptitude in coming to grips with this problem. One might normally think that a lawyer would disqualify himself from any transaction by his corporate client where his former public office is involved. Indeed, as one looks at corporate codes and senses the concern of enterprises to avoid exploiting proprietary information from an employee coming from another company—as well as to protect its own proprietary data—one is struck by the apparent indifference of both corporations and the law profession to meet squarely this problem of the lawyer's revolving door. If that profession does not move, should corporations prohibit lawyers from preparing applications or briefs to be used in appeals before regulatory agencies where the lawyer has recently had important connections? A District of Columbia proposal to bar a lawyer who has left a government agency from participating for a five-year period in any transaction with that agency has caused a furor. One might confidently predict the proposal will not be sustained. No extensive recapitulation is necessary to emphasize the dangers of present practices.

Unlike lawyers who are expected to play advocacy roles for their clients, accountants are presumed to act in the public interest; a further presumption in the public mind is that the profession is governed by rather precise mathematical rules which offer little room for personal judgment or deviations. In point of fact there exists a rather flexible "consultation" ethic which gives room for moral evasion. In a *Saturday Review* article of November 1, 1975, Professor Abraham Briloff of Baruch College illustrated this point by recalling the role of accountants toward firms promoting recreational land development in Florida, Arizona and California. By entering on the books, essentially as payments in full, customer pledges to pay for lots over the next decade it was made to appear that the developers were earning a fantastic profit. While this incident may be exceptional Briloff insisted that the leeway offered to accountants in determining the value of inventories on hand, plant depreciation or good-will is so ample that the "great book" called Generally Accepted Accounting Procedures can permit two plus two to equal some rather unexpected sums.

Recent court cases (Continental Vending, National Student Marketing and Penn Central) have combined to curb this sort of behavior but Briloff feels that the "Big Eight" in accounting maintain an oligopolistic stranglehold on the American Institute of Certified Public Accountants. Only they can bring voluntary reform. The Professor insisted that unless the AICPA especially stop serving as a trade association and playing the role of ostrich regarding transgressions of those within the power structure government regulation is inevitable.

The Outward Look

If *accountability* is the key word for assessing managers within a company, *performance* is the key word when it comes to their company's behavior in the market place. Performance itself is influenced by the economic goals established, the philosophy which permeates it and, when it surfaces as a major issue of conflict, obligations to the existing organization or to the stockholders.

GOAL-SETTING

So far as goal-setting is concerned, Fred Allen said a good place to start is with sensible sales and profit objectives so that subordinates will not feel inordinate pressure to make unrealistic objectives and to take an "anything goes" attitude. The same thinking was revealed by Fletcher Byrom, Koppers' chairman, when he said that profit and capital growth may determine the quality of performance but they can never be viewed as ends in themselves. The philosophy which animates the performance ethic is critical.

Strategic planners are primarily concerned with the impact of their decision on market shares and on antitrust laws. Might not the corporation routinely ask—as Purcell has suggested—that in addition to the usual legal, financial, and marketing questions, ethical questions be raised: How will the proposed action affect the rights of employees? The welfare of the community? The moral tone of society itself?

Three examples—A few examples illustrate how the performance ethic is shaped by an underlying philosophy. When Mark Toys was a subsidiary of Quaker Oats it returned an especially good profit on the sale of toy machine guns. It was an item which did not depend on seasonal demand, was easy to manufacture and distribute, was desired by retailers because of its rapid turnover—and obviously sought by youngsters. When the question of violence was raised as an ethical issue there was a tendency for some to heed the plea that nothing be changed. Here was a "hot item." In the face of strong consumer demand, someone would sell the product anyhow; further, no one really had assessed the reliability of evidence that use of the toy adversely affected child behavior. But the company, not wishing to engage in anything that might be suspect in so serious a matter, withdrew. An interesting question arises: If Quaker Oats decided to stay in the toy gun market would it have been unethical? If the answer is yes, what are the ethical implications for others—and for society at large? In an analogous situation, Milton Perlmutter reported that Supermarkets General had received occasional requests from distributors of pornographic literature which could be sold, so the vendor argued, safely within an "adult" area of the store. But management refused flatly such overtures—even though the profit margin was substantial.

Ethical sensitivity appears in other guises. For example, in the IBM guidelines a fictional story was told regarding a new product which, for security purposes, was developed under the code name CRUSH—an anacronym for Calculating Regressions Under Standard Hypotheses. It was expected that the program product, when announced, would compete very favorably with the successful program marketed by a smaller enterprise. But IBM said that the code itself was inappropriate because it could be interpreted as an intention to "crush the competition."

Proposed mergers—Often a very vexatious ethical question occurs when a board member or an executive is torn between loyalty to stockholders' interest and loyalty to the present organizational format. It has already been noted (in the Rotunda essay) how difficult this is for a responsible corporate office who feels the merger would be good for shareholders and that management's resistance was due to self-interest. Handling proposed merger issues *is* becoming more ethically sensitive. It becomes doubly so when one management group accuses the other of raiding expeditions.

Are there ways to resolve the issue other than inflated rhetoric, name-calling, media bombardment and the like? The day may not be far off when such issues will be resolved in some kind of public forum before both stockholder groups. Suppose a debate were carried over educational television during a sufficient time frame before five knowledge-able external jurors, and further, suppose that when the debate were concluded the jurors would make their assessments known to the stockholders *before* they voted on the issue. Each management would retain the right to sustain—or withdraw—from the original positions but the conclusions would be reached after genuine full disclosure. Far fetched? So was the thought of unions in 1875 and so was the thought of reaching the moon in 1940.

The Larger Society

ADVOCACY AND CRITICISM

Meanwhile, as inner corporate restructuring is considered, corporate executives will likely be concerned with the shape and nature of the American society. If Lodge's prediction (see Chapter 2) comes true and government activity actually increases, what is the proper ethical posture for corporations *qua* corporations? Should corporate resources be used to shape public policy? Mobil Oil has acted positively to run a series of advertisements during the 1977 energy crisis which criticized short-sighted public policy. Some congressmen were upset and publicly criticized Mobil. But the corporation stuck to its guns. But advocacy is not easy. Professor Milton Friedman remarked that

> if you are a businessman at the head of a great corporation you would think three times before you spoke out on major public issues. You would look over your left shoulder and see the IRS getting ready to come and audit your accounts and you would look over your right shoulder and see the Department of Justice standing only too ready to launch an antitrust suit against you. And then, if you have more shoulders than two, you would ask what the FTC is going to do about the products you produce, and what is the Safety Council going to do about this and that and other things. You are not free to speak if you are in this position.

Silence means forfeiture of the game. There are areas where the business community is ethically obligated to speak out and take a stand. The operation of regulatory agencies is one. Regulators must be vigorous in defense of public interests, but motives are not always above reproach. Should a prosecuting agency be obliged to pay costs in some cases of obviously egregious judgment when the government loses a case? Such a practice would discipline the crusading ardor of bureaucrats who see "winning a big one" as the way to fame and power. It could equally result in an overly cautious approach. The point is not that the answer is provided but, rather, that the problem exists. There has been widespread negative criticism. There have been less constructive approaches.

Universities are another important agency. Presumed to be the critics of society, they themselves are hypersensitive to external criticism of the type mounted by Max Ways. When David Packard, William Simon and Henry Ford III criticized some faculty's hostility to free enterprise (or the Ford Foundation for its operations) the result was a volley of angry retorts from the academic community. Yet it seems to me that in the marketplace of ideas, the businessman has a role to play and that in his commitment to democratic government and to free enterprise he had better take his stand at this critical moment. Playing it safe tactically may be playing it wrong ethically.

INTERMEDIATE ORGANIZATIONS

Should business seek to assist in building other intermediate organizations created to improve the moral tone of business behavior? Carl Madden has censured professional schools of business for being too cautious in dealing with ethical problems. But Harvard's Robert Ackerman recently expressed a rather common view when he said that

> the literature on ethics and corporate social responsibilities began to be so full of rhetoric and so void of sensitivity to the problems of managing the large corporation that I fully intended to let the matter drop. Then one afternoon that 1971 summer, a proposition came into focus that I had only dimly perceived before: the difficulty corporations were having in satisfying their social critics might lie precisely in the organizational innovations that had permitted them to cope effectively with diversifications and competitive conditions. Ironically, the genius of American business might be flawed, not because of dubious intentions or its interests in profits, but because it could not implement responses to social change with sufficient speed and competence.

Certainly since that date the Harvard Business Faculty has been very active in exploring the role of ethics in corporate affairs.

There is a new movement within universities that might well commend themselves to positive support by business and the following note is appended to suggest the growing range of possibilities. The proposition offered here is that if business has often found faculties hostile toward them, they could support autonomous centers that refrain from ideological warfare against free enterprise yet criticize those whose own behavior tends to subvert the values of that system. Examples come to mind.

The University of Virginia has attempted to develop greater ethical sensitivity through its School of Business and under the leadership of Stuart Shepherd. Fred Allen of Pitney-Bowes and Fletcher Byrom of Koppers are spearheading efforts to bring other new organizations into being.

In January 1977 The Catholic University of America announced a new Center for Organizational Ethics. Funded by seed money from the National Endowment for the Humanities, the Center plans to tackle initially four major projects:

1. *Concept-building* which provides ethical responses to imperatives brought on by ecology, consumerism, minority claims, third-world views and the like.
2. *Case-writing* not only for use in professional schools of business but for use in liberal arts courses as well.
3. *Comparative analyses* of professional codes to determine common assumptions, explore differences, and to contrast them with practices in other countries. For example: conflicts of interest seem to have significantly

different meanings to accountants and lawyers in America and both differ
from prescribed professional behavior in England.

4. *Counselors-for-Business*—a project which, because of its novel nature,
requires additional explanation.

Drawing on the experiences of the Hague International Court of
Justice, plans are underway to create a distinguished panel of experts
from business and law, moral theology and social science, government
and journalism, etc., who would be on call to review different ethical
issues as these arise. A "jury" of four or five of them could, with adequate staff help, issue advisory opinions on certain problems which
come to light. Such opinions would, therefore, add the force of external
moral suasion. Successful performance over a period of time would
bring to it a greater recognition by courts and Congress—and by business itself. Further if a corporation is taxed by a particularly vexatious
issue, the center could—providing no clear violations of the law are
involved—offer opinions on request and on a confidential basis which
management is free to accept or reject. Help in assessing guidelines
could come and, very importantly, the whole state of the art could be
advanced. Will these distinguished counselors be a success? The answer
is as ambiguous as the project is risky. Ideally, the center should be
eventually so successful that it would be no longer needed.

Why a new agency when we have the Business Roundtable? Because
an autonomous nonbusiness center in a university setting would be
viewed as more objective. Why not a regulatory agency? Because it must
act within the strict meaning of the law. Why not consultants since big
corporations can buy the talent it needs? Because consultants are con-
stricted by the nature of their contract with the corporate employer.

Vintage Years

The offering of savouries to tempt palates of the minds is complete.
The savoury is not the meal; it provides an after-taste only. How it will
be received and digested depends on the American who is sitting at the
table. For there are, in truth, many Americans. When George Cabot
Lodge speaks of a new ideology he speaks of those who might properly
be called the "Emersonian intellectuals." These are the upper middle
class who reside in suburbs and in university towns, fear industrial
growth, serve as custodians of the culture, manage the technology, form
the government bureaucracies, dominate the universities, control foun-
dations, direct international affairs, and favor social improvement.

Against this is the competitive entrepreneurial American pushed forward by a sense of mission and a desire to find a place in the sun. This is the terrain for small business and for ethnic groups, a domain peopled by individuals who, from the vantage point of the elite, remain essentially uncultured and parochial. In a practical way it is the Polish and Italian Catholics who are more Calvinistic in their work ethic than the Anglo-Saxon Protestants.

Normally one should be able to predict with confidence that the upper-class values will come to dominate but, in America, no one can be sure. All that we can be sure of is that whether it is General Motors Chairman Thomas Murphy who warns against oversimplifications or Trappist monk, Thomas Merton, who warns of the same danger, the road will not be easy. The latter's views are worth recalling. Shortly before his death, Merton looked back at the fame brought to him in 1948 with publication of the tale of his religious conversion in the book *Seven Storey Mountain:*

> It is a book too simple in many ways, too crude. Everything is laid out in black and white [with] cleancut division between the natural and the supernatural, God and the world, sacred and secular—with boundary lines that were supposed to be quite evident. Since those days I have acquired a little experience, I think, and have read a few things, tried to help other people with their problems. Life is not so simple as it once looked in the *Seven Storey Mountain.*

"Life is not so simple" marks the beginning of ethical wisdom. When life has become so complex that it literally spews forth problems, we have great difficulty—and great opportunity. Seizing the opportunity is the current challenge. Yet harvesting creative ideas and noble thoughts comes infrequently in history. Vintage years are scarce. But they do occur: 1685 was a vintage year for music when Bach, Scarlatti and Handel were born; 1776 was a vintage year for freedom because of Thomas Jefferson, Adam Smith and Richard Arkwright.

Will 1977 and beyond be vintage years for corporate ethics? Interesting question, *n'est-ce pas?*

Index

The American Assembly

COLUMBIA UNIVERSITY

About The American Assembly

The American Assembly was established by Dwight D. Eisenhower at Columbia University in 1950. It holds nonpartisan meetings and publishes authoritative books to illuminate issues of United States policy.

An affiliate of Columbia, with offices in the Graduate School of Business, the Assembly is a national educational institution incorporated in the State of New York.

The Assembly seeks to provide information, stimulate discussion, and evoke independent conclusions in matters of vital public interest.

AMERICAN ASSEMBLY SESSIONS

At least two national programs are initiated each year. Authorities are retained to write background papers presenting essential data and defining the main issues in each subject.

A group of men and women representing a broad range of experience, competence, and American leadership meet for several days to discuss the Assembly topic and consider alternatives for national policy.

All Assemblies follow the same procedure. The background papers are sent to participants in advance of the Assembly. The Assembly meets in small groups for four or five lengthy periods. All groups use the same agenda. At the close of these informal sessions, participants adopt in plenary sessions a final report of findings and recommendations.

Regional, state, and local Assemblies are held following the national session at Arden House. Assemblies have also been held in England, Switzerland, Malaysia, Canada, the Caribbean, South America, Central America, the Philippines, and Japan. Over one hundred thirty institutions have co-sponsored one or more Assemblies.

ARDEN HOUSE

Home of the American Assembly and scene of the national sessions is Arden House, which was given to Columbia University in 1950 by W. Averell Harriman. E. Roland Harriman joined his brother in contributing toward adaptation of the property for conference purposes. The buildings and surrounding land, known as the Harriman Campus of Columbia University, are 50 miles north of New York City.

Arden House is a distinguished conference center. It is self-supporting and operates throughout the year for use by organizations with educational objectives.

The background papers for each Assembly are published in cloth and paperbound editions for use by individuals, libraries, businesses, public agencies, nongovernmental organizations, educational institutions, discussion and service groups. In this way the deliberations of Assembly sessions are continued and extended.

The subject of Assembly programs to date are:

1951——United States-Western Europe Relationships
1952——Inflation
1953——Economic Security for Americans
1954——The United States' Stake in the United Nations
——The Federal Government Service
1955——United States Agriculture
——The Forty-Eight States
1956——The Representation of the United States Abroad
——The United States and the Far East
1957——International Stability and Progress
——Atoms for Power
1958——The United States and Africa
——United States Monetary Policy
1959——Wages, Prices, Profits, and Productivity
——The United States and Latin America
1960——The Federal Government and Higher Education
——The Secretary of State
——Goals for Americans
1961——Arms Control: Issues for the Public
——Outer Space: Prospects for Man and Society
1962——Automation and Technological Change
——Cultural Affairs and Foreign Relations
1963——The Population Dilemma
——The United States and the Middle East
1964——The United States and Canada
——The Congress and America's Future
1965——The Courts, the Public, and the Law Explosion
——The United States and Japan
1966——State Legislatures in American Politics
——A World of Nuclear Powers?
——The United States and the Philippines
——Challenges to Collective Bargaining
1967——The United States and Eastern Europe
——Ombudsmen for American Government?
1968——Uses of the Seas